Studies in the Legal History of the South

Edited by Paul Finkelman and Kermit L. Hall

This series explores the ways in which law has affected the development of the southern United States and in turn the ways the history of the South has affected the development of American law. Volumes in the series focus on a specific aspect of the law, such as slave law or civil rights legislation, or on a broader topic of historical significance to the development of the legal system in the region, such as issues of constitutional history and of law and society, comparative analyses with other legal systems, and biographical studies of influential southern jurists and lawyers.

Local Matters

Local Matters

Race, Crime, and Justice in the Nineteenth-Century South

EDITED BY *Christopher Waldrep* & *Donald G. Nieman*

The University of Georgia Press   *Athens & London*

© 2001 by the University of Georgia Press
Athens, Georgia 30602
All rights reserved
Designed by Walton Harris
Set in 10.5/14 Ehrhardt by G&S Typesetters
Printed and bound by Thomson-Shore, Inc.
The paper in this book meets the guidelines for
permanence and durability of the Committee on
Production Guidelines for Book Longevity of the
Council on Library Resources.

Printed in the United States of America

05   04   03   02   01   C   5   4   3   2   1

Library of Congress Cataloging-in-Publication Data

Local matters : race, crime, and justice in the nineteenth-
century South / edited by Christopher Waldrep and
Donald G. Nieman.
p.   cm. — (Studies in the legal history of the South)
Includes bibliographical references and index.
ISBN 0-8203-2247-4 (alk. paper)
I. Slavery—Law and legislation—Southern States—
History—19th century.   2. Discrimination in justice
administration—Southern States—History—19th
century.   3. Afro-Americans—Legal status, laws,
etc.—Southern States—History—19th century.
4. Afro-American criminals—Southern States—
History—19th century.   5. Southern States—Race
relations—History—19th century.   I. Waldrep,
Christopher, 1951–   .   II. Nieman, Donald G.
III. Series.
KF4545.S5 L63 2001
342.75'087—dc21   00-044725

British Library Cataloging-in-Publication Data available

CONTENTS

INTRODUCTION

Alexis de Tocqueville, the great French observer of American life, viewed law and constitutionalism as central to democracy's success in the United States. De Tocqueville noted that Americans saw virtually every political issue as a legal question, using judicial ideas and language to express their thinking. He took hope from this phenomenon, believing that lawyers, by the very tenacity with which they valued order and guarded established procedures, restrained the force of popular opinion and mitigated the tyranny of the majority. But was de Tocqueville correct? How effective were lawyers and the rule of law in quieting majoritarian tyranny and guaranteeing justice? Perhaps the best test of de Tocqueville's analysis is criminal law and its application. As in the twentieth century, those accused of crime were generally marginal persons who had transgressed community norms—often in ways that outraged the community. In the face of an aroused public opinion, only judges, lawyers, and the rule of law stood in the way of arbitrary violence perpetrated by the community against those charged with crimes.[1]

This book examines crime, justice, and community in the nineteenth-century American South, a region better known for honor and vigilantism than the rule of law. Bringing together new research by nine social historians of the law, it explores how effectively law mitigated tyranny in the face of the greatest threat to American democracy—slavery and racism. Each of the contributors takes a local perspective, addressing these broader issues from the vantage point of one county, community, or (in one case) individual. This approach allows the authors to explore rich but hard-to-use local records that illuminate the day-to-day operation of the law and its social and political context and consequences.

While the essays that follow are tightly focused, they ask big questions and offer rich insights into the nature of law in a highly racialized polity. They by no means minimize the importance of legal culture and the rule of law, but they do suggest that de Tocqueville overstated his case. In the southern context, at least, law, lawyers, and judges often supported slaveholders' demands for absolute power over their human property and too frequently succumbed to white demands for security at the expense of due process. But this was not always the case. In the last decades of slavery and in the first years after emancipation, the rule of law probably did, in some cases, mitigate the worst excesses of slavery. In the 1840s and 1850s more slaves accused of major felonies went to court than before. Once in court, judges sometimes surrounded even these slave defendants with real due process protections. At the end of the Civil War, whites created many inferior courts to prosecute freed slaves charged with minor crimes. The justice African Americans received in these minor courts was undoubtedly fairer than the plantation justice common in the slavery era. Later in the Reconstruction period, the very democracy that de Tocqueville feared served to make law and the legal process more responsive to the demands of justice.

The essays span the nineteenth century, a period of dramatic change that witnessed the flowering and demise of chattel slavery, the flowering of a biracial democracy that sought to establish the rule of law during Reconstruction, and the triumph of white supremacy with its disregard for the rule of law in the 1880s and 1890s. In the antebellum era, the law could plausibly stand as a neutral force—at least for white male citizens. Women and blacks constituted only a tiny percentage of the defendants or complainants who found their way into the criminal justice system.[2] Most regulation of slaves occurred on farms and plantations, outside the law and according to the whim of whites. Slaveowners and their managers punished what they defined as misconduct with little supervision from governmental authorities. Some slaveowners overlooked theft while others punished it cruelly. Some masters punished their slaves for drunkenness and profanity; few hesitated to administer a whipping to a lazy or recalcitrant slave. Bennet Barrow of Louisiana sometimes had whole gangs of his slaves whipped for such "crimes" as "shallow ploughing." In one two-year period, Barrow administered 156 whippings on his plantation for 331 offenses, most often for faulty work.[3] Slaveowners were often above the law and had almost complete license to decide what constituted "crime" on their plantations and who should be punished.

In theory, the law challenged such autonomy for precisely the reasons de Tocqueville outlined. Law and lawyers, because of their devotion to due process, were supposed to make tyranny difficult. White southerners debated just how much the state could intervene between whites and slaves. In courthouses across the South, in ordinary criminal cases, judges, justices, and magistrates articulated the values they thought most vital, most important to their society. Often these cases were too trivial to reach any state appeals court. In the routine, day-to-day operations of southern trial courts, judges, lawyers, and jurors tested the limits of judicial power in society. Just what role the courts and law should play in regulating relations between slaveowner and slave, or between nonslaveowners and slaves, or even between slaves and other slaves, had to be worked out in ordinary courts.[4]

Slaveowners found it difficult to keep plantation discipline entirely outside the courts—especially when their slaves were accused of acts that affected the lives, property, and well-being of other whites, that threatened public order, or that seriously offended community norms. In these instances, slaves often found themselves facing prosecution in the criminal courts. Most slave encounters with the law took place in special slave courts. Presided over by magistrates and planters, these courts administered justice to slaves charged with noncapital offenses. The records of one South Carolina slave court operating between 1830 and 1865 document cases in which authorities charged slaves with such crimes as gambling, consuming liquor, disorderly conduct, theft, insolence, assault, arson, rape, and insurrection. The records of a similar court in Tennessee reveal the same range of crimes, and the defendants in that court rarely escaped a guilty verdict. Almost all the guilty were sentenced to be whipped, with half receiving 39 lashes, the maximum allowed by the law.[5]

Indeed, as time passed, slaves were more likely to find themselves in court. During the nineteenth century, the United States moved from a culture hardly touched by governmental institutions to a place where the state reached the most intimate aspects of citizens' lives. In the 1820s English and American judges revived an old legal doctrine called the police power, which authorized public officials to regulate the public's health, safety, welfare, and morals. Constitutionally rooted in the Tenth Amendment, the police power doctrine encouraged intrusive action by local officials because it suggested that the rights of the individual must yield to the whole.[6]

Southern courtrooms were hardly immune from these powerful intellectual currents. In the 1830s, a more robust understanding of police power led southern states to curb or limit the sale of alcohol. In 1839, the Mississippi legislature, for example, passed a law against selling liquor in quantities less than a gallon. Grand juries across the South strove for a well-regulated society by indicting those who used their property in ways that harmed or were obnoxious to the public. In this environment, judges and lawyers increasingly directed their attention to the relations between slave and master. Allowing a slave with a penchant for drinking and stealing to roam free was a nuisance to the community just as surely as an obstructed road. During the 1840s and 1850s most slaves remained outside the legal system, just as they had before, but slave cases occupied a growing portion of the docket. In these last two decades of southern slavery, authorities moved to "modernize" the peculiar institution, regulating and legalizing the relationship between enslaved and enslaver.[7]

When de Tocqueville wrote that American lawyers functioned as a kind of aristocracy, few state constitutions allowed for the popular election of judges. Most were appointed. It seemed reasonable to view such unelected men as defenders of order and the rule of law against the "actions of the multitude." At the same time as legal professionals increasingly asserted abstract legal doctrine, other developments undermined jurists' isolation from the public even as they confirmed judges' commitment to white supremacy. Every state that joined the Union prior to 1845 entered with a constitution that called for the appointment, not the popular election, of state judges. The idea that law should be immune from popular whims and the public clamor remained strong. But every state that came into the Union between 1845 and 1912 mandated the popular election of state judges. The Jacksonian notion that courts should be guided by popular sovereignty had taken hold.[8] This meant white popular sovereignty, of course, and public election of judges probably made southern courts even more responsive to the imperatives of white supremacy than had been the case with appointed judges.

Yet even appointed judges who insisted that law must be autonomous were sometimes driven by the hard logic of slavery to minimize the law's power to mitigate the authority of masters over their slaves. Thomas Ruffin's life illustrates the tension between abstract judicial ideals, like the police power doctrine, and the demands of white supremacy, enforced by elected officials. Sally Hadden's contribution takes a close look at Ruffin, a North Carolinian who was perhaps the South's most famous state judge. A slave-owner himself, he argued against allowing the rule of law to endanger the existing social structure. Judges, he wrote, should not "rashly" decide slave cases with abstract truths derived from common law precedents. The judiciary, Ruffin thought, owed a greater allegiance to slavery—and the arbitrary authority upon which it rested—than to the common law.

Whites' demand for security did not always trump the rule of law, even when slaves were concerned. Tim Huebner's essay shows how legal, social, political, and personal circumstances led the North Carolina Supreme Court to overturn one slave's conviction for murdering a white man, albeit over Ruffin's strenuous dissent. As Huebner points out, a statute written by the North Carolina legislature played a decisive role. Without a law in place guaranteeing slaves the right to appeal, officials in Martin County would have swiftly hanged Caesar for the murder of Kenneth Mizell, a poor, shiftless white man. The most important reason Caesar did not hang was that whites feared no slave insurrection at the time Caesar committed his crime. Whites felt comfortable allowing normal due process procedures to advance. Thus Huebner underscores the relationship between law and community that shaped the contours of criminal justice—often far more than the influence of the legal aristocracy in which de Tocqueville had placed his faith.

Louisiana law enforcement perhaps best illustrates the implications of Ruffin's idea that the requirements of due process and the common law ought not be allowed to restrain the authority of masters over their human chattels. Judith K. Schafer examines the operation of criminal justice in New Orleans. The Louisiana legislature exempted slaves from the common law and even said that no error of form would be allowed to imperil the prosecution of a slave. The consequences were devastating, she shows, removing even the limited protection due process afforded slaves in other jurisdictions.

White authorities expected to use civil law as well as the criminal code to control African Americans. In her study of antebellum Natchez, Mississippi, Ariela Gross shows how whites manipulated the forms of the law to preserve hegemony over African Americans. In southern cities, slaveowners commonly gave their slave property considerable liberty to hire themselves out and manage their own time. Gross documents a case in which a slave actually bought another slave and then planned to sell his slave to a white man.

The white slaveowner filed a civil lawsuit against the white purchaser to reclaim the slave his own slave had sold. The slaveowner intended the suit to
humble his own "quasi-free" slave, to keep him in his place. Civil law as well
as criminal law could be used to keep blacks in a subordinate position.

The Civil War and emancipation revolutionized southern law enforcement. When Union and Confederate armies occupied southern soil, they
thoroughly disrupted the courts. But it was the end of slavery that had the
greatest impact, ending a formal and informal legal system that had governed
most black southerners. After the war, the white conservatives that President Andrew Johnson had restored to power proposed nothing less than a
revolution in the role of law in society. These men attempted to use the criminal justice system to control former slaves, a function previously performed
by slaveowners. Under their leadership, state legislatures passed harshly discriminatory laws and set up new inferior courts to try blacks charged with
the sort of minor crimes generally punished before the war outside court,
without due process. Northerners condemned the new laws as "black codes,"
designed to nullify emancipation and create a new form of slavery. In a way,
these black codes reflected trends already in place before the war, when state
legislatures and trial courts had tried to formalize black-white relations. But
the black codes essayed an unprecedented regulation of the lives of freed
slaves. Never before had African American life come within the purview of
the courts to such an extent.

For the most part, whites found the black codes and the new courts un-
wieldy tools, ill-suited to reestablish control over African Americans. Lawyers insisted on due process protections, even for black clients, and judges
often proved reluctant to simply trample over centuries of precedent. In addition, former slaves demanded the right to vote and serve on juries. Many
African Americans actually preferred to be defendants where they could appeal to the rule of law and have the opportunity to escape whites' extralegal
"justice." Even the right to be prosecuted in court can seem a sacred privilege to those long the victims of white caprice unrestrained by law.

Despite the failure of the black codes, state power continued to expand,
challenging patriarchy and the autonomy of the household and regulating
domestic relations in new ways. Laura Edwards explores this development,
showing how black and white North Carolina women agitated for greater
protections from abusive white male elites. At first the North Carolina Supreme Court tried to retain antebellum notions that the state should not in-

trude into the family and the household. But poor white and black women insisted that law must protect them. Their persistence enlarged the state's role in domestic relations.[9]

With the courts moving to protect the poor from impositions by the elite, and the law playing a generally expanded role in the lives of ordinary Americans, many white southerners turned to vigilantism. Perhaps nothing testifies so convincingly to the failure of black code courts to discipline blacks as the rise of the Ku Klux Klan. While the Klan's principal purpose was clearly to smash African American political activity, thereby blunting their effort to influence the political and legal systems, many historians have contended that Klansmen had an important secondary purpose: disciplining black labor. Mike Fitzgerald's essay challenges this view. Rather than a group dominated by planters and intent on reestablishing labor discipline, Fitzgerald insists that whites created the Klan because they feared black criminality. With no confidence in their courts, whites turned to vigilantism to control crime.

White authority over African Americans was challenged by the national government as well as by the states during Reconstruction. This represented a dramatic change in American constitutionalism and law, which had traditionally given states almost complete authority to define and protect the rights of individuals. Three Civil War – era amendments to the Constitution and a host of new statutes promised federal protection of civil rights. Lou Falkner Williams's careful reconstruction of the prosecutions that grew out of the 1876 Ellenton, South Carolina, riots shows the profound limits of the federal government's efforts to enforce the rule of law in the South. While supreme court decisions limited national authority over civil rights, federal prosecutors did retain broad authority to prosecute those who used violence and chicanery to keep African Americans away from the polls. But one great continuity in southern life ultimately frustrated federal efforts to prosecute violators of the civil rights laws. Although civil rights cases were prosecuted in federal courts, they were nevertheless heard by southern jurors. When called for jury duty, few South Carolinians could even claim to be racially impartial. With whites still so strongly committed to white supremacy, even racially mixed federal juries failed to muster the unanimity required to convict Ku Klux Klan malefactors.

During and even after Reconstruction, there were places in the South where African Americans used the political rights conferred by the Reconstruction Act and the Fifteenth Amendment to bring the rule of law closer to reality. In Washington County, Texas, and Vicksburg, Mississippi, African Americans enjoyed unprecedented access to the political process and used their newly won political power to place blacks on juries and in other strategic positions in the criminal justice system. In his essay, Donald Nieman shows that blacks used the ballot to win a powerful voice in local government and to create a legal system that was fairer and more responsive to their claims for impartial justice. In Vicksburg, Mississippi, as Chris Waldrep shows, whites responded to black political empowerment and an expanded rule of law by pursuing the politics of the white line and forming a powerful racial bloc. As whites organized to control blacks through extralegal means, dueling among whites disappeared. The factionalism among whites that had led to dueling before the Civil War was no longer tolerable in the new environment. In a racially unified society, law was less necessary, encouraging whites to act against blacks outside the law.

By the end of the century, the legal system remained central to American life, just as de Tocqueville had found in the 1830s. Aubrey Lee Brooks, a North Carolina lawyer who began practice in the 1890s, reminisced that when the circuit court met, the whole county turned out to see the show, "the most important event in their lives." It was a social event, with lots of liquor, storytelling, patent medicine selling, and socializing. But the court remained at the center. People went to hear the judge charge the jury, watch the lawyers make their closing arguments, and witness the drama and tragedy of human lives played out before them. These rituals had been going on for two centuries. But at the end of the nineteenth century, the law seemed even more pervasive, more actively involved in the affairs of ordinary people.[10]

And the law presented itself as a neutral force, offering protection against tyranny. For a time after the Civil War, poor women, both black and white, had believed they could seek protection from judges under this new regime. African Americans believed they could make the system work for them. Some dared hope that de Tocqueville's view of the law as a buffer against tyranny would finally be realized for the whole population. Yet many white men thought the courts too impartial and resisted the expansion of the rule of law by turning for relief to the Ku Klux Klan and other vigilante groups.

By the 1890s they had largely succeeded. When whites met for court week, the stories they told and laughed at revealed the realities to be found at the court house. In the 1890s Albion Tourgée, the carpetbagger judge who had attempted to bring the rule of law to Reconstruction North Carolina, had become the butt of white jokes. Whites enjoyed remembering how Tourgée had once charged a grand jury to investigate a lynching. Tourgée gave a forceful speech on the power and majesty of the law, lecturing the jurors on their duty under the law. After retiring to the jury room, the jurors asked the prosecutor if, under the law, a juror had to indict himself. "No," the lawyer answered, "A juror is not required to present or indict either himself or his wife." Whereupon one juror in the back quipped, "Mr. Foreman, if that is so, I will be damned if that don't let a majority of this grand jury out of that lynching." [11]

African Americans understood such realities. James Weldon Johnson described court week much as Brooks, as a spectacle, with crowds flooding streets and sidewalks. "We had an exciting day," Johnson wrote, "we met some old friends and made some new ones." The actual work of the court, however, troubled Johnson. Visiting the trial of a black man charged with theft, the prosecutor hardly pressed his case. He did not need to, as the whites in attendance stood ready to vote guilty with or without evidence. The production resembled a Roman circus more than a court of justice, Johnson wrote, with white spectators cheering for the conviction of black defendants. [12]

Whether reported by Brooks or Johnson, court week exposed whites' attitudes toward the law. More pervasive law did not translate into more due process or respect for constitutional principles. As the essays in this volume document, at the close of the Civil War there was a moment when (contrary to de Tocqueville's analysis) political democratization gave those previously shut out of the legal system greater access to the courts. They used their newly won access to demand application of the rule of law, seeking to use it to curb tyranny. But, in the Reconstruction South, whites sought to enforce order outside the law, through vigilantism and Ku Klux Klan violence. The law expanded into the lives of ordinary southerners in new ways. But at the end of the nineteenth century, white southerners knew the limits of law as well. Many jurors, and the lawyers and the judges as well, sided with the lynchers. Some actually rode with them. De Tocqueville's faith in the law ultimately proved elusive in a society more devoted to protecting white privilege than to the rule of law.

NOTES

1. Alexis de Tocqueville, *Democracy in America*, 2 vols. (New York: Knopf, 1953), 1: 272–87.
2. Christopher Waldrep, *Roots of Disorder: Race and Criminal Justice in the American South, 1817–80* (Urbana and Chicago: University of Illinois Press, 1998), 32.
3. Charles Joyner, *Down by the Riverside: A South Carolina Slave Community* (Urbana and Chicago: University of Illinois Press, 1984), 53; Edwin Adams Davis, ed., *Plantation Life in the Florida Parishes of Louisiana, 1836–1846: As Reflected in the Diary of Bennet H. Barrow* (New York: Columbia University Press, 1943); Peter Kolchin, *Unfree Labor: American Slavery and Russian Serfdom* (Cambridge, Mass., and London: Belknap Press, 1987), 122–23; John Spencer Bassett, *The Southern Plantation Overseer as Revealed in His Letters* (1925; reprint, Westport: Negro Universities Press, 1968), 52–53; Fletcher M. Green, ed., *Ferry Hill Plantation Journal, January 4, 1838–January 15, 1839* (Chapel Hill: University of North Carolina Press, 1961), 17–118; James O. Breeden, ed., *Advice Among Masters: The Ideal in Slave Management in the Old South* (Westport: Greenwood Press, 1980), 50–60, 78–88; Theodore Rosengarten, *Tombee: Portrait of a Cotton Planter* (New York: Morrow, 1986), 457, 500–520, 561–84, 606–37; Phillip Racine, ed., *Piedmont Farmer: The Journals of David Golightly Harris, 1855–1870* (Knoxville: University of Tennessee Press, 1990), 119–25.
4. Thomas D. Morris, *Southern Slavery and the Law, 1619–1860* (Chapel Hill: University of North Carolina Press, 1995).
5. William C. Henderson, "The Slave Court System in Spartanburg County," *The Proceedings of the South Carolina Historical Association* (1976): 24–38; Arthur F. Howington, *What Sayeth the Law: The Treatment of Slaves and Free Blacks in the State and Local Courts of Tennessee* (New York and London: Garland, 1986), tables 6, 7, 8; Alan D. Watson, "North Carolina Slave Courts, 1715–1785," *North Carolina Historical Review* 60 (January 1983): 24–36.
6. William J. Novak, *The People's Welfare: Law and Regulation in Nineteeth-Century America* (Chapel Hill and London: University of North Carolina Press, 1996), 1–50; Hendrik Hartog, "Pigs and Positivism," *Wisconsin Law Review* (1985): 899–935; Christopher L. Tomlins, *Law, Labor, and Ideology in the Early American Republic* (Cambridge: Cambridge University Press, 1993), 19–59.
7. Waldrep, *Roots of Disorder*, 37–58; Daniel H. Calhoun, *Professional Lives in America: Structure and Aspiration, 1750–1850* (Cambridge: Harvard University Press, 1965), 59–87; Bertram Wyatt-Brown, "Modernizing Southern Slavery: The Proslavery Argument Reinterpreted," in *Region, Race, and Reconstruction: Essays in Honor of C. Vann Woodward*, ed. J. Morgan Kousser and James M. McPherson (New York and Oxford: Oxford University Press, 1982), 27–49.

8. Caleb Nelson, "A Re-Evaluation of Scholarly Explanations for the Rise of the Elective Judiciary in Antebellum America," *American Journal of Legal History* 37 (April 1993): 190–224.

9. On this point, see also Peter Bardaglio, *Reconstructing the Household: Families, Sex, and the Law in the Nineteenth-Century South* (Chapel Hill: University of North Carolina Press, 1995).

10. Aubrey Lee Brooks, *A Southern Lawyer: Fifty Years at the Bar* (Chapel Hill: University of North Carolina Press, 1950), 21–27. For court day in the eighteenth century, see A. G. Roeber, *Faithful Magistrates and Republican Lawyers: Creators of Virginia Legal Culture, 1680–1810* (Chapel Hill: University of North Carolina Press, 1981), 73–111.

11. Brooks, *A Southern Lawyer*, 79–80.

12. James Weldon Johnson, *Along This Way* (New York: Viking, 1933), 115.

Local Matters

Judging Slavery: Thomas Ruffin and *State v. Mann*

Sally Hadden

One of the most noteworthy judges of the antebellum South was Thomas Ruffin, whose work on the North Carolina Supreme Court made him both famous and infamous. Among North Carolinians, Ruffin was esteemed a fair and hardworking jurist, who labored long hours writing far more opinions than his colleagues on the bench. This reputation persisted even after Ruffin died, when the institution of slavery and the antebellum South were gone and Ruffin's writings mostly forgotten. In the central foyer of the Supreme Court Building in Raleigh, the state capital, Ruffin's statue still stands alone, a marble tribute to the judge who sat on the supreme court bench for more than 20 years. Of all North Carolinians who served on that state's high court, he has repeatedly been called "greatest of our chief justices" and Roscoe Pound singled out Ruffin as one of the ten most eminent judges in American history.[1]

Yet Ruffin's career, to legal historians of the twentieth century, is recalled most for his authorship of the North Carolina Supreme Court opinion *State v. Mann*. The 1829 case began with a horrific confrontation, in which a slave named Lydia tried to avoid a beating and was consequently shot in the back by her temporary master, John Mann, who had rented Lydia from her true owner. In his opinion for the court, Ruffin held that the renter of the slave, Mann, had the same right as her true owner to punish the slave: Lydia's attacker was innocent in the eyes of the law. Ruffin's opinion stated that "[w]e cannot allow the right of the master to be brought into discussion in the Courts of Justice . . . [t]he danger would be great indeed, if the tribunals of justice should be called on to graduate the punishment appropriate to every temper, and every dereliction of menial duty." So long as slavery existed, Ruffin claimed, "it will be the imperative duty of the Judges to recognize the full dominion of the owner over the slave, except where the exercise of it is forbidden by statute." [2]

State v. Mann became a *cause célèbre* among northern abolitionists like novelist Harriet Beecher Stowe, who modeled Judge Clayton and his slavery opinions in *Dred: A Tale of the Great Dismal Swamp* upon the actions of Thomas Ruffin and *State v. Mann.* Stowe's most famous statement about Ruffin has often been repeated: "No one can read this decision [*Mann*], so fine and clear in expression, so dignified and solemn in its earnestness, and so dreadful in its results, without feeling at once deep respect for the man and horror for the system." [3] For legal historians, *Mann* has come to represent (along with *Souther v. Commonwealth*) the acceptance among southern jurists that the law gave slaves virtually no recourse from a master's punishments and decisions. [4] This form of judicial restraint where slaves were concerned, however, did not spring fully formed into Ruffin's mind in 1829. While we know much about Ruffin's writings after 1829, which have dominated the study of *State v. Mann*, little has been written about Ruffin's earlier views on slavery, or what attitudes he held at the time he penned *State v. Mann.* [5] After learning more about Ruffin's character and early views on slavery, as well as certain key events in 1829–30, we may discover that the traditional interpretation of *State v. Mann* has lacked sufficient attention to detail. [6]

Thomas Ruffin was born in Virginia in 1787 and later moved to North Carolina, but during his long life he continued to write and visit his Virginia relations. He was educated at Princeton from 1803 to 1805, where he kept a diary, the only time during his life when he would do so. [7] From this early period, our best sources for Ruffin's beliefs are to be found in his diaries and the letters he received from home. His sojourn in Princeton was probably his "first exposure to Northern sentiment regarding slavery" and this may have raised great moral questions for the young man. [8] In 1805, at a time when Ruffin's health was failing, he wrote a letter (no longer extant) to his family in which he expressed his reluctance to rely upon slave laborers, or as his father put it, "those unhappy fellow mortals the Africans, whom our ancestors have entail'd on us." [9] Ruffin and his father, in the early national period, could still imagine that their slaveholding was not the result of conscious choice, but a consequence of actions taken by their ancestors and the rest of southern society. Neither they, nor others, had yet entered into the full-fledged defense of slavery that would become more common in the 1830s and afterward.[10]

Ruffin's father, a Methodist minister, sympathized with the young Thomas, whose letter revealed how he felt "for them, lament[ed], greatly lament[ed] their uncommon hard fate, without being able to devise any means by which it [might] be ameliorated." His father responded to some of Thomas's questions, in particular, "You will perhaps ask why we do not treat them with more humanity? The answer (according to the elder Ruffin) was obvious: the fewer there are of this discription intermix'd with the Whites, the more they are under our immediate eye, and the more they partake of the manners and habits of the whites, and thereby require less rigidness of treatment."[11] The need to treat slaves with kindness through personal supervision, while still remembering that slaveownership was a trust passed from generation to generation and a legal part of civil society, became a firmly held tenet of Thomas's thought from an early age.

The sense that one had a personal responsibility for the well-being of others and the development of one's own moral standards grew more important for Ruffin once he himself became a parent. Historian James Carlson asserts that "Ruffin's letters to his children attest to his strong personal belief in a moral perspective on life."[12] He thought that all people needed to develop strong moral sensibilities in order to practice virtues and avoid baneful temptations. In 1824, Ruffin wrote to his eldest daughter that she should carefully select her books and then "apply the moral considerations arising out of them, by reflection, to [her] own heart and improvement."[13] This careful attention to moral growth and stewardship motivated Ruffin to resign from the state supreme court in 1859; he believed that performing public duties was a moral task, which should be given the most careful attention. His failing health moved him to put aside public office for the good of the state.[14]

Both natural law and legislative intention made a strong impact on Ruffin's judicial decisions. In at least one 1830s case, Ruffin used natural law to validate society's right to take private property by eminent domain, and he spoke about the "laws of nature and nations" which gave the government this theoretical and historical right to invade private property.[15] Yet Ruffin also saw that natural law could protect private property as well—its safeguard gave both the government and individuals conflicting rights.[16] In either case, the judge must refuse to render an opinion based solely upon his personal values; maintaining one's own moral vision meant not extending private values into the public sphere. Natural law must not be used to cloak and implement one's individual beliefs in weighty matters like a high court opinion.

Disinterested justice, for Ruffin, meant that the judge must seek the legislative meaning of a statute, even when the law clashed with a principle of moral right.[17] Individual opinions must give way to greater social needs, like those promoting and protecting slavery—the legislature would provide guidance about which social needs required the greatest protection.[18] Ruffin's extreme attentiveness to his state legislature's views may have evolved from North Carolina's peculiar government structure; North Carolina did not have a true state supreme court until the early nineteenth century, and at the time of Ruffin's appointment, the legislature dominated the process of judicial selection.[19] The state supreme court still seemed very young, and relatively weak, when compared with other branches of the state government.[20] And deferring to the state legislature on the issue of protecting slavery may not have taxed Ruffin too much, for as his family and financial interests became more dependent upon the economic success of slavery, Ruffin's early qualms about slavery's immorality seem to have faded into the background.

Despite his youthful understanding of the moral wrongness of slavery, Ruffin did not continue to reveal that more compassionate side of his character as he grew to manhood and began practicing law in the 1820s. Even to men who knew him well, Ruffin was remote, distant, and less than humane—and these were opinions about how he dealt with whites. Ruffin's manner in the courtroom as an attorney was notorious. A judge who had seen Ruffin practice for years wrote that "notwithstanding Ruffin's ability and reputation as a lawyer there were objections to him which many thought were well founded. His manner at the bar towards opposing litigants and opposing [w]itnesses was rough and often offensive, hardly ever courteous and not always respectful and frequently abusive. As a consequence he was unpopular with the common people and with many who were not very common." Ruffin's coldness toward others while still a lawyer became habitual, and was noted even when he became a judge. In comparing Ruffin with Archibald Murphey, another celebrated jurist of North Carolina, a man who had known both judges wrote that "Ruffin though not repulsive or displeasing in manner did not seem to possess that outflowing love of human kind which so greatly distinguished Murphey. . . . And while it may be truly said that Ruffin was honored and respected, it may be said that Murphey was equally honored and respected, as well as *universally beloved.*"[21] As a lawyer and close observer of people and events in Raleigh, William Valentine was elated when a new judge was selected to serve with Ruffin on the supreme court in the 1840s. Judge Richmond Pearson's presence on the court would be, in Valentine's words, "a wholesome check on the Chief Justice, Ruffin, who is complained [of] in being overbearing, and too much discarding practical common sense."[22]

Although Ruffin's long and illustrious career as lawyer and judge is well remembered, Ruffin the slaveowner and agriculturalist is routinely forgotten. His earliest slaveholdings were modest: ten slaves, given to him by his father and father-in-law, to commence married life in 1811.[23] Ruffin's profits from the courtroom he shrewdly reinvested in land and slaves to establish financial independence. By 1830, Ruffin owned thirty-two slaves, which he divided between his two plantations.[24] Ruffin held lands scattered in Rockingham County, Haywood County, and Alamance County. In the late 1820s he even owned land near Nashville, Tennessee, and considered speculating in land along the Cape Fear River.[25] Ruffin did not set out to become a planter, but as the son of a farming minister he understood the workings of a farm and enjoyed seeing his lands sustain his family.[26] Yet in the 1820s, 1830s and 1840s Ruffin left his Rockingham and Alamance plantations in the hands of overseers while he pursued his legal career; his work as an attorney kept him away from home weeks at a time, even as the number of slaves he owned gradually increased.

Although Ruffin believed himself to be a kind master, and his father had admonished him to be kind to his slaves and give them his personal attention, his plantations were ruled with fear and the lash. During one harvest, he hired additional slaves to do extra work, but one bondsman fled Ruffin's place and ran back to his true owner, Dr. James Webb, a friend of Ruffin's. Even though Webb returned the slave, in a letter to Ruffin he made it clear that he "really felt unwilling that Dan'l should return" because of his illtreatment.[27] Among the more unusual letters Ruffin received was one written by his teacher, mentor, and close friend Archibald Murphey, in June 1824.[28] Murphey found brutal treatment of slaves abhorrent, but he also was reluctant to "interfere in other People's business" and heartily disliked intruding into the affairs of a man like Ruffin, a man he admired.[29] Despite his qualms, Murphey summoned the courage to write Ruffin about "the evil and barbarous Treatment of your Negroes by your overseer." Murphey related how the slaves were "worked to death" and how some of the atrocities were "too revolting to be put on paper"—for example, the slave Will had been "literally barbecued, peppered and salted." To discover the truth of the matter, Murphey recommended that rather than relying on the words of the overseer, Ruffin look himself "to the Book of the Negro," namely, that he should examine the bodies of his slaves to find out what the overseer was really doing.[30] Webb and Murphey were not the only ones who notified the absent Ruffin about his overseer's callous behavior: Ruffin received letters from his wife, Anne Kirkland Ruffin, describing how the overseer mistreated Ruffin's slaves and how likely it was several of them would run away.[31] Twice a dissatisfied slave tried to burn the Ruffin home in 1835, an indication of the level of that slave's dissatisfaction and desire for revenge.[32]

Ruffin's precarious financial situation, throughout much of the 1820s and the early 1830s, required him to be absent from his farms for long stretches of time. Lawyers who wanted business had to ride circuit from court to court. On circuit, a lawyer might be "busy at all hours, for at night the lawyer had to consult clients and study for his cases the following day."[33] Ruffin regularly worked forty and fifty weeks per year, handling cases before county and circuit courts, and he routinely appealed lost cases to the state supreme court, which generated even more weeks of practice away from home.[34] The pace did not slacken once he joined the bench. After Ruffin became a judge, his workload did not diminish very much because of his insistence on writing the majority of opinions issued by the supreme court.[35] Yet Ruffin struggled with contradictory impulses: he wanted to contribute his full share of work on the bench, and yet he also wanted to be home, supervising operations on his farms. Money, or the lack of it, made Ruffin's choice to continue in law a clear one. Much as he desired the life of a full-time planter, Ruffin realized that "I cannot give up the income arising from my personal exertions . . . for my estate will not educate and provide for [my children]."[36]

As a mostly absentee owner in the 1820s, it should not surprise us that Ruffin's relations with the slaves on his own plantation were not close and chummy, although Ruffin clearly thought of himself as a paternalistic master and probably remembered the injunctions of his father to be an attentive, caring slaveowner.[37] He firmly subscribed to the principle of unconditional slave obedience, and he viewed truancy as a personal affront to what he supposed were ties binding slave to master: when one runaway was captured in 1858, Ruffin delayed the slave's punishment until he could administer it personally.[38] Yet Ruffin was distant from his own slaves; when questioned about the distinguishing marks of a captured runaway who might be his property, Ruffin responded, "I am not in the habit of examining the persons of my slaves minutely, and therefore am not able to give an exact description of this man."[39] Ruffin remained convinced of his paternal duties, even when he did not fulfill them. Years later, Ruffin delivered the presidential address to the state's agricultural society, describing his paternalistic outlook. "[T]he feelings between masters and their slaves . . . is kindly on the part of the former, and affectionately faithful on the part of the latter" and "the comfort, cheerfulness, and happiness of the slave should be, and generally is, the study of the master."[40] Hidden behind this open declaration of masterly affection was the dark secret each slaveowner knew. While Ruffin might believe that his slaves loved him as a father, he did not discuss in public the hidden underside of master-slave relations: the very real possibility that slaves would be sold from their families to another part of the South. Although Ruffin might act the paternalist's part, he did not do so consistently.

The most obviously unpaternalistic acts committed by Ruffin included interstate slave-trading in the 1820s, before his elevation to the North Carolina Supreme Court. Ruffin began trading in slaves in 1821 and continued this practice until 1826. He established a partnership with Benjamin Chambers, who actually bought and transported slaves from the Upper South to Alabama. Ruffin's original contribution was $4,000, the initial capital needed to buy the first groups of slaves who would be moved and then resold. The profits and the partnership ended after five years when Ruffin's trading partner, Chambers, died. One curious point is why Ruffin did not resume trading in slaves after Chambers's death. Certainly it was among the most profitable of all his enterprises, and his failure to renew it might suggest that he thought his neighbors or colleagues found his activities in the trade distasteful.[41] Although records of the partnership are scanty, Ruffin's notes show that the partnership turned more than a $6,000 profit during a three-year period; his plantation earnings were so doubtful in the 1820s that the profits from slave-trading must have seemed providential. The partners were paid in cash or in cotton, which could appreciate in value between the date of payment and their sale abroad. In 1825 alone, the Ruffin-Chambers profits were over $1,200, even including the loss of runaway slaves, slaves not sold, and expenses for food, shelter, wagons, horses, and transportation.[42] In addition to the profits gained, Ruffin also had first pick of the strongest slaves to add to his own North Carolina plantations, rather than have them sold in Alabama.[43]

Ruffin's involvement in slave-trading, even if only financial at heart, raises a difficult question: could Ruffin be sincere in his paternalism, and still engage in the sale of slaves for profit to the Deep South? Although I am skeptical that Ruffin's paternalism was more than skin-deep and a convenient emotion to be paraded among his agricultural peers, one recent chronicler of slave-trading would have had no trouble reconciling Ruffin's supposedly deep and abiding interest in his slaves with his repeated participation in the sale of slaves for profits. Historian Michael Tadman has suggested that slaveowners engaged in selective paternalism, by focusing on close relationships with "key" slaves while remaining aloof from other slaves they owned, creating a paternalistic series of relations with a few slaves while holding all others at arm's length, ready for sale.[44] This selective paternalism would later allow Ruffin to craft the *State v. Mann* opinion in such a way as to deny the basic humanity of bondsmen. Ruffin's close interest in specific slaves, like Jerry who supervised his gristmill, is evidence that he was concerned about some of the slaves he owned. He asked about them by name in the letters he wrote home.[45] However, Ruffin's long absences weakened the emotional connections between the master and his growing slave workforce.

When *State v. Mann* appeared as part of the supreme court's December 1829 docket, Ruffin must have been reminded of some events in his own life. After all, he too had rented slaves as seasonal workers, and his autocratic tendencies could have made him favor John Mann, the renter who shot Lydia as she tried to run away to her true master. *State v. Mann* was also one of Ruffin's earliest court cases as a justice. Ruffin was a new judge on the supreme court, having only been commissioned by the governor to join it in mid-January 1830.[46] The justices finally heard *State v. Mann* on February 15, 1830, the last day of the court's December 1829 term.[47]

On its surface, the case must have seemed unusual, even to a judge like Ruffin who had seen and heard a lot on the legal circuit: *State v. Mann* commenced as a criminal action when a Chowan County district attorney indicted John Mann for assault and battery against the slave Lydia. Assault and battery by a white man against a slave was a crime unknown in North Carolina's statutes; only at common law might the offense exist, and the supreme court would have to determine whether Mann's indictment could hold. Whether or not common law could be used to indict whites who attacked slaves was hotly debated in the South. Virginia and South Carolina rejected any claim that assault and battery upon a slave was indictable at common law, while Alabama and Texas endorsed the idea of common law crimes committed against slaves.[48] That a local official indicted Mann in the first place probably resulted from one of two reasons: Lydia's owner pressed for the indictment (but why would she not file a civil suit for damages?), or the offense seemed so heinous—a slave woman shot in the back—that it shocked local sensibilities.[49] Local officials rarely intervened when an owner struck or shot a slave, but Mann's situation was different; as the renter of Lydia, Mann might not automatically assume all the rights and controlling authority that belonged to her genuine owner. Whether the renter held the same rights as the true owner would be determined by Ruffin's opinion, in a case of first impression for North Carolina about the extent of renter's rights over slave property.

State v. Mann allows the historian unusual access to Justice Ruffin's evolving ideas about slavery, society, and the courts. He actually wrote three drafts of the *State v. Mann* opinion, and all three are reprinted in J. G. Hamilton's edition of Ruffin's papers. The three versions bear strong similarities to each other, each having five lengthy sections that are repeated almost verbatim in every draft.[50] The opinion that Ruffin delivered was the last of three handwritten copies that he created, two of which contain many similarities to the eventual printed version found in the state's reporters.[51] However, the earliest handwritten version of the *State v. Mann* opinion shows Ruffin's ideas in the raw, and it provides a clear view of which ideas he felt should be discarded or enhanced as he revised his opinion.

Between the first and second drafts of the *Mann* opinion, Ruffin deleted the only language that celebrated slavery's "benevolent" aspects. The entire last paragraph of his first draft spoke of the shared "pride as Citizens and sincere joy as men" that North Carolinians felt in the "every day improvements in the condition of slaves." Ruffin praised the legislature for making laws compelling owners to provide for their slaves, and he paid tribute to courts that protected slaves "from the cruelty and abuse of a stranger." He also wrote about the generally improved condition of slaves, how the "rigors of slavery" had been ameliorated by public opinion and common humanity through the years—he even focused on the benevolence of masters who practiced "as much indulgence" toward their slaves as public safety would allow.[52] This paean to the positive aspects of slavery did not resurface in the two later versions of the opinion; possibly Ruffin recalled his youthful letters to his father, in which he lamented the hardships of slavery. Alternatively, Ruffin may have removed this tribute to slavery's beneficial aspects when he considered how ironic it would sound given *State v. Mann*'s verdict, which acknowledged the court's incapacity to protect a slave from an owner's or renter's cruelty. And quite possibly Ruffin's own words, elsewhere in the opinion, may have spurred him to omit any commendation for slavery. Ruffin's gloomy appraisal of slavery's realities (the slave was "doomed in his own person and his posterity, to live without knowledge and without capacity to make anything his own"), found in all three drafts of the opinion, must have caused him to reconsider and remove this early tribute to slavery's nobler aspects.[53]

Ruffin also removed language which emphasized the severe punishments the master must inflict upon the slave, and the effect of slavery upon southern society. This time, the language he deleted between the first and second drafts discussed how masters suffered under the regime of slavery. "[C]onstant, vigilant, not unfrequently severe and exemplary and painful punishment of the slave is the unwelcome, and the necessary task of the master."[54] Given that slaves suffered physical chastisement, while the master's pain was only psychological, Ruffin chose to drop this sentence, and instead focus on slavery as a "curse to both the bond and free portions of our population."[55] His language recalls the views of his minister father, who would doubtless have taught Ruffin about the biblical "curse of Canaan" as a divine justification for slaveholding.

Despite the legal literature's portrayal of Ruffin as a moral monster, the drafting process allows us to see how Ruffin tried to expose the dilemma posed by this case. Rather than muffling his conscience, Ruffin's second and third drafts expound upon his own moral difficulties in *Mann*. Ruffin reined in his sympathies for slaveholders—much more vitally expressed in his first draft—and in his later drafts focused on John Mann's unseemly behavior, a person who would stoop to shooting a woman in the back. This shift in focus is highly ironic, given that Ruffin had already decided to clear Mann from criminal charges even in his earliest draft opinion. In the second draft, he reorganized the introduction to begin his opinion by emphasizing how repulsed he was by the particulars of *State v. Mann*. His now-famous line "A judge cannot but lament when such cases as the present are brought into judgment" found its origins in similar wording that he inserted at the beginning of the second draft. The entire first paragraph, including "the struggle in the judge's own breast" between his humanity and legal obligations, contained sentiments that Ruffin felt compelled to express rather than hide.[56] Ruffin's attitude toward the physical correction of slaves and the legal standing of whites who harmed them seems to be "that if the slave was still alive, the degree of correction could not have exceeded legal limits; if the slave died, it was indeed evidence that the punishment had gone beyond legal bounds." It may have been necessary for Ruffin to parade his sympathy for the victim here, since he knew that sympathy, and not legal redress, would be all she could obtain from the high court.[57]

As his drafting progressed, Ruffin inserted additional comments about how he abhorred the outcome toward which logic compelled him. In language deleted from the final version of *Mann*, Ruffin particularly emphasized that, as a judge, he preferred not to have to say anything about the brutality of slavery. "Courts are often compelled to act on principles, which outrage individual feeling."[58] In the final opinion, Ruffin found a more moderate way to articulate this sentiment: after stating that the power of the master must be absolute, he added, "I most freely confess my sense of the harshness of this proposition."[59] As the son of a minister who taught his son to care for his slaves personally but whose job forced him to leave them in the hands of brutal overseers, Ruffin's conscience must have been pricked, just a little, by the *Mann* opinion.

Logic overrode any sentimental appeals to what a judge *might* do—for Ruffin, the judiciary had a limited role, one defined by its relation to the legislature. If courts began prosecuting white owners and renters for assaulting their slaves, the state's intrusion into the master–slave relationship would eventually overwhelm the docket. But if Ruffin felt that the judiciary's hands were tied, those of the legislature were not. In his second draft (and continued in the final version of *Mann*), Ruffin wrote that judges could not simply impose their views on social relations: "We can not set our notions in array against the judgment of everybody else and say that this or that authority may be safely lopped off." His escape, if you will, from personal responsibility, was to invoke the language of judicial restraint, claiming that the legislature should take action, not the courts. North Carolina had no laws at this time which protected the slave from abuse at the hands of his master, a situation unlike South Carolina, Georgia, Louisiana, and Mississippi.[60] In each successive draft of the opinion, Ruffin increased the rhetoric of judicial restraint while pointing the finger at the legislature. Indeed, if any changes were needed in slave law, they must come from the legislature and most decidedly not from the bench, for Ruffin believed that the legislature's work would be "much more rationally expected" than any "rash expositions of abstract truths" expounded by the judiciary. That the supreme court had decided many cases relating to slaves in the preceding thirty years perhaps explains why Ruffin thought slave law should be defined by the legislature. Of the 1,156 cases heard by the supreme court between 1800 and 1830, a steadily rising number related to slaves (1800–1810: 31; 1811–1820: 63; 1821–1830: 82).[61] It seemed likely, to Ruffin, that the law could intervene in selected situations if masters acted barbarously, but "[t]he difficulty is to determine where a Court may properly begin." To interpose the court's authority and punish a cruel master would be "to redress an acknowledged evil by means still more wicked and appalling than even that evil," namely judicial activism.[62] Ruffin's reluctance to interpose the judiciary's views into slave matters may also have stemmed from the relative weakness of the state supreme court in North Carolina of the 1830s, or possibly Ruffin's very recent appointment to the bench.

While Ruffin drafted his opinion in *State v. Mann*, remarkable events in North Carolina and the surrounding region must have come to his attention. Surprisingly, the potential that these events had to influence Ruffin's thoughts has been overlooked by earlier scholars, who may have been misled by the dating of *State v. Mann* as an 1829 opinion.[63] The supreme court did not hear the case until mid-January 1830, and the published version of Ruffin's final opinion did not emerge until 1831. Ruffin's drafting process must have been under way by late January 1830, although the precise date when Ruffin delivered his opinion in the case cannot be ascertained either from court records or newspapers of the time. However, newspaper evidence suggests that Ruffin probably delivered the oral version of his *Mann* opinion on February 24; it seems unlikely that he had the written version completely drafted before the end of February 1830.[64]

Ruffin authored his *Mann* opinion in a strife-filled atmosphere fueled by insurrection rumors and an increasingly large, hostile free black community. The late 1820s witnessed explosive growth in North Carolina's black population, which contributed to a significant period of unrest among free blacks and slaves. The number of free blacks living in North Carolina had been growing rapidly in the first thirty years of the nineteenth century (rising from 7,043 in 1800 to more than 19,000 in 1830), increasing many whites' growing sense of unease.[65] Not only was the black population swiftly expanding, but many rumors circulated at the end of the 1820s, suggesting that free blacks might gain greater political rights and slaves could be liberated soon. These rumors probably stemmed from political activity in western Virginia, where white agitators resented the stranglehold that eastern Virginians had on state politics. Efforts to create greater equity between eastern and western whites generated a flood of literature discussing equal rights and fair representation, which hopeful slaves and free blacks could easily misinterpret as signaling a willingness by whites to accept blacks politically. In 1829–1830, Virginians finally met in a constitutional convention to iron out their east-west differences; bondsmen believed that the meeting was a discussion about freeing slaves, "and there were widespread reports of plots to free themselves if they were not emancipated."[66] Rumors circulated in Gloucester, Mathews, and the Isle of Wight counties that slaves planned to rise up against their masters.[67]

All along the eastern seaboard, slaves appeared restless from early 1829 to 1830, which made many southern whites nervous about the prospect of imminent slave insurrections.[68] In December 1829, inhabitants of Lenoir County petitioned North Carolina's legislature asking that they create a special task force to curb the activities of runaway slaves; before its second reading, twelve state senators asked that their counties also be added to the bill.[69] The widespread activity of runaway slaves in twelve different counties is likely to have been connected with Virginia's concurrent discussions of liberty and equality. In any case, whites and blacks were on edge at the end of 1829, anxious about political developments and the possibility of slave rebellion.

The nervousness of whites increased dramatically following the publication of David Walker's *Appeal*, which encouraged slaves to rise up against their masters and use violence to achieve their freedom.[70] Originally printed in Boston in September 1829, the *Appeal* began circulating among free blacks as early as December 1829 in Savannah, Georgia, and "[o]nly a week or two after first appearing in Georgia, the *Appeal* arrived in Virginia."[71] "[T]he mayor of Richmond found a copy of the dreaded publication in the home of a free Negro" in late January 1830.[72] Although the *Appeal* was much slower in arriving in North Carolina, Ruffin probably knew of the *Appeal*'s existence in Virginia before its arrival in North Carolina. Ruffin had close ties to Richmond through his family and, in particular, one cousin, Thomas Ritchie, who was editor of the *Richmond Enquirer*, to which Ruffin had a subscription. Ritchie penned a forthright editorial on January 28, 1830, about Walker's pamphlet, stating that he thought the *Appeal* was deliberately designed to stir up slave discontent in the South.[73] Walker's attacks on slave owners— "Are they not the Lord's enemies? Ought they not to be destroyed?"— echoed the language of Denmark Vesey, who also used language to sanction brutality against whites in the South in his 1822 South Carolina uprising.[74] One can only speculate about whether or not Walker's pamphlet actually reached North Carolina slaves in early 1830, but Ruffin, through letters or the newspaper of his cousin in Richmond, almost certainly knew about David Walker's pamphlet while drafting the *State v. Mann* opinion.

In the face of such outspoken race-based rhetoric, either by Vesey in 1822 or by Walker in 1829, Ruffin's writings about the absolute rights of owners to discipline their slaves without interference from the state's judiciary seem well attuned to the late 1820s racial climate.[75] In the greatest change between the second and the final drafts of *State v. Mann*, Ruffin inserted two lengthy sentences near the end of the opinion that hypothesized about how slaves might be encouraged by others to revolt against their masters. The first of these sentences seems to speak directly to Walker's influence: "No man can anticipate the many and aggravated provocations of the master which the slave would be constantly stimulated by his own passions or *the instigation of others* to give; or the consequent wrath of the master, prompting him to bloody vengeance upon *the turbulent traitor*—a vengeance generally practiced with impunity by reason of its privacy."[76]

Ruffin's suggestion that the slave might be prompted to rebel, and the master to retaliate, reveals what he thought would likely result from Walker's *Appeal* reaching southern communities. The outcome would be continued white supremacy, Ruffin confidently predicted, and the cost would be the lives of deluded slaves who suffered at the hands of vengeful owners. Nor did Ruffin wish for his writings to be misunderstood. If Walker's pamphlet reached the hands of slaves, Ruffin would not add the authority of the North Carolina Supreme Court to sanction a slave's violent outburst. Ruffin's opinion in *Mann* must be so clear, so plain, that it could never be blamed for "instigating" a slave to cross swords with his master. This may also explain the severity of *Mann*'s language regarding slave self-defense, which pervades all three versions Ruffin drafted. For that reason, Ruffin deferred again to the legislature: "The court, therefore, disclaims the power of changing the relation in which these parts of our people stand to each other."[77]

Aside from Walker's *Appeal*, and Ruffin's personal experiences as a planter and slave trader, another influence shaping Ruffin's opinion in *State v. Mann* can be traced to slave cases in other states. In 1985, historian Andrew Fede identified the intellectual connection between *State v. Mann* and a Virginia case of two years earlier, *Commonwealth v. Turner*.[78] He noted strong similarities that existed between the Virginia case's dissenting opinion, in which the judge explicitly noted that a slave's personal rights must be balanced against the necessity of punishment in a slave society, and Ruffin's majority opinion in *State v. Mann*, in which he balanced the needs of slavery as an institution against the slave's injuries at the hands of his master.[79] What Fede did not uncover was an even closer connection between *Commonwealth v. Turner* and *State v. Mann*: the author of the *Turner* dissent, Judge William Brockenbrough, and Thomas Ruffin were cousins who had known each other for decades.[80] Even though there is no extant correspondence to prove that Ruffin knew of Brockenbrough's specific dissent in that case, Ruffin's legal library was reputed to be vast, and the exchange of reporter volumes between neighboring states was quite common, particularly when family members were concerned. Even if he had not heard directly of *Turner*, Ruffin might have learned of its implications from *Fields v. State*, an 1829 Tennessee case that discussed Brockenbrough's dissent (mistakenly labeled as a North Carolina opinion).[81]

The balancing test Brockenbrough employed in his dissent relied upon the distinction between the slave as a thing and the slave as a person. He saw "no incompatibility" between "the full enjoyment of the right of property" by a master, and protecting a slave from "all unnecessary, cruel, and inhuman punishments."[82] According to Brockenbrough, because of the slave's unusual status as unfree, the common law protection extended to a bondsman might be modified and reduced when compared to the rights of other subservient persons (like servants, children, or pupils), but the common law would still recognize his basic humanity and protect him from abusive punishment: the master's right extended so far, and no farther. The slave's personhood trumped other factors Brockenbrough might have thrown in the balance, but chose not to. With his scales firmly tipped in the slave's favor, Brockenbrough turned to the "consequences of the doctrine which I have supported." He discounted any competing considerations when evaluating his solution: slaveholders would not be injured from protecting slaves in this fashion, nor would the "peace of society" suffer either.[83] On the contrary, Brockenbrough foresaw the salutary effects that his opinion might have had on Virginia society. "[W]hilst kindness and humane treatment are calculated to render [slaves] contented and happy, is there no danger that oppression and tyranny, against which there is no redress, may drive them to despair?"[84] By indicting the occasional Simon Legree, Brockenbrough believed it would discourage slaves from rising up and revolting against cruel masters.

In crafting *State v. Mann*, Ruffin refused to balance competing claims in the same manner as Brockenbrough had. How far should the master's power extend? Ruffin looked not to the slave's abstract rights as a person but instead to community practice and the basic truth of lifetime service to others. "The established habits and uniform practice of the country in this respect, is the best evidence of the portion of power, deemed by the whole community, requisite to the preservation of the master's dominion."[85] Rejecting any comparison of slaves to children, pupils, or apprentices, Ruffin focused on the difference between slavery and freedom. The difference in status between slaves and others also gave them a different purpose, one unlike the subservience of children or students to their masters: "With slavery it is far otherwise. The end is the profit of the master, his security and the public safety," Ruffin wrote, and this explained why slaves could be beaten to extremity. His language, which focused on the master's security and public safety, seems to echo Brockenbrough's dissent in *Commonwealth v. Turner*. How could slavery, which had as its chief purpose the master's profit, permit any interference in how the master controlled his slaves? Ruffin the slave trader certainly knew that slaves created economic benefits. And his statement about the absolute obedience of slaves was not based upon blind faith in Sambos, but in the iron necessity of servitude. The master's lash, not the slave's docility, gave slave society order. "Such obedience is the consequence only of uncontrolled authority over the body. There is nothing else which can operate to produce the effect."[86] Only later, at the very end of the opinion, when Ruffin is backpedaling from his result by focusing on the benign nature of slavery, does he refer to the affection and love masters and slaves had for one another.[87]

Ruffin's deliberate decision to turn away from the "slave as person" analysis explains his cruel rhetoric in *State v. Mann*, and made it far simpler to ignore the possibility of common law protection for slaves.[88] The subjugation of the slave could only be complete if he were treated as pure property, for to see it otherwise would be to change the very nature of what it meant to be a slaveowner. Being a master of slaves meant more than just the conversion of money into human flesh; for Ruffin and other southern whites, the ownership of another person conferred status, power, and in some circumstances, a degree of dignity. One could not lessen the degree of a slave's obedience without undermining the authority and power of the master. "The power of the master must be absolute, to render the submission of the slave perfect. . . . This discipline belongs to the state of slavery. They cannot be disunited, without abrogating at once the rights of the master, and absolving the slave from his subjection."[89] And with David Walker's pamphlet at the door, Ruffin would view unquestioning slave obedience and continued white domination as the paramount objectives of southern justice.

Almost twenty years later, when he heard *State v. Caesar*, Ruffin would scold his fellow justices for their failure to condemn the slave Caesar when he killed a white man who attacked his friend.[90] Using exactly the same phrase he had employed in *State v. Mann*, Ruffin proclaimed that judges must refrain from rendering "rash expositions" about abstract truths and slavery: their positions required them to promote "the stability of national institutions, and the common welfare."[91] Although he preferred the legislature to act, so that the judiciary could "merely interpret" their statutes, Ruffin would employ the language of judicial restraint while still judging, still choosing between different legal outcomes—for a judge must choose. For Ruffin, these difficult decisions reaffirmed the judiciary's commitment to sustaining and upholding the "peculiar institution."

Ruffin had several subsequent opportunities to abandon his *Mann* position, but he used them only to modify his opinion in the most limited circumstances. When *State v. Will* was decided in 1834, Ruffin remained silent while Justice Gaston found a slave not guilty of murder, for he had been provoked by an overseer whose hostile actions toward the slave bordered on homicide. Gaston said, "There is no *legal* limitation to the master's power of *punishment*, except that it shall not reach the life of his offending slave." This case is frequently cited as rebuffing *State v. Mann*'s severe dictum about the absolute power of the master over the slave, but in fact, Gaston clearly saw the right of self-preservation as a singular exception to the slave's duty of obedience to his master and claimed that *Mann* did not apply to the situation. "Unconditional submission," Gaston stated, "is the *general* duty of the slave; unlimited power is, in general, the *legal* right of the master." As to why Ruffin did not write a concurring or dissenting opinion in *Will*, he may have agreed with Gaston that *Mann* had no bearing on the outcome of *Will*. Ruffin's choice in *State v. Mann* would sum up his beliefs about slavery, and express them at a time when many southerners felt great fear about David Walker's pamphlet and the threat of racial warfare.[92]

Mixed among Ruffin's notes about supreme court cases there is a short list of biblical epigrams related to the law, scrawled in Ruffin's own distinctive handwriting. The first, from Ecclesiasticus, speaks about the nature of judging: "Deliver him that suffereth wrong from the hand of the oppressor; and be not fainthearted when thou sittest in judgement."[93] That Ruffin chose to keep this particular text among his legal papers tells us much about how he trusted Bible verse. Abrupt, stern, and capable of being severe with those around him, Ruffin's attitudes toward slaves were adequately reflected in the *State v. Mann* opinion: he might lament the brutality of slavery (as he had done at Princeton in his youth and as he acknowledged in his paternalist writings later on), but he recognized that a slave society must command a slave's absolute submission to authority. The master must make hard-nosed decisions about hiring overseers (even when brutal) and selling slaves (mostly for profit). Although Ruffin might be tempted to deliver a slave "from the hand of the oppressor" because he understood slavery's basic immorality, the unpleasant realities of slavery did not allow him to be "fainthearted" when he sat in judgment.

NOTES

Portions of this essay were originally presented as "The Worldview of Thomas Ruffin: Before *State v. Mann*" at the American Society for Legal History annual meeting, 1997. I thank Robert F. Berkhofer III, Alfred Brophy, Timothy Huebner, Mary McCormick, the commentators, William W. Fisher III and Stephen Siegel, and members of the conference audience for their insightful remarks, which assisted me as I revised this paper. Research on this article was funded by an Archie K. Davis Fellowship and the Florida State University History Department.

1. Robert C. Lawrence, "Thomas Ruffin: Greatest of the Chief Justices," Greensboro Daily News, December 22, 1940 in *North Carolina Collection Clipping File through 1975: Biography*, 127: 519, North Carolina Collection, University of North Carolina Chapel Hill (NCC); Roscoe Pound, *The Formative Era of American Law* (New York: Little, Brown, 1938), 4. Pound also selected John Marshall, James Kent, Joseph Story, John Gibson, Lemuel Shaw, Thomas Cooley, Charles Doe, Oliver Wendell Holmes, and Benjamin Cardozo.

2. *State v. Mann*, 13 N.C. 167, 170–71, 2 Devereaux 263, 267–68 (1829). See also *State v. Hale*, 9 N.C. 325, 328, 2 Hawks 582, 585 (1823).

3. Harriet Beecher Stowe, *Key to Uncle Tom's Cabin; presenting the original facts and documents upon which the story is founded* (Boston: J. P. Jewett, 1853), 78. Stowe, *Dred: A Tale of the Great Dismal Swamp*, 2 vols. (Boston: Phillips, Sampson, 1856). For analyses of Stowe's novelization of Ruffin and *Mann*, see Brook Thomas, *Cross-examinations of Law and Literature: Cooper, Hawthorne, Stowe and Melville* (New York: Cambridge University Press, 1987); Alice Crozier, *The Novels of Harriet Beecher Stowe* (New York: Oxford University Press, 1969); Alfred Brophy, "Humanity, Utility, and Formalism in Southern Legal Thought: Harriet Beecher Stowe's View in *Dred: A Tale of the Great Dismal Swamp*," paper delivered to the Harvard University, History of American Civilization Dissertation Colloquium, December 9, 1996.

4. *Souther v. Commonwealth* 48 Va. 338, 7 Gratt. 673 (1851).

5. On Ruffin's later opinions, see Thomas Morris, *Southern Slavery and the Law, 1619–1860* (Chapel Hill: University of North Carolina Press, 1996); Julius Yanuck, "Thomas Ruffin and North Carolina Slave Law," *Journal of Southern History* 21 (1955): 456–475; Mark Tushnet, *The American Law of Slavery 1810–1860: Considerations of Humanity and Interest* (Princeton: Princeton University Press, 1981). Only three studies have attempted to describe Ruffin's life in any detail: Blackwell P. Robinson, [Thomas Ruffin], unpublished manuscript, 1992, NCC; James Carlson, "The Iron Horse in Court: Thomas Ruffin and the Development of North Carolina Railroad Law" (master's thesis, University of North Carolina, 1972); and Sean C. Walker, "'The Lawyer May Be Altogether Sunk in the Farmer': Thomas Ruffin, Planter of Ante Bellum North Carolina" (honors thesis, University of North Carolina, 1994), NCC. Robinson's work is strangely silent about his legal writings and career as a judge, Carlson concentrates on his railroad jurisprudence, while Walker's study focuses specifically on his life as a planter.

6. The tangled scholarly web of slave law has been well described by Reuel Schiller, "Conflicting Obligations: Slave Law and the Late Antebellum North Carolina Supreme Court," *Virginia Law Review* 78 (1992): 1207–51. For *Mann* as an anomaly, see A. E. Keir Nash in "A More Equitable Past? Southern Supreme Courts and the Protection of the Antebellum Negro," *North Carolina Law Review* 48 (1970): 197–242, esp. 221–27; A. E. Keir Nash, "Fairness and Formalism in the Trials of Blacks in the State Supreme Courts of the Old South," *Virginia Law Review* 56 (1970): 64–100, esp. 70–76; John Kellam, "The Evolution of Slave Law in North Carolina: Supreme Court Decisions, 1800–1860," (master's thesis, Wake Forest University, 1992).

7. Basic information about Ruffin found in Blackwell Robinson's entry "Thomas Ruffin," in *Dictionary of North Carolina Biography*, ed. William S. Powell (Chapel Hill: University of North Carolina Press, 1994), 5: 266–67. Ruffin diary entry for March 26, 1805, states, "This day wrote to my father to inform him of my indisposition & of my determination on having Negroes." The subsequent entry suggests that Ruffin reconsidered his position almost immediately: "the feelings thoughts and opinions of one who is sick are to a well man almost inconcievable [*sic*]." 1805 diary, Thomas Ruffin papers, Southern Historical Collection, University of North Carolina (SHC).

8. Walker, "'The Lawyer May Be Altogether Sunk in the Farmer,'" 10. At Princeton, Ruffin also made friends who held antislavery attitudes, like Virginian William Garnett, with whom he maintained a correspondence for almost fifteen years. See Garnett to Ruffin, December 17, 1805, J. G. Hamilton, ed., *The Papers of Thomas Ruffin*, 4 vols. (Raleigh: Edwards and Broughton, 1918), 1: 93 (hereafter *Ruffin Papers*).

9. Sterling Ruffin to Thomas Ruffin, May 9, 180[5], Hamilton, ed., *Ruffin Papers*, 1: 53. Either Ruffin's diary or his father's letter must be misdated, and I have assumed that the father's letter is incorrect.

10. See Peter Kolchin, *American Slavery: 1619–1877* (New York: Hill and Wang, 1993), 87–92, on evolving attitudes among southern critics and defenders of slavery. For an elaborate discussion of the variant proslavery defenses developed in the 1830s and afterward, see Drew Faust, ed., *The Ideology of Slavery: Proslavery Thought in the Antebellum South, 1830–1860* (Baton Rouge: Louisiana State University Press, 1981). Ruffin's father may have sensed some rebuke from his son, for his comment in the June 1804 letter reveals his defensiveness on this subject: "You will not pretend to throw blame on the present generation, for the situation of these unhappy domestics, for as they are impos'd on us, and not with our consent, the thing is unavoidable." Hamilton, ed., *Ruffin Papers*, 1: 54.

11. Hamilton, ed., *Ruffin Papers*, 1: 54–55.

12. Carlson, "The Iron Horse in Court," 14.

13. Thomas Ruffin to Catherine Ruffin, February 10, 1824, Hamilton, ed., *Ruffin Papers*, 1: 290.
14. Thomas Ruffin to Governor John W. Ellis, November 5, 1859, ibid., 3: 49–50.
15. *Railroad v. Davis*, 19 N.C. 431, 435–37, 2 Dev. and Bat. 451, 456–58 (1837).
16. Carlson, "The Iron Horse in Court," 67–68.
17. *State v. Mann*, 13 N.C. 171, 2 Dev. 268.
18. Ruffin's great tragedy is that he refused to apply natural law when it came to the institution of slavery and balancing the needs of the individual against those of society. See pp. 16–17 for an analysis of his balancing test in *State v. Mann*.
19. Ruffin's later slave law opinions seem not to have the same rhetoric of judicial deference to the legislature.
20. Carlson, "The Iron Horse in Court," 15–18.
21. Judge Jesse Turner to Judge Archibald Murphey Aiken, undated, William H. Hoyt, ed., *The Papers of Archibald D. Murphey* (Raleigh: Uzzell, 1914), 2: 427, 429.
22. December 20, 1848, diary volume 9 (1848–1849), 113, William Valentine collection, SHC. It should be noted that Valentine's diaries reflect that he was a "very miserable, introspective man" with a "disagreeable disposition." Editor's survey note, William Valentine collection, SHC.
23. Walker, "'The Lawyer May Be Altogether Sunk in the Farmer,'" 31.
24. Ibid., 32.
25. Ibid., 52–53.
26. "His farming was not that of a mere *amateur* in the art, designed . . . to dignify retirement, to amuse leisure or gratify taste. . . . This he could not, or did not think he could afford, but to realize subsistence and profit, to make money." William Graham, "Life and Character of the Hon. Thomas Ruffin, Late Chief Justice of North Carolina" (Raleigh: Nichols and Gorman, 1871), repr. Hamilton, ed., *Ruffin Papers*, 1: 31.
27. Webb to Thomas Ruffin, January 16, 1823, Thomas Ruffin papers, SHC.
28. On the close relationship between Ruffin and Murphey, see "Thomas Ruffin," Samuel Ashe, ed., *Biographical History of North Carolina, from Colonial Times to the Present* (Greensboro: Van Noppen, 1906), 5: 351. Ruffin's willingness to tolerate such brutality in a person responsible for overseeing his slaves during his lengthy absences, and Murphey's insistence that Ruffin make a change of supervisor, run directly counter to Yanuck's interpretation that "Ruffin's papers reveal no ill-treatment of slaves." "Thomas Ruffin and Slave Law," 475. Murphey to Ruffin, June 3, 1824, Thomas Ruffin papers, SHC.
29. Murphey to Thomas Ruffin, March 27, 1824, Thomas Ruffin papers, SHC.
30. Murphey to Ruffin, June 3, 1824, Thomas Ruffin papers, SHC. The eventual editor of the Murphey papers, William Henry Hoyt, kept extensive correspon-

dence about how both the Ruffin and Murphey families wanted this letter suppressed—which it was—in the early twentieth century. Copy of letter from Murphey to Ruffin marked in Hoyt's handwriting "Cameron et al would not permit publication" in Archibald Murphey papers, North Carolina Department of Archives and History (NCDAH). "I would not publish . . . a letter of Judge Murphey to Judge Ruffin about his overseer maltreating his negroes. That was very much censured by all decent people. And of course Ruffin did not know of it. But I do not think I would bring that to view again. Let it sleep with the past." B[ennehan] Cameron to William Henry Hoyt, September 20, 1910, William Henry Hoyt collection, NCDAH. In response, Hoyt wrote, "If we are to print only the nice things about the men of the past, and say nothing about their shortcomings as public servants, how are historians to tell us who are our great men of the past? I feel almost dishonest in keeping from view facts which enable us to form a true estimate of the ability of men in public life." Hoyt to "Cousin Bennehan" [Cameron], September 23, 1910, William Henry Hoyt collection, NCDAH.

31. Webb to Ruffin, January 16, 1823, Thomas Ruffin papers, SHC. Anne K. Ruffin's letter described in Jean Anderson, *The Kirklands of Ayr Mount* (Chapel Hill: University of North Carolina Press, 1991), 52. The original letters from Anne K. Ruffin have not been located by this author.

32. Anderson, *The Kirklands of Ayr Mount*, 53.

33. Fannie M. Farmer, "Legal Practice and Ethics in North Carolina, 1820–1860," *North Carolina Historical Review* 33 (1953): 331. For a description of the circuits' physical size and how that affected justice, see Walter F. Pratt, "The Struggle for Judicial Independence in Antebellum North Carolina: The Story of Two Judges," *Law and History Review* 4 (1986): 136.

34. Farmer, "Legal Practice and Ethics in North Carolina, 1820–1860," 343.

35. In his first term on the bench, December 1829, Ruffin authored six of the ten written opinions. He shared the bench with Justices John Hall and Leonard Henderson. Hall wrote the other four opinions in that year. This pattern of authorship continued during the next twenty years Ruffin served on the bench.

36. Thomas Ruffin to Catherine Ruffin, January 14, 1836, Hamilton, ed., *Ruffin Papers*, 2: 154.

37. See references in his letters to his family "white and black," or references to "*my own* family," which included slaves, in Ruffin to Joseph Roulhac, October 3, 1846, and December 15, 1850, ibid., 2: 306, 246.

38. Richard M. Abbott to Thomas Ruffin, November 13, 1858, Thomas Ruffin Papers, SHC.

39. Ruffin to James Renfro, June 24, 1852, Hamilton, ed., *Ruffin Papers*, 2: 331. This letter was not written by Ruffin, but was instead edited and then signed by him,

suggesting that Ruffin merely endorsed a draft written by his overseer, since Ruffin wrote the vast majority of his own correspondence. The original handwriting is similar to that of his overseer. The draft and editing (in two different handwritings) would explain why Ruffin disclaimed any direct knowledge of the captured runaway, and then went on to give an extremely detailed description of the slave: "He is about 38 years of age; with a round face; wide mouth, strong teeth, and jaws, well set together; stout beard; dark Colour, but not fully black, and with enough yellow to show a slight admixture of white blood; is between (I think) 5 feet 6 and 5 feet 8 inches high, weighs, probably, about 160 lbs; and has a coarse or hoarse voice, with a surly countenance and gruff aspect, when not decidedly laughing." Ruffin Papers, SHC. Yanuck interprets Ruffin's lack of knowledge about the slave's features in a positive light, suggesting that his unwillingness to descend into descriptions of a slave's body markings gave the slave "such a measure of dignity." Yanuck, "Thomas Ruffin and Slave Law," 475.

40. "Address of Hon. Thomas Ruffin, of Alamance," October 18, 1855, *The Carolina Cultivator* 1 : 311, repr. Hamilton, ed., *Ruffin Papers*, 4: 323–37. For Ruffin, if a master was cruel, he was an aberration. "There are instances of cruel and devilish masters, and of turbulent and refractory slaves, who cannot be controlled and brought into subjection but by extraordinary severity. But these are exceptions, and rare exceptions." Ibid., 311. Ruffin's opinion that, overall, slaves in North Carolina generally experienced a more benign form of slavery than those living elsewhere has been debated by historians as eminent as Kenneth Stampp and Eugene Genovese. Genovese would contend that slaves living on small farms, which predominated in North Carolina, might fare better in treatment than those living on large plantations such as those found in the Deep South. Genovese, *Roll, Jordan, Roll: The World the Slaves Made* (New York: Vintage Books, 1972), 7–11.

41. Partnership papers, October 26, 1821, June 15, 1825, Thomas Ruffin papers, SHC. We know very little about Chambers except for the few brief papers connecting him to Ruffin in the SHC papers.

42. Volume 19, series 2, subseries 2.4 (1825–26, 1829), Thomas Ruffin papers, SHC. Ruffin's determination to make a profit would not keep him from selling an elderly slave away from his spouse. Ruffin's daughter wrote of how a longtime slave of Ruffin was sold against his will to a neighbor, in what appeared to be straight profit-making by Ruffin. Anderson, *The Kirklands of Ayr Mount*, 52–53.

43. Walker, "'The Lawyer May Be Altogether Sunk in the Farmer,'" 35.

44. Michael Tadman, *Speculators and Slaves: Masters, Traders, and Slaves in the Old South* (Madison: University of Wisconsin Press, 1989), passim.

45. Ruffin came into possession of the mill and Jerry when Archibald Murphey sold

them to him in 1821. Murphey to Ruffin, June 10, 1821, Hamilton, ed., *Ruffin Papers*, 1: 250. Other specific slaves in whom Ruffin showed particular interest include Jesse, the wagon driver who conveyed him to and from court sessions, and Henry, who was skilled in repairing mechanical implements. Walker, "'The Lawyer May Be Altogether Sunk in the Farmer,'" 48.

46. Although Ruffin was selected by the legislature to be a member of the court beginning with its December 1829 term, he was not officially commissioned as a judge by the governor until January 1830. Commission by Governor Jno. Owen to Thomas Ruffin, January 9, 1830, Governor's Letter Book 28, 154, NCDAH, repr. Hamilton, ed., *Ruffin Papers*, 2: 3. Ruffin's mind may have also been distracted from his work in late January because of escalating disagreements with William Kirkland Ruffin, his eldest son, who temporarily considered dropping out of college in January 1830. William K. Ruffin to Bryan [?], January 10, 1830, and William K. Ruffin to My Dear Father [Thomas Ruffin], January 25, 1830, Thomas Ruffin papers, SHC; William K. Ruffin to Thomas Ruffin, June 12, 1830, Hamilton, ed., *Ruffin Papers*, 2: 15.

47. Supreme Court Minute Docket, vol. 254, December 1827–June 1830, NCDAH.

48. *Commonwealth v. Turner*, 26 Va. 564, 5 Rand. 689 (1827), *State v. Maner*, 9 S.C.L. 249, 2 Hill 453, 454 (1834), *State v. Jones*, 5 Ala. 666 (1843) and *State v. Flanigin*, 5 Ala. 477 (1843), *Chandler v. State*, 2 Tx. 305, 309 (1847). In North Carolina, *State v. Hale* distinguished between a master's and a stranger's right to assault a slave. While "the law secures to the master a complete authority over [the slave]," the stranger had no right under the law to beat a slave at random. The stranger's recourse must be to go to court if the slave committed an offense. 9 N.C. 328, 2 Hawks 585. See Tushnet, *The American Law of Slavery*, 90–121.

49. That a slave's master could sue a renter for shooting the slave and damaging his or her value was later settled by *Copeland v. Parker*, 25 N.C. 340, 3 Ired. 513 (1843). Ruffin himself thought that a civil suit (brought by the owner against the renter) would succeed if the hirer inflicted a permanent injury by an "unreasonable and dangerous blow" instead of relying upon moderate correction, presumptively a whipping. *Jones v. Glass* 35 N.C. 209, 211, 13 Ired. 305, 308 (1852), Ruffin concurrence.

50. Hamilton, ed., *Ruffin Papers*, 4: 249–57.

51. A clear, final copy in Ruffin's handwriting, identical to the printed version, is in Supreme Court, Opinions, *State v. Mann* (No. 1870), NCDAH. The two earlier versions, much more heavily annotated and corrected, are in the Ruffin papers, SHC. The same pattern of early drafts in his private papers and the finished version in the state archives is repeated with *State v. Caesar*, 31 N.C. 269, 9 Ired. 391 (1849).

52. Hamilton, ed., *Ruffin Papers*, 4: 251.

53. Compare language on the lifelong drudgery of servitude in all three versions, ibid., 4: 250, 252–53, 256.

54. Ibid., 4: 250–51.

55. *State v. Mann*, 13 N.C. 170, 2 Dev. 266–67.

56. Here, the insights of Robert Cover, *Justice Accused: Antislavery and the Judicial Process* (New Haven: Yale University Press, 1975), 78, regarding Ruffin's unwillingness to obscure the "iron fist beneath the law's polite, neutral language" seem very clear.

57. Yanuck, "Thomas Ruffin and North Carolina Slave Law," 465. For a tabular summary of North Carolina's cases and their outcomes, see Tushnet, *The American Law of Slavery*, 106.

58. Hamilton, ed., *Ruffin Papers*, 4: 253–54.

59. Ibid., 4: 256.

60. For a review of protective statutes and their general ineffectiveness, see Morris, *Southern Slavery and the Law*, chapter 8.

61. Statistics from tables 3 and 4 of Kellam, "The Evolution of Slave Law in North Carolina." Of the cases heard between 1800 and 1830, twenty-five related to violent crimes committed upon African Americans by others. Table 9, Kellam, "Evolution of Slave Law in North Carolina." The North Carolina Supreme Court was called the "Court of Conference" from 1801–1811. William Adams, "Evolution of Law in North Carolina," *North Carolina Law Review* 2 (1924): 138.

62. *State v. Mann* 13 N.C. 171, 2 Dev. 268.

63. My analysis of *State v. Mann* comes closest to a reliance on Ruffin's judicial biography and ideology, merged with specific events of the period. Thus, it rejects the systemic analyses suggested by Fede, Nash, and Tushnet, while claiming kinship with the work of Schiller and Fisher.

64. Supreme Court Records, vol. 33, June 1829–1831, give brief transcripts of each case heard, followed by the official opinion entered by one of the judges. The handwriting is of such even and elaborate character as to suggest that the official record was created after all business had concluded and the clerk had time to recopy his notes (which are no longer extant). There is no official entry for *State v. Mann* recorded in vol. 33 by the clerk of court. The printed version of *State v. Mann* recorded in 2 Devereaux was published in 1831, and that volume contained opinions penned as late as December 1830. A brief notation in the *Raleigh Register* of February 25, 1830, states that the judgment of the lower court in *State v. Mann* was reversed, suggesting that at least a preliminary opinion may have been delivered, or the court's judges may have reached agreement on the case's

outcome, but no opinion is recorded in the newspaper. Ruffin's final written verdict in the case may have been delivered to Devereaux several months later. *Raleigh Register* microfilm, NCC.

65. Data on North Carolina's free black population from 1800–1860 drawn from the U.S. Census, summarized with maps showing distribution in John Hope Franklin, *The Free Negro in North Carolina, 1790–1860* (New York: W. W. Norton, 1943), 15–16.

66. Derris Raper, "The Effects of David Walker's *Appeal* and Nat Turner's Insurrection on North Carolina," (master's thesis, University of North Carolina, 1969), 9.

67. H. W. Fournoy, ed., *Calendar of Virginia State Papers* (Richmond, 1892), 10: 567–69, cited in Clement Eaton, "A Dangerous Pamphlet in the Old South," *Journal of Southern History* 2 (1936): 326.

68. Herbert Aptheker, *American Negro Slave Revolts* (New York: Columbia University Press, 1943), 281.

69. Discussions on December 28 and 30, 1829, and January 1 and 5, 1830, in state Senate, *Journals of the Senate and House of Commons of the General Assembly of the State of North Carolina, Session of 1830*, 91, 96, 100–101, 109, 125. Although the state Senate passed the bill, the state House of Commons indefinitely postponed taking action on the proposed law.

70. *David Walker's Appeal, in Four Articles; Together with a Preamble, to the Coloured Citizens of the World, But in particular, and very expressly, to those of the United States of America* (1829; reprint, with an introduction by Sean Wilentz, New York: Hill and Wang, 1995).

71. Peter Hinks, *To Awaken My Afflicted Brethren: David Walker and the Problem of Antebellum Slave Resistance* (University Park, Penn.: Pennsylvania State University Press, 1997), 134.

72. Eaton, "A Dangerous Pamphlet in the Old South," 329.

73. Editorial, "The Pamphlet," *Richmond Enquirer*, January 28, 1830. On Ritchie, see Hamilton, ed., *Ruffin Papers*, 1: 51, fn.1, and "Thomas Ruffin," Ashe, ed. *Biographical History of North Carolina, from Colonial Times to the Present*, 5: 350. Hinks speculates that the *Appeal* only arrived in Wilmington in August 1830. *To Awaken My Afflicted Brethren*, 137. Corroborating evidence for this view is found in James McRee (Wilmington Magistrate of Police) to Governor J. Owen, August 7, 1830, Governor's Letter Book, NCDAH. See also Raper, "The Effects of David Walker's *Appeal* and Nat Turner's Insurrection on North Carolina," 19–23.

74. Walker, *Appeal*, 25; Hinks, *To Awaken My Afflicted Brethren*, 33.

75. Obviously, the tension of the late 1820s and early 1830s became pronounced when Nat Turner's rebellion (which was followed by many more insurrection

threats, both imagined and real) sparked a wave of repressive legislation targeted at both slaves and free blacks across the South in the early 1830s.

76. Emphasis added. *State v. Mann*, 13 N.C. 170, 2 Dev. 267.

77. *State v. Mann*, 13 N.C. 170, 2 Dev. 267.

78. *Commonwealth v. Turner*, 26 Va. 560, 5 Rand. 678 (1827). The scholar who has attempted to contextualize *Mann* most closely to its social and cultural surroundings is Andrew Fede, "Legitimized Violent Slave Abuse in the American South, 1619–1865: A Case Study of Law and Social Change in Six Southern States," *American Journal of Legal History* 29 (1985): 93–150, esp. 126–42, although his contextualization has focused on the plantation system at large and its economic impact on southern society, rather than specific events of 1829–30. In the end, Fede reads Ruffin's *Mann* opinion as fully in keeping with other slave case verdicts that denied basic protections to bondsmen. Scholars who have shown Fede's limitations include Schiller, "Conflicting Obligations," 1249–50, and William W. Fisher III, "Ideology and Imagery in the Law of Slavery," *Chicago-Kent Law Review* 68 (1993): 1051–83.

79. *Commonwealth v. Turner*, 26 Va. 563, 5 Rand. 686 (Brockenbrough, dissenting).

80. Ruffin was related to Brockenbrough and Spencer Roane, who were his mother's first cousins. Family records, series 3.7, Ruffin-Roulhac-Hamilton Family papers, SHC. Brockenbrough and Ruffin exchanged letters on both legal and family matters in the 1830s, see Brockenbrough to Ruffin, February 7, 1831, January 4, 1835, January 21, 1835, Hamilton, ed., Ruffin Papers, 2: 27, 139. In the letter of February 7, 1831, Brockenbrough drew Ruffin's attention to *Commonwealth v. Turner*, calling it the most important Virginia case "touching the relation of Master and slave."

81. 9 Tenn. 141, 149, 1 Yer. 156, 165 (1829).

82. *Commonwealth v. Turner*, 26 Va. 564, 5 Rand. 689.

83. Ibid., 564, 5 Rand. 690. Others have interpreted Brockenbrough's balancing test to include slaveholder protection and societal peace, but the wording of his opinion makes it clear that these are not weights thrown in the balance but afterthoughts that he may have had to justify to other southerners. Having concluded his balancing test between the slave as person or property, he begins a new paragraph to discuss the consequences of his dissent.

84. Ibid.

85. *State v. Mann*, 13 N.C. 169, 2 Dev. 265.

86. Ibid., 13 N.C. 169, 2 Dev. 266.

87. Ibid., 13 N.C. 170, 2 Dev. 267–68.

88. At the 1997 ASLH conference, Professor William Fisher wondered if part or all of the *Mann* opinion was insincere, since its elements are not necessarily consistent with one another logically. I think that Ruffin's selective paternalism allowed

him to distance himself from the greater mass of enslaved persons, and support an extreme position that would deny the humanity of bondsmen. In the tension between instrumentalism and judicial restraint, Ruffin saw no inconsistency in urging the judiciary to support an existing societal structure (by telling slaves to mind their masters) while simultaneously advocating judicial restraint. For Ruffin, judicial restraint could extend so far as approval of social arrangements that masters (and slaves) had previously constructed.

89. Ibid., 13 N.C. 169–70, 2 Dev. 266.

90. *State v. Caesar*, 31 N.C. 269, 9 Ired. 391.

91. "Rash expositions," *State v. Mann*, 13 N.C. 268, 2 Dev. 171, and *State v. Caesar*, 31 N.C. 287, 9 Ired. 415.

92. 18 N.C. 173, 1 Dev. and Bat. 165–66. Thus, the various biographers of Gaston who have touted his apparent humanity in contrast to Ruffin's apparent inhumanity (as revealed in their opinions) have overstated Gaston's sympathies for the enslaved. Certainly Bartholemew Moore, counsel for the slave Will, presented Gaston with the opportunity to refute *Mann*'s absolute logic, but he declined. J. Herman Schauinger, *William Gaston, Carolinian* (Milwaukee: Bruce, 1949), 167. See also Patrick S. Brady, "Slavery, Race, and the Criminal Law in Antebellum North Carolina: A Reconsideration of the Thomas Ruffin Court," *North Carolina Central Law Journal* 10 (1979): 251–53. It is also possible that events at home drew Ruffin's attention away from the courtroom. Both his wife and daughter were hovering near death when *Will* was decided, and Ruffin was distracted from his work for one of the few times in his entire legal career. In *State v. Hoover*, Ruffin adopted the logic of *State v. Will*'s formulation, in a case where the master killed the slave through repeated beatings. Combining *Mann* and *Will*, Ruffin wrote that "A master may lawfully punish his slave; and the degree must, in general be left to his own judgment . . . [but] the master's authority is not altogether unlimited. He must not kill." *State v. Hoover*, 20 N.C. 500, 503 4 Dev. and Bat. 503 (1839).

93. Ecclesiasticus 4:9. The surrounding verses of this chapter describe ways in which man should improve himself through interaction with others: "Get thyself the love of the congregation, and bow thy head to a great man. Let it not grieve thee to bow down thine ear to the poor, and give him a friendly answer with meekness. Deliver him that suffereth wrong from the hand of the oppressor; and be not fainthearted when thou sittest in judgment. Be as a father unto the fatherless, and instead of an husband unto their mother: so shalt thou be as the son of the most High, and he shall love thee more than thy mother doth." *The Apocrypha: or, Non-Canonical Books of the Bible: The King James Version*, ed. Manuel Komroff (New York: Tudor, 1937), 162. In the 1800s, when Ruffin read the Bible, the Apocrypha would have been part of his text.

The Roots of Fairness: *State v. Caesar* and Slave Justice in Antebellum North Carolina

Timothy S. Huebner

Late on a warm summer night in 1848 in Jameston, North Carolina, two intoxicated white men, after napping for a while at a friend's house, headed across an open field and into town.[1] Drinking from a common bottle as they went, the two men soon stumbled upon two unfamiliar slaves lying on the ground near a storehouse. One of the white men, referred to in court records simply as Mr. Brickhouse, falsely identified himself and his friend as slave patrollers, and the two proceeded to harass the slaves and to inflict upon them a few "slight blows" with a "piece of board." Brickhouse and his companion, Kenneth Mizell, then asked the slaves if they might be able to "get some girls for them." Brickhouse added that he and his friend had plenty of money. The two slaves, named Caesar and Dick, refused to comply with the men's request, and at that moment another slave, named Charles, approached.[2]

The slaves' refusal to accede to the wishes of the white men prompted a violent confrontation. After again identifying himself and his friend as patrollers, Brickhouse grabbed Charles and ordered Dick to find a whip with which to beat him. Dick began to obey the order but then stopped and refused. The drunken white men reacted angrily to Dick's impudence. Brickhouse released Charles, and both of the men then focused their anger on the recalcitrant slave. Mizell grabbed Dick by the hand, and Brickhouse began to beat him about the head and side with his bare fists. As the blows continued and as Dick begged the two to stop battering him, Caesar and Charles looked on helplessly. Remarking to Charles that he "could not stand" to watch his friend being beaten, Caesar grabbed a nearby fence rail and, grasping it with both hands, struck Brickhouse in the head, breaking the "tolerably rotten" rail in two.[3] Still left with a piece of the rail in his hands, Caesar then hit Mizell once in "the left jaw and the left side of the neck," whereupon Mizell immediately fell to the ground.[4] No doubt terrified over what had transpired, for Caesar was by all accounts "obedient to white persons," the rail-wielding slave and his two companions fled.[5] A few hours later, after the two stunned white men had managed to return to their friend's house, Mizell lost consciousness and "blood and froth" began to run from his mouth and nose.[6] Caesar had killed Kenneth Mizell.

Two weeks after the incident, on August 29, 1848, a large crowd gathered at the county courthouse, a crude yet "venerable" old building elevated on posts or pillars just off the main street in Williamston, the county seat.[7] As the assemblage looked on, authorities ushered Caesar, "a man of ordinary size," before Judge John M. Dick, who brought this session of the Martin County Superior Court to order. A day earlier, a grand jury had issued an indictment charging Caesar with "feloniously, willfully and of his malice aforethought" killing and murdering Mizell, and Caesar now stood before the judge to respond to the charges.[8] Because the defendant's owners were children, Simon Latham, the father of the two boys who owned Caesar, played the legal role of the master in these proceedings. Acting in accordance with North Carolina law, Latham affirmed that he had been duly notified of the charges against his slave and that he had procured counsel for the defendant. The following morning, Caesar pleaded not guilty, and the judge and the attorneys spent the rest of the afternoon selecting and swearing in a twelve-man jury. The next day, August 31, Caesar stood trial for murder.[9]

Caesar's subsequent encounter with the justice system in Martin County and eventually with the state supreme court offers insights into the contours of slave justice in late antebellum North Carolina.[10] Most historians of the law of slavery have focused solely on the published reports of the appellate cases they have examined.[11] This approach neglects the proceedings at the trial level, as well as the specific local origins and context of appellate cases. Examining the experiences of individual slaves in the criminal justice system from beginning to end allows historians to view how the law of slavery functioned in antebellum southern society—that is, how local circumstances affected trial and appellate outcomes. Caesar's journey through the justice system demonstrates that, in some instances, "fairness and formalism" triumphed in North Carolina slave cases.[12] The state's relatively humane laws regarding slaves and free blacks, combined with the specific local circumstances and personalities involved in this case, afforded Caesar a measure of justice rarely found in the antebellum South.

At the time Caesar stood trial, the institution of slavery was a significant part of the social and economic fabric of Martin County and the entire northeastern region of North Carolina. In 1850, 3,367 slaves lived in the county, comprising 40.5 percent of the total population. Another 323 free blacks resided there, bringing the total share of the black population to 44.4 percent. The slave population had risen from 2,816 in 1840, an increase of 19.6 percent, compared to a corresponding 4.0 percent increase in the white population over the same period. All of the surrounding counties, moreover, had similar or even higher proportions of African Americans in their respective populations, and a few of these stood above 50 percent.[13] A large majority of Martin County's white residents, of course, did not own slaves, and most slaveholders, with a few notable exceptions, owned only a few. Still, the numbers reveal that slavery in Martin County and the surrounding area thrived well into the antebellum period.[14] Aside from agriculture, many of the county's slaves were employed in the area's timber industry, as well as in the fishing and commercial trades in the county's three small towns, all of which rested along the Roanoke River. Fairly typical of slaves in the region, Caesar, according to the record of his trial, "was employed in getting timber."[15]

The relative strength and significance of slavery in northeastern North Carolina, however, did not translate into a comparatively harsh or oppressive legal climate for African Americans. Measured against the other old seaboard states—Virginia, South Carolina, and Georgia—North Carolina's slave code was by far the most lenient.[16] Beginning in the 1790s, the state began "humanizing" its laws so as to grant slaves a greater degree of rights in criminal trials. During the eighteenth century, "Negro courts" had meted out hard justice for slaves accused of crimes, but the state abolished these tribunals in 1807 and began gradually to extend procedural guarantees to slaves. Trial by jury, benefit of clergy, and eventually the right of a full common law trial, conducted as if the accused were a free white man, were all granted to slaves by the 1820s.[17] Free blacks, moreover, enjoyed many legal rights and privileges in North Carolina. The state boasted many large property holders (including several slaveholders) among its free black population, and until 1835, free African Americans even retained the right to vote. Most important, North Carolina's free black population, the third largest of any state in the South, was unique in its overwhelmingly rural and agricultural character. In a state with no urban centers to speak of, whites apparently tolerated a significant degree of interaction among free blacks and slaves across the countryside.[18]

This comparatively loose pattern of race relations—where free blacks retained a degree of liberty and associated closely with slaves—apparently prevailed in Martin County. The fact that Caesar and his friend Dick could be "lying on the ground near a storehouse" at about 11:00 P.M. and that another slave could wander up to them upon hearing their conversation suggests that none of these slaves feared that their behavior violated local convention. Caesar, after all, was "obedient to white persons," and he likely did not aim to defy white authority by talking and resting with his friend at the end of the workday.[19] Moreover, there probably was no need for, or no recent activity on the part of, the local slave patrol. The three slaves involved in this incident, given their reaction, must have known that the drunken Brickhouse and Mizell were lying when they identified themselves as patrollers. As there had not been a serious insurrectionary scare in that part of the state in nearly half a century, the patrol was probably rarely active in Martin County.[20] Caesar's killing of Mizell, therefore, caused no hysteria among the local white population. Martin County whites feared neither that slaves were on a rampage nor that rebellion was at hand. Instead, the wheels of justice began to turn, and Caesar's case came before the superior court.

Attorney General Bartholomew F. Moore, appointed to his position just a few months earlier after a distinguished legal career, led the effort to prosecute Caesar. A graduate of the University of North Carolina, Moore had been practicing law since 1823 and had taken part in the North Carolina constitutional convention of 1835. Afterward, he served in the state House of Commons, where he advocated internal improvements, public education, and improved care for the mentally ill and orphans.[21] Moore was best known, however, for his argument before the North Carolina Supreme Court in *State v. Will* (1834). In that case fourteen years before, Moore had contended on behalf of the defendant that a slave had the right to protect himself from unlawful violence at the hands of an overseer. Impressed with the forceful logic of his argument, the state supreme court held that if, in the defense of his life, a slave killed his overseer—or his master—the homicide was to be mitigated to manslaughter. In the case of Caesar, ironically, Moore found himself on the other side, condemning the slave on behalf of the state for the murder of a white man.[22]

Asa Biggs, one of the most renowned lawyers in the eastern half of the state and a friend of Simon Latham, Caesar's master, defended the accused. Born, raised, and educated in Martin County, Biggs had entered the practice of law in 1831 and over the next several years succeeded in both the legal profession and the political arena. He served in the state House of Commons, the state Senate, as well as the U.S. House of Representatives, and, at the time of Caesar's trial, was actively involved in the 1848 presidential campaign of Democratic candidate Lewis Cass.[23] Coincidentally, one of Biggs's own slaves, named Peter, was arraigned and tried for murder during the same court session as Caesar, although Peter stood accused of killing another's slave rather than a white man, a crime of considerably less magnitude. Still, Biggs, fearing his own loss of property at the hands of the state, could no doubt sympathize with Latham's desire to see Caesar acquitted. Latham, a man of local prominence and the owner of thirteen slaves, had hired Martin County's best attorney to defend his slave.[24]

The State's case was relatively simple, for there was little disputing the facts of what had occurred late that night near the storehouse in Jameston. Attorney General Moore called Brickhouse (the companion of the deceased Mizell), as well as the two other slaves, Dick and Charles, to the stand, and all testified that Caesar had struck both the white men with a fence rail. Moreover, another slave named Whitmell, to whom Caesar had run after he had hit Mizell, testified that Caesar told him he had taken a rail and knocked the two men down, "one for dead." In light of the overwhelming evidence that Caesar had attacked Mizell, the attorney general insisted that the slave was guilty of murder.[25]

In Caesar's defense, Biggs contended that the charge of murder ought to be reduced to manslaughter. Under common law, manslaughter was defined as "the unlawful killing of another without malice either express or implied" and without premeditation or deliberation. Voluntary manslaughter, which occurred "upon a sudden heat," usually arose from provocation. Murder, in contrast, depended upon the existence of malice, "the dictate of a wicked, depraved, and malignant heart." Biggs argued that these common law definitions ought to apply to slaves. This was a particularly controversial point, for under existing precedent an "ordinary assault" by a white man upon a slave did not constitute grounds for mitigating a charge of murder to manslaughter.[26] Yet, given the peculiar circumstances of this incident, Biggs claimed, "the time, the manner, the drunken situation of the white men, their conduct on that occasion, being utter strangers to the Negroes and the Negroes to them, were naturally calculated to provoke a well-disposed slave into a violent passion." This was no ordinary assault, Biggs argued, and Caesar's crime therefore was not murder. The slave swung the fence rail in a sudden burst of passion caused by the injuries being inflicted upon his friend, not in a malicious attempt to end the life of Mizell. In a final effort to convince the jury of the impulsiveness rather than the malevolence of Caesar's actions, Biggs contended that the fence rail could in no way be considered a deadly weapon.[27]

At the conclusion of testimony and argument, Judge Dick issued a charge to the jury that clearly favored the prosecution. First, the judge instructed the jury that if the evidence satisfied them beyond a reasonable doubt that Caesar had slain Mizell with a fence rail in the way described by witnesses, then it was a clear case of murder. This, of course, was the same argument made by the attorney general. Second, Judge Dick directly challenged the defense's claim that the fence rail was not a deadly weapon by describing the rail as "an instrument in the hands of a stout man, calculated to produce death or great bodily harm." It was, therefore, in the judge's words, "in law, a deadly weapon." Finally, the judge took issue with Biggs's central contention—that the circumstances of the incident mitigated the charge from murder to manslaughter. Instead, Judge Dick described what had occurred that night between the two white men and the three slaves as "nothing more than ordinary assaults and batteries" that, under existing precedent, "would not amount to legal provocation so as to extenuate the killing from murder to manslaughter." In his instructions to the jury, in short, the judge destroyed the foundations of Caesar's defense.[28]

Though Judge Dick was well aware of the precedent relevant to this case, his questionable interpretation of the law might have resulted from incompetence on his part.[29] A gentleman planter of moderate wealth from nearby Guilford County, Judge Dick had gained his position on the bench more for political reasons than because of his legal expertise. At least a few observers within the North Carolina legal community severely criticized him for his "muddy and halting" knowledge of the law. "He seems not to have a legal mind," wrote William D. Valentine, a lawyer in the eastern part of the state, "and shuns conversation on law when he can."[30] Another lawyer, James W. Bryan, confided to his brother John Heritage Bryan, "It would make you split your side to hear [lawyer George E.] Badger talk about his qualifications." Judge Dick, in short, left much to be desired as a jurist, though he undoubtedly did the best he could in light of his lack of training. Nevertheless, his charge in Caesar's trial clearly damaged the defense.[31]

With the judge's instructions in mind, the jury not surprisingly rendered a guilty verdict, though at least one of the jurors took no joy in condemning Caesar. In a letter describing his service on the jury, William Slade, a local attorney, concluded, "I never before had to perform a like painful duty, and I earnestly hope I never may again." After the verdict had been announced at the end of the day (Caesar's entire trial lasted only a day), authorities took the convicted slave back to the county jail.[32] Two days later when Caesar again appeared before the judge for sentencing, Biggs moved for a new trial, citing Judge Dick's charge as a "misdirection of the Court as to the law applicable to the circumstances of the case." Biggs also contended that a technical error had taken place in the process of jury selection. After listening to arguments on these points by both attorneys, Judge Dick overruled the motion for a new trial. Then he ordered that the slave be escorted back to the county jail until Friday, October 20, when he was to be taken "to the place of execution" to "be hanged by the neck between the hours of twelve o'clock noon and four P.M. until he be dead."[33]

Acting on Caesar's behalf, Biggs immediately requested an appeal to the North Carolina Supreme Court, a right which slaves retained under North Carolina law. Judge Dick granted the appeal upon Caesar's "entering into bond of $200 with W. K. A. Williams and William C. Eborn." While the relationship between these two men and Caesar's master is unclear, Eborn was the second wealthiest man in Martin County, and his generosity in covering these court costs undoubtedly assisted Latham and his attorney in their efforts to overturn the conviction. Having for the time avoided the noose, Caesar returned to jail and waited to find out what would happen to him next. On November 30, 1848, Biggs formally filed the appeal with the supreme court.[34]

The following summer, during its June term, the North Carolina Supreme Court met in Raleigh to decide Caesar's fate.[35] Chief Justice Thomas

Ruffin, a former speaker of the House of Commons and president of the State Bank, was the court's dominant personality. During his career as a lawyer, Ruffin had been renowned for his toughness—almost belligerence—in the courtroom, and in his twenty years as a justice he had developed a reputation for carefully considering the broad public policy implications of his decisions. His most famous opinion in a slave case, for example, had allowed a white man to shoot a fleeing slave in the back, a ruling necessary, Ruffin believed, "to render the submission of the slave perfect." [36] Frederick Nash, a member of the court since 1844 and a long-time superior court judge, and Richmond M. Pearson, an eminent North Carolina law teacher appointed only six months before Caesar's case, labored in the shadow of the indomitable chief justice. [37]

Upon reviewing the grounds for the appeal, the supreme court heard arguments in the case of *State v. Caesar, a Slave*. After Attorney General Moore again made the case against Caesar, Biggs countered with a compelling argument criticizing Judge Dick for his charge at the trial. Specifically, Biggs questioned why the judge had taken it upon himself to instruct the jurors that the attack on Caesar's companion was nothing more than an "ordinary battery," and, moreover, why the judge had defined the fence rail as a deadly weapon. As no settled law existed as to what constituted an "ordinary battery" or a "deadly weapon," Biggs claimed, the jurors would have been fairer judges of such matters. "Their personal security has influence on one hand and the protection of the right of slave owners has the influence on the other," he argued. "There is nothing inconsistent with public policy or security in reference to slavery that ought to take from the jury the decision of these questions." [38]

Biggs then took aim at the content of Judge Dick's charge. Contending that the assault upon Caesar's friend was not just an ordinary battery, Biggs launched into a scathing attack on the conduct as well as the social position of the two aggressors, Brickhouse and Mizell. "Here are two drunken, worthless white men found at a late hour of the night . . . placing themselves below the rank which the law assigns them in deference to their color," he argued, "appealing to the slaves to become their pimps and assisting in acts of lewdness and prostitution, and because [the slaves] refuse, assuming the . . . position of patrollers." In light of the peculiar sequence of events surrounding the killing, Caesar's actions were not those of a murderer. "What was better calculated to excite the anger of a well disposed Negro than the circumstances of this case," Biggs concluded. As precedents had established no clear rule as to the rights of slaves in such instances, Biggs urged the court ought to adopt the same rule had all the parties to this incident been white men.[39] Were that the case, the crime clearly would be reduced to manslaughter.

Rarely did members of the nineteenth-century North Carolina Supreme Court deliver their opinions separately, but in this remarkable case, owing to the significance of the issues involved, all three justices wrote opinions. Justice Pearson, for his part, sympathized with Caesar's plight. The attack by Brickhouse and Mizell, in Pearson's view, was not an ordinary battery on a slave, permissible under law. Instead, taking his cue from Biggs, Pearson evaluated the case as if all those involved had been white men and applied common law principles. Under common law, the charge of murder was reduced to manslaughter when one killed "because of the passion which is excited when one sees his friend assaulted." Moved by Biggs's description of the circumstances surrounding the killing, Pearson portrayed Caesar as an "obedient slave, submissive to white men," who had patiently endured the initial beating and harassment inflicted by Brickhouse and Mizell. In subsequently hitting the two men with the fence rail, Caesar had merely yielded to a "generous impulse and come to the rescue" of his friend. Brickhouse and Mizell, in sharp contrast, were "two drunken ruffians," in Pearson's words, whose "fury and disappointed lusts" had incited them to harm the slaves. Concluding, Pearson asked, "Are we not forced, in spite of stern policy, to admire, even in a slave, the generosity which incurs danger to save a friend?" Swayed by Biggs's compelling characterization of the incident, Pearson ruled that Judge Dick had erred in charging the jury that there had been no legal provocation in this case.[40]

Still, Pearson expressed concern about the policy implications of his decision, and he noted that "any departure from the known and ordinary rule of the law of homicide" was "called for to a very limited extent." He went to great lengths to make clear that, in order for the killing to be extenuated to manslaughter, it had to take place "at the instant" and that the instigating blows upon the slave had to be "severe" rather than "slight." Moreover, not wanting to send the message that he was condoning Caesar's violent behavior, Pearson concluded his opinion with a plain reminder of its meaning: "A conviction of manslaughter is far from being an acquittal; it extenuates on account of human infirmity, but does not justify or excuse. Manslaughter is a felony. For the second offense life is forfeited."[41] Perhaps befitting his status as the court's newest member, Pearson maneuvered carefully through this potentially explosive case.

In a more succinct opinion, Justice Nash also ruled in Caesar's favor. Nash centered his analysis on the question of whether Caesar was entitled to the same consideration as if he himself were being victimized. Under *State v. Will* (1834) and *State v. Jarrot* (1840), both of which involved slaves who had killed whites while excessive violence was being inflicted upon them, the court had reduced the charges to manslaughter. Nash pointedly criticized Judge Dick for failing to take full account of these precedents in his instructions to the jury. For that reason, Nash held that there was error in the charge and that Caesar deserved a new trial.[42] But the question remained: could Caesar claim the same rights as a slave who was being assaulted?

Lacking any precedents adaptable to the exact factual situation of Caesar's case, Nash hesitated to formulate a new legal rule. Instead, like Pearson, Nash turned to the common law for guidance. As Biggs had demonstrated in his argument and Pearson had wholly accepted in his opinion, under common law, if all the parties in this incident had been white men, Caesar's crime would have been mitigated to manslaughter. Because neither the court nor the legislature had previously considered the case of a slave killing a white man while coming to the aid of his friend, Nash refused to abandon common law principles and create a distinct rule that applied to slaves. "I fully admit that the degraded state of our slaves requires laws different from those applicable to white men," he reasoned, "but I see no authority in the courts of justice to make the alteration." Instead, Nash devoted much of his opinion to praising the common law for shedding "a steady light upon the path of the jurist." "Why should I desert this safe guide to wander in the mazes of judicial discretion?" he asked.[43] Although neither seemed ready to champion the cause of a slave who had murdered a white man, both Pearson and Nash viewed Caesar as an individual and attempted to understand his predicament. Both justices ruled in his favor, and Caesar won a new trial.

Rendered uncharacteristically powerless by the ruling of his colleagues, Chief Justice Ruffin vigorously dissented. Pearson and Nash had conferred upon Caesar all the rights that a white man would have assumed under the common law in an identical situation. Ruffin, in contrast, began by arguing that fundamental differences existed between the legal rights of slaves and whites. About these distinctions Ruffin was adamant. "It has been repeatedly declared by the highest judicial authorities, and it is felt by every person, lay as well as legal," Ruffin argued, "that the rule for determining what is a mitigating provocation cannot, in the nature of things, be the same between persons . . . who stand in the very great disparity of free whites and black slaves." All efforts by Pearson and Nash, therefore, to extend common law principles to Caesar's case were nonsense. Slaves were not the same as white men, and to argue that they were denied, as Ruffin quoted his predecessor Chief Justice John L. Taylor, the "actual condition of society and the difference between a white man and a slave."[44]

Ruffin believed that what had occurred between the two white men and three slaves that night in Jameston was nothing more than ordinary battery. The best evidence for this, he contended, was the behavior of Dick, the slave under assault. "Did [the blows of the white men] make his blood boil and transport him," Ruffin asked, "so that, being wrought into a tempest of passion, he attempted in retaliation to slay his assailant, or even to join battle with him?" Because the beleaguered slave did not resist his assailant, but instead begged and pleaded that he stop battering him, Ruffin argued that Caesar's actions on behalf of his friend were unjustified. How, Ruffin wondered, could the battery upon Dick be considered a provocation to kill, "when, from the evidence of the man upon whom it was made, we see clearly that in fact it was not, and produced in him no such impulse."[45]

Dick's fainthearted reaction, moreover, simply confirmed, in Ruffin's mind, the Sambo nature of most slaves and highlighted the uncharacteristic cruelty of Caesar's act. Dick behaved just as slaves usually did under such circumstances, which proved, according to Ruffin, that slaves were inherently docile beings. "It is an incontestable fact that the great mass of slaves— nearly all of them—are the least turbulent of all men," Ruffin wrote, "that, when sober, they never attack a white man; and seldom, very seldom, exhibit any temper or sense of provocation at even gross and violent injuries from white men." To Ruffin, slaves were Sambos, and because Caesar violated this notion of normative behavior, Ruffin could in no way sympathize with his actions. Caesar's behavior did not arise from a "generous impulse," as Pearson had claimed, but "from a bad heart—one intent upon the assertion of an equality, social and personal, with the white, and bent on mortal mischief in support of the assertion."[46] In short, Ruffin's narrow conception of acceptable slave behavior permitted no deviation. To Ruffin, Caesar was not just a murderer—he was a potential revolutionary.

Given his ideas about the differences between slaves and whites, as well as his narrow notion of slave behavior, Ruffin was shocked and dismayed at the opinions rendered by his colleagues. Throughout his opinion, Ruffin implied that Pearson and Nash had overstepped the bounds of judicial discretion and, in the process, had lost touch with the reality of southern society. Judges, Ruffin warned, "should be and are proportionally cautious against rash expositions, not suited to the actual state of things and not calculated to promote the security of persons, the stability of national institutions, and the common welfare."[47] While Pearson and Nash had approached the case by viewing Caesar as an individual, with whom they could sympathize, Ruffin kept policy considerations at the forefront of his mind. In other words, whereas Pearson and Nash were willing to consider the case of the individual slave, Ruffin focused relentlessly on the institution of slavery.

The irritated chief justice concluded his opinion with an ominous warning to his brethren against the "dangerous" implications of their decision. "First denying their general subordination to the whites," he wrote of the slave population, "it may be apprehended that they will end in denouncing the injustice of slavery itself, and, upon that pretext, band together to throw off their common bondage entirely." Clearly exasperated with the reasoning of his colleagues, Ruffin lastly commented, "I have never heard such a position advanced before, either as a doctrine of our law or as an opinion of a portion of our people."[48]

Despite Ruffin's vehement protests, Caesar had won a new trial. Two months after the supreme court's decision, on August 28, 1849, almost a year to the day after his arraignment, Caesar again appeared at the courthouse in Williamston before the Martin County Superior Court. While the record of this second trial is extremely brief and the judge's name is not stated, Caesar pleaded not guilty to the charge of murder. Upon instructions from the judge, apparently revised in light of the supreme court's recent decision, a new twelve-man jury found Caesar "not guilty of the felony of murder as charged in the bill of indictment, but guilty of the felonious slaying of the said Kenneth Mizell."[49]

When asked by the judge why he should not be sentenced to die, Caesar, according to the record, "prayed the benefit of clergy," which the court extended to him. English tradition had permitted a person condemned to death to claim this privilege, whereupon the court would present the criminal with a Bible and ask him to read a specific verse invoking the mercy of God. This reading averted the death penalty. During the eighteenth century the concept of benefit of clergy found its way into the American legal system as an expeditious means of dealing with convicted felons before the rise of penitentiaries, though American jurisdictions usually abolished the reading test. After a felon prayed benefit of clergy, the court would order some form of punishment, usually either a public whipping or branding. Even with the growth of the penitentiary, in the South it was advantageous to neither slaveholders nor the state to imprison slaves convicted of felonies, and benefit of clergy continued to exist for slaves well into the antebellum period. North Carolina maintained the privilege for slaves until 1854, longer than any other state except South Carolina. Under North Carolina law, slaves were entitled to "the benefit of clergy, in like manner with a free man."[50]

After granting benefit of clergy, the court ordered that "the prisoner Caesar be branded on the brawn of the left thumb with the letter 'm' and be discharged on payment of all costs." Caesar was then "branded in open court," according to the record, forever marked as guilty of manslaughter. He then presumably returned to his master, Simon Latham. As Caesar walked out of the old courthouse that day in Williamston, free from any additional punishment at the hands of the state, so too did he step off the pages of history and into obscurity.[51]

Caesar's experience with the justice system in North Carolina reveals that a multiplicity of legal, social, political, and personal circumstances—all related to one another—combined to produce the outcome in this case. At the most basic level, the slave code of North Carolina afforded Caesar procedural guarantees throughout his journey through the justice system. A trial in the local superior court, a twelve-man jury, the right to counsel, the opportunity for Caesar's slave companions to testify, and the benefit of clergy, all arose out of the state's relatively humane slave code. Most important in this case, the right of appeal to the state supreme court meant that Caesar's case did not come to an end after the Martin County jury had rendered its verdict. Without laws specifying these guarantees—particularly the right of appeal—Caesar's fate certainly would have been different.

The social context within the local community played an even more significant role in determining the outcome in this case. The absence of a fear of slave insurrection among whites in northeast North Carolina during this period created a sense of security that allowed the guarantees of the state's slave code to be implemented and permitted Caesar to receive a fair trial in

Martin County. Community opposition never threatened the legal process, and jurors neither reveled in Caesar's conviction nor demanded his execution. Indeed, had it not been for the charge of a marginally competent judge, who seemed eager to convict the slave, the verdict rendered at the trial might have been different.

Within this local environment, the social status of Caesar's master as well as that of his victim also played a pivotal part in the legal treatment of the slave. Latham's reputation as a property holder and slaveowner, coupled with his connection to local notables like Asa Biggs, undoubtedly assisted him in his efforts on behalf of Caesar. Brickhouse and Mizell, on the other hand, apparently lacked any meaningful connections to the community. Neither was listed in the 1840 or 1850 census, and neither appeared in the Martin County deed books. Biggs described them as "worthless vagabonds" and Pearson referred to them as "drunken ruffians." Indeed, no one involved in this case, not even Chief Justice Ruffin, had anything positive to say about the two men. Although Mizell was a prominent family name in the region, Kenneth Mizell's killing prompted no familial or community mobilization on his behalf. In short, Latham's high social standing, combined with the lowly status of Brickhouse and Mizell, surely worked to Caesar's advantage.[52]

In a related vein, Latham's ability to acquire the skillful counsel of Biggs proved significant as well, for the lawyers in this case proved vastly different in their effectiveness. Beginning with the case at trial, but especially before the supreme court, Biggs offered compelling arguments on behalf of Caesar that took full advantage of both the legal and social evidence surrounding the case. Biggs's criticism of the trial judge's interpretation of existing law, as well as his ability to portray Brickhouse and Mizell as the villains, successfully persuaded the supreme court to order a new trial. Attorney General Moore, on the other hand, although records of his arguments in *Caesar* do not survive, probably did not demonstrate the argumentative mastery of Biggs. Moore had made his reputation, after all, in a case that had *expanded* the rights of slaves to defend themselves. In his famous argument in *State v. Will*, Moore had urged the supreme court to "foster the enlightened benevolence of the age," while he had sharply criticized "the barbarian who is guilty of savage cruelty" against slaves. Moore's skillful work in *Will* undoubtedly made his job more difficult in *Caesar*.

Existing precedent regarding the treatment of slaves in similar situations, as well as the makeup of the supreme court, constituted a final factor affecting Caesar's fate. Although neither Pearson nor Nash relied heavily on precedent, the supreme court had a recent history of handing down relatively liberal and humane decisions regarding the rights of slaves. Despite all the attention scholars have devoted to *State v. Mann*, an important 1829 case in which Ruffin had upheld the legal authority of the master to shoot a fleeing slave in the back, two more enlightened decisions, *State v. Will* and *State v. Jarrot*, provided a legal foundation for extenuating Caesar's charge from murder to manslaughter. Combined with the justices' willingness to see Caesar as an individual to whom common law rights might apply, Pearson and Nash had ample grounds on which to mitigate the charge. Ruffin proved to be the only obstacle to such a ruling. Although he had remained silent in each of the above decisions, in *Caesar* Ruffin could keep quiet no longer. As he witnessed his colleagues pronounce what he believed to be dangerous doctrines, the chief justice made a final effort to elaborate his position. The court's ruling in *Caesar*, however, rendered Ruffin's protests irrelevant.[53]

The decision in *State v. Caesar* marked the high point of the North Carolina Supreme Court's recognition of slave humanity, and the opinion stood out as one of the most humane slave decisions to emerge from an antebellum southern state supreme court.[54] According to historian Thomas D. Morris, only the Tennessee Supreme Court ever expressly agreed that a homicide of a white man by a slave could be reduced to manslaughter. A year after the decision in *Caesar*, Tennessee's high court held in *Nelson v. State* that if a slave, after being assaulted and beaten by a stranger having no authority over him, killed the person beating him, such a killing would be extenuated to manslaughter if the blows of the stranger were inflicted with a weapon and in a cruel and excessive manner. Tennessee Judge Nathan Green, author of the opinion in *Nelson*, looked to the North Carolina Supreme Court for support, and he specifically cited the court's opinion in *State v. Will*. Had the recent decision in *Caesar* been available in Tennessee in 1850, Green no doubt would have cited that case as well, as the facts were more applicable than those in *Will*.[55] In the final analysis, the favorable treatment of Caesar was a rare occurrence in the operation of the southern criminal justice system.

The type of fairness exhibited in Caesar's case, one historian correctly notes, was completely compatible with a "healthy, vigorous, and expanding institution" of slavery.[56] Indeed, neither Pearson, Nash, nor Biggs favored anything even remotely resembling abolition; all held slaves and none publicly challenged the institution's existence. At the end of the 1840s, North

Carolinians were probably as deeply committed to the institution of slavery as they ever would be. Yet Caesar benefited from a unique combination of legal and social circumstances. In a state with a relatively humane slave code and in a community where whites were secure in their dominance, a slave owned by a prominent master who killed a socially marginal white man could receive justice and escape death. Scholars debate whether such a ruling merely grew out of white masters' commitment to protecting their slave property or whether judges in such cases actually recognized the humanity of the slave.[57] Regardless of the motives of white jurors and judges, Caesar, a slave, reaped the benefits.

NOTES

The author wishes to thank H. G. Jones and the North Caroliniana Society for a 1993 Archie K. Davis Research Fellowship, which helped make possible the research for this essay. In addition, the author acknowledges the helpful criticisms and suggestions of Eric W. Rise, Paul Finkelman, Kermit L. Hall, Stuart Streichler, Bertram Wyatt-Brown, Whittington B. Johnson, Michael LaRosa, Elizabeth Roberson, and Christopher Smith.

1. Jameston, the second oldest town in Martin County, in northeastern North Carolina, was first incorporated in 1785 as "Jamestown," but in 1803 an act of the legislature dropped the "w" and referred to the town as "Jameston," as it appears in the record of this case. On February 10, 1855, the General Assembly adopted an act officially changing the town's name to "Jamesville," by which name it has been known ever since. During the antebellum period, the town was noted primarily for its production of shingles and lumber. Francis M. Manning and W. H. Booker, *Martin County History*, vol. 1, (Williamston, N.C., 1977), 103–4.

2. This account is a composite based on the testimony of those involved in the Monday, August 14 incident, described in *State v. Caesar, a Slave*, 31 N.C. 391, 391–96 (1849). Quotations are from 31 N.C. 393–94. Much of the reported opinion is a copy of the original case file for North Carolina Supreme Court Case No. 4630, *State v. Caesar, a Slave*, (1849), North Carolina Division of Archives and History (NCDAH), Raleigh, North Carolina.

3. 31 N.C. 391, 395.

4. This description comes from the bill of indictment, 31 N.C. 391, 392. The indictment in its original form can be found in *Minutes, Martin County Superior Court*, Fall Term, 1848, Williamston, N.C., entry for August 29, 1848, NCDAH

(hereinafter cited as *Minutes*). The blow inflicted by Caesar upon Mizell caused a bruise "the breadth of two inches and of the length of six inches."

5. 31 N.C. 391, 396.

6. 31 N.C. 391, 393.

7. James Ross, *Life and Times of Elder Reuben Ross*, (Philadelphia, n.d.; reprint, 1977, Nashville, Tenn.), 85; Manning and Booker, *Martin County History*, vol. 1, 85; *Minutes*, entry for Tuesday, August 29, 1848.

8. 31 N.C. 391, 396; Bill of Indictment, *Minutes*, entry for August 29, 1848.

9. Caesar's actual owners were John and Thomas Latham, but because they were "infants," Simon Latham, presumably the boys' father, played the role of guardian in these proceedings. North Carolina law provided that a slaveowner be given ten days' notice before a trial, in order to give the master time to hire counsel. In this instance, Latham, having already hired Asa Biggs to defend Caesar, waived the ten days. See Chapter 111, Section 48, *Revised Statutes of the State of North Carolina*, vol. 1, (Raleigh, 1837), 583; *Minutes*, entries for August 29–31, 1848; Cushing Biggs Hassell, *Autobiography*, vol. 4, 218, Southern Historical Collection (SHC), Library of the University of North Carolina at Chapel Hill.

10. The main character of this entire drama is the one about whom the least can be discovered. Caesar is, quite simply, a mystery. His name does not appear in any of the numerous deeds detailing sales of slaves and property by any of the Lathams during this period. Moreover, the name of neither John nor Thomas Latham, the slave's juvenile owners in 1848, appears in the slave schedule for 1850. Although John had by that time reached the age of 21, he apparently no longer owned Caesar. Simon Latham does appear in the slave schedule as owning 13 slaves at that point, four of whom—aged 45, 33, 30, and 30—might possibly have been Caesar. See deeds negotiated by Simon J. Latham and John Latham, January 1, 1848, and January 1, 1849, Martin County Deeds, Book O, Martin County Governmental Center, Williamston, North Carolina; *Population Schedules of the Seventh Census of the United States, 1850, North Carolina, Slave Schedules, Martin County*.

11. See, for example, Mark V. Tushnet, *The American Law of Slavery: Consideration of Humanity and Interest* (Princeton, 1981); Andrew Fede, *People Without Rights: An Interpretation of the Fundamentals of the Law of Slavery in the U.S. South* (New York, 1992); A. E. Keir Nash, "A More Equitable Past? Southern Supreme Courts and the Protection of the Antebellum Negro," *North Carolina Law Review* 48 (February, 1970): 197–242; Nash, "Fairness and Formalism in the Trials of Blacks in the State Supreme Courts of the Old South," *Virginia Law Review* 56 (February, 1970): 64–100; Nash, "Reason of Slavery: Understanding the Judicial Role in the Peculiar Institution," *Vanderbilt Law Review* 32 (Janu-

ary, 1979): 7–233; Mason W. and D. Grier Stephenson, "'To Protect and Defend': Joseph Henry Lumpkin, the Supreme Court of Georgia, and Slavery," *Emory Law Journal* 25 (1976): 579–608.

12. Nash, "Fairness and Formalism in the Trials of Blacks," 64–100. Daniel Flanigan hints at North Carolina's uniqueness in its procedural treatment of slaves, but does not develop the idea. See Flanigan, "Criminal Procedure in Slave Trials in the Antebellum South," *Journal of Southern History* 40 (November, 1974): 546–47.

13. Harold Sugg, "Race Relations in Pitt County, N.C.: Slavery, 1700–1860," 46–47, unpublished paper in Harold G. Sugg Papers, East Carolina Manuscript Collections, J. Y. Joyner Library, East Carolina University, Greenville, North Carolina.

14. The institution of slavery was perhaps healthier in Martin County than in the rest of the state. Between 1820 and 1860, almost 3,000 slaves were sent each year from North Carolina to the Deep South. This development helps account for the only modest increases in the proportion of slaves in the state's population over the years. Slaves accounted for 32.6 percent of North Carolina's population in 1840 and 33.3 percent in 1860, an increase of just .7 percent. In contrast, the proportion of the enslaved population in Alabama, Mississippi, and Georgia increased by 2.2 percent, 3.1 percent, and 3.4 percent, respectively, over the same period. See James H. McCallum, *Martin County During the Civil War* (Williamston, N.C., 1971), 3; Reuel E. Schiller, "Conflicting Obligations: Slave Law and the Late Antebellum North Carolina Supreme Court," *Virginia Law Review* 78 (August, 1992): 1243–44; Rosser Howard Taylor, *Slaveholding in North Carolina: An Economic View* (New York, 1969), 65–66.

15. McCallum, *Martin County During the Civil War*, 4; Manning and Booker, *Martin County History*, 72–73, 103; 31 N.C. 391, 396.

16. Flanigan, "Criminal Procedure," 540–47; Michael S. Hindus, "Black Justice Under White Law: Criminal Prosecutions of Blacks in Antebellum South Carolina," *Journal of American History* 63 (1976): 575–99; Philip J. Schwarz, "Forging the Shackles: The Development of Virginia's Criminal Code for Slaves," in David J. Bodenhamer and James W. Ely Jr., *Ambivalent Legacy: A Legal History of the South* (Jackson, Miss., 1984), 125–46; Philip J. Schwarz, *Twice Condemned: Slaves and the Criminal Law of Virginia, 1705–1865* (Baton Rouge, La., 1988); Nash, "Reason of Slavery," 104–23. Famous traveler Frederick Law Olmsted commented that in North Carolina slavery was "less lamentable" than in Virginia. "There is not only less bigotry upon the subject, and more freedom of conversation, but I saw here, in the institution, more of patriarchal character than in any other State. The slave more frequently appears as a family servant—a member of his master's family, interested with him in his fortune, good or bad.

This is a result of the less concentration of wealth in families or individuals, occasioned by the circumstances I have described. Slavery thus loses much of its inhumanity." Olmsted, *A Journey in the Seaboard Slave States*, vol. 1 (New York, 1904), 408.

17. Flanigan, "Criminal Procedure," 540–46; Alan D. Watson, "North Carolina Slave Court, 1715–1785," *North Carolina Historical Review* 60 (January, 1983): 24–36; Marvin L. Michael Kay and Lorin Lee Cary, *Slavery in North Carolina, 1748–1775* (Chapel Hill, N.C., 1995), 52–95; R. H. Taylor, "Humanizing the Slave Code of North Carolina," *North Carolina Historical Review* 2 (July, 1925): 323–31; John Spencer Bassett, *Slavery in the State of North Carolina* (Baltimore, Johns Hopkins Studies, Series 177, Nos. 7 and 8, 1899), 12–13. Slaves, of course, could not serve on juries. Benefit of clergy, discussed later in this essay, was a request for mercy on the part of the defendant, in order to avoid the punishment of death.

18. John Hope Franklin, *The Free Negro in North Carolina, 1790–1860* (Chapel Hill, N.C., 1943), 222–37. Franklin notes that "at no time during the period did more than one tenth live in the population centers" (222). Moreover, he concludes that North Carolina's treatment of free blacks "suggests a type of liberalism that existed in few other states in the South" (225). Martin County had three free blacks who owned slaves, including John Critchion, who held twenty-four bondsmen (236). North Carolina's free black and mulatto population in 1850 stood at 27,463. Maryland's was 74,723 and Virginia's was 54,333. See Jessie Smith and Carnell Horton, eds., *Historical Statistics of Black America* (New York, 1995), vol. 2, 1819–1820.

19. 31 N.C. 391, 394, 396. North Carolina law prohibited slaves leaving "the plantation or seat of land where such slave shall be appointed to live, without a certificate of leave in writing for so doing, from his or her master or overseer." Chapter 111, Section 24, *Revised Statutes*, 578. Still, enforcement of this act was apparently selective. According to surviving records, no one at the trial or appellate level ever mentioned this fact, with the exception of Justice Thomas Ruffin. He made only brief reference to it in his opinion: "They were from home without passes from their owners and associated in the street of a village in the middle of the night. They were, thus, subject to be taken up by any one, and might be looked on as the first transgressors." 31 N.C. 412.

20. R. H. Taylor, "Slave Conspiracies in North Carolina," *North Carolina Historical Review* 5 (1928): 31; Randall Lathan, "The Slave Insurrection of 1802," *The State* (May, 1995), 40–42; Jeffrey J. Crow, "Slave Rebelliousness and Social Conflict in North Carolina, 1775–1802," *William and Mary Quarterly*, 3rd Series, 37 (1980): 79–102; Thomas C. Parramore, *Carolina Quest* (Englewood Cliffs, N.J., 1978), 181–85. Based upon strong evidence of an insurrectionary

plot in 1802, authorities executed twenty-three African Americans, including two in Martin County.

21. Moore signed Caesar's indictment (*Minutes*, August 29, 1848). Moore had been appointed attorney general by Governor William A. Graham, May 20, 1848, and was subsequently elected to a regular term by the general assembly on December 1, 1848. See John L. Cheney Jr., *North Carolina Government, 1585–1979: A Narrative and Statistical History* (Raleigh, 1981), 182, 196; "Moore, Bartholomew Figures," in *Dictionary of North Carolina Biography*, ed. William S. Powell (Chapel Hill, 1979), vol. 4, 294; "Bartholomew Figures Moore," in *Biographical History of North Carolina*, vol. 5, ed. Samuel A. Ashe (Greensboro, N.C., 1906), 275–77; "Bartholomew Figures Moore," in *Lives of Distinguished North Carolinians, with Illustrations and Speeches*, ed. W. J. Peele (Raleigh, 1898), 378–79.

22. *State v. Will*, 18 N.C. 121 (1834). For the text of Moore's famous argument, see 18 N.C. 121, 124–45 and Peele, ed., *Lives of Distinguished North Carolinians*, 389–412. Historians and legal scholars have recognized *State v. Will* as one of the most liberal appellate opinions in the antebellum South. See Patrick S. Brady, "Slavery, Race, and Criminal Law in Antebellum North Carolina: A Reconsideration of the Thomas Ruffin Court," *North Carolina Central Law Journal* 10 (1979): 251–55; Eugene D. Genovese, *Roll, Jordan, Roll: The World the Slaves Made* (New York, 1972), 36; Helen Catterall, ed., *Judicial Cases Concerning American Slavery and the Negro*, vol. 2 (Washington, D.C., 1936), 2–3; Taylor, "Humanizing the Slave Code," 327; George Gordon Battle, "The State of North Carolina v. Negro Will, A slave of James S. Battle; A Cause Celebre of Antebellum Times," *Virginia Law Review* 6 (1919–1920): 515–30.

23. "Biggs, Asa," in Powell, *Dictionary of North Carolina Biography*, vol. 1, 151–52; *History of North Carolina* (Chicago, 1919), vol. 6, 67–68; R. D. W. O'Connor, ed., *Autobiography of Asa Biggs* (Raleigh, 1915); "Memorial Proceedings and Tributes of Respect to the Memory of the Late Asa Biggs" (Norfolk, Va., 1878), University of North Carolina, Chapel Hill, library, general collection.

24. Peter, in fact, was arraigned with Caesar, for the murder of a slave named Sawny, belonging to Anna Hyman. See *Minutes*, entry for Tuesday, August 29, 1848; Hassell, *Autobiography*, v. 4, 216. Simon Latham and Biggs numbered among the county's leading citizens. Both played important roles, for example, in a parade honoring Martin County volunteers returning home from service in the Mexican War. See *Tarborough Press*, September 9, 1848. See *Population Schedules of the Seventh Census of the United States, 1850, North Carolina, Slave Schedules, Martin County*.

25. 31 N.C. 391, 392–96. Chapter 111, Section 50, *Revised Statutes*, vol. 1, 583, pro-

vided that blacks (slave or free) could testify in cases where the defendant was black, Indian, or mulatto.

26. William Blackstone, *Commentaries on the Laws of England*, Book 4, Thomas Cooley, ed., 3rd ed., rev. (Chicago, 1884), 190–94; *State v. Jarrot, a slave*, 23 N.C. 76 (1840).

27. 31 N.C. 391, 396–97.

28. 31 N.C. 391, 397–98. See *State v. Jarrot*, 23 N.C. 76 (1840).

29. Dick had been the trial judge in the case of *State v. Jarrot* (1840), where the supreme court held that to rule a killing manslaughter instead of murder, a slave had to prove that the white victim was committing an unjustified and excessive battery upon him.

30. John M. Dick was elected superior court judge by the North Carolina general assembly on November 30, 1835, and served until his death in October, 1861. See Cheney, ed., *North Carolina Government*, 361, 370; John M. Dick to Weldon Edwards, July 21, 1859, in Katherine Clark Pendleton Conway Collection, Correspondence, 1817–1859, NCDAH; Will of John M. Dick, 1861, *Guilford Wills*, NCDAH; *William D. Valentine Diaries*, vol. 14, entry for June 2, 1855, in SHC. Valentine remarked disparagingly that Dick's ascension to the bench had been "by accident," while James W. Bryan similarly noted that politics, rather than legal acumen, had been the principal factor in Dick's election (see note 31). To Dick's credit, however, Valentine noted, "He possesses . . . two requisites for a judge, patience and firmness. . . . He does what he thinks is right to the best of his knowledge."

31. James W. Bryan to John Heritage Bryan, December 1, 1835, Bryan Family Papers, Special Collections Library, Duke University, Durham, N.C. A survey of the reported North Carolina Supreme Court cases on appeal from trials where Dick had presided reveals a reversal rate of nearly 50 percent. The supreme court found no error in the trial proceedings seventy-six times, while Dick was found to be in error seventy-one times. See *North Carolina Reports*, vols. 21–31, 36–39.

32. William Slade to James Slade, September 9, 1848, William Slade Papers, Special Collections Library, Duke University, Durham, N.C.; *Minutes*, entry for August 31, 1848. The jury was composed entirely of slaveholders, as required by North Carolina law in cases involving slaves. This did not mean, though, that slaveholders were particularly inclined to condemn slaves accused of crimes. As slaveholders, they could perhaps sympathize both with Latham's desire to retain his property and the State's wish to keep slaves from challenging white authority. See Chapter 111, Section 45, *Revised Statutes*, vol. 1, 582.

33. *Minutes*, entry for September 2, 1848; Hassell, *Autobiography*, v. 4, p. 219. The

error in jury selection involved the appearance of a juror, named Terri Jones, in both the original panel of prospective jurors, as well as in the "special venire," or expanded jury pool. Jones did not serve as a juror in the case, and the error was apparently harmless, as the supreme court never mentioned the issue.

34. *Minutes*, entry for September 2, 1848; Eborn listed as second wealthiest man in Martin County in "Occupations: Lawyers," file in Francis Manning History Room, Martin Community College, Williamston, North Carolina.

35. The date of argument is unknown. The official records of the court give no dates, only the vague reference, "June Term." *Records of the North Carolina Supreme Court*, June Term, 1849, 419–21, NCDAH. As the *Raleigh Register* makes brief note of the case (along with several others) in its edition of July 25, 1849, the case was probably argued in the first two weeks of that month.

36. Timothy S. Huebner, *The Southern Judicial Tradition: State Judges and Sectional Distinctiveness, 1790–1890* (Athens: University of Georgia Press, 1999), 15–159; Blackwood Pierce Robinson, "Thomas Ruffin, 1787–1870," unpublished manuscript in North Carolina Collection, Wilson Library, University of North Carolina, Chapel Hill; Channing C. Carpenter, "The Influence of Justice Thomas Ruffin on American Constitutional Law" (Ph.D. diss., University of Nebraska, 1972); William A. Graham, "The Life and Character of the Hon. Thomas Ruffin, Late Chief Justice of North Carolina, A Memorial Oration" (Raleigh, 1871), University of North Carolina, Chapel Hill, library, general collection; *State v. Mann*, 13 N.C. 263 (1829); Julius Yanuck, "Thomas Ruffin and North Carolina Slave Law," *Journal of Southern History* 21 (1955): 456–75.

37. Both Pearson and Nash eventually served as chief justices of the North Carolina Supreme Court. On Pearson, see "Pearson, Richmond Mumford," in *Dictionary of North Carolina Biography*, vol. 5, ed. William S. Powell, 49–51; "Richmond M. Pearson," in *Biographical History of North Carolina*, vol. 5, ed. Samuel A. Ashe (Greensboro, N.C., 1905), 295–309; "Memorial Address on the Life and Character of Richmond Mumford Pearson, Chief Justice of North Carolina" (Raleigh, 1881), 1–21, University of North Carolina, Chapel Hill, library, general collection; James Albert Hutchens, "The Chief-Justiceship and the Public Career of Richmond M. Pearson, 1861–1871," (master's thesis, University of North Carolina, Chapel Hill, 1960). On Nash, see "Nash, Frederick," in *Dictionary of North Carolina Biography*, vol. 4, ed. Powell, 359–60; "Frederick Nash," in *Biographical History of North Carolina*, vol. 1, ed. Ashe, 405–10; John M. Bryan, "Memoir of Hon. Frederick Nash, L.L.D., Late Chief Justice of the Supreme Court of North Carolina" (Chapel Hill, N.C., 1859), 1–7.

38. "*State v. Caesar*, Mr. Biggs' Argument," in Thomas Ruffin Papers, SHC. Unfortunately, there is no surviving copy of the attorney general's arguments, and an analysis is therefore impossible.

39. "*State v. Caesar*, Mr. Biggs' Argument," in Ruffin Papers.

40. Pearson cited 12 Coke 87 as the applicable English precedent. 31 N.C. 391, 400, 405, 406.

41. 31 N.C. 391, 398–99, 403, 405, 406.

42. 31 N.C. 391, 406–9. Nash wrote: "His Honor ought to have instructed the jury that an assault made by a white man upon a slave, which endangers his life or threatens great bodily harm, will amount to legal provocation. . . . The prisoner was entitled to have the law bearing upon the case fully and correctly laid down by the court" (408). The irony, of course, was that Dick had been the trial judge for *Jarrot* and was very familiar with the court's decision. His interpretation of the facts in Caesar's case, however, did not square with the interpretation given by Nash.

43. 31 N.C. 391, 409, 410, 411.

44. 31 N.C. 391, 413; *State v. Hale*, 9 N.C. 582 (1823).

45. 31 N.C. 391, 420.

46. 31 N.C. 391, 423, 424. Ruffin did not use the term "Sambo," but the type of slave which Ruffin described definitely fit the Sambo profile. On the Sambo personality, see Stanley Elkins, *Slavery: A Problem in American Institutional and Intellectual Life* (Chicago, 1959), esp., 81–139. While there is little if any validity to the idea that slaves were actually Sambos, there is no doubt that many slaveholders—like Ruffin—conceived of their slaves in this way.

47. 31 N.C. 391, 415.

48. 31 N.C. 391, 427, 428. For Ruffin's most complete extrajudicial statement on slavery, see Ruffin, "Address of Thomas Ruffin, Delivered before the State Agricultural Society of North Carolina, October 18th, 1855," as published in J. G. de Roulhac Hamilton, *The Papers of Thomas Ruffin* (Raleigh, 1920), vol. 4, 323–37.

49. *Minutes*, entry for August 28, 1849.

50. *Minutes*, entry from August 28, 1849; Lawrence M. Friedman, *A History of American Law*, 2nd ed. (New York, 1985), 71; Lawrence M. Friedman, *Crime and Punishment in American History* (New York, 1993), 43–44; George W. Dalzell, *Benefit of Clergy in America and Related Matters* (Winston-Salem, N.C., 1955); William K. Boyd, "Documents and Comments on Benefit of Clergy as Applied to Slaves," *Journal of Negro History* 8 (October, 1923): 443–47; Chapter 111, Section 47, *Revised Statutes*, 583. The Bible verse read was the so-called neck verse, Psalm 51:1: "Have mercy upon me God, according to your lovingkindness; according unto the multitude of thy tender mercies blot out my transgressions."

51. *Minutes*, entry for August 28, 1849. This type of branding was common for clergyable offenses. "M" signified that one had been convicted of manslaughter (not murder—for a murderer would not have gotten off so easily), while "T" meant

that one had been convicted of theft. In North Carolina, the legislature even passed a law in 1787 that dealt with horse theft by prescribing that a convicted thief be branded on the right cheek with an "H" and the left cheek with a "T." See Dalzell, *Benefit of Clergy in America*, 221–22, 258. A defendant could only plead benefit of clergy once in his lifetime; the brand indicated that an individual had already used this privilege.

52. "*State v. Caesar*, Mr. Biggs' Argument," in Ruffin Papers; 31 N.C. 391, 405. Literally nothing is known of Brickhouse or Kenneth Mizell. Jamestown was originally founded upon the lands of a Luke Mizell in 1785, and a number of Mizells appear in the census. Still, Brickhouse and Mizell must have been either drunkards or other such outcasts, or they were the wanderers that Biggs made them out to be. There is no record of anyone mobilizing against Caesar or the slave population to avenge Mizell's death.

53. On *State v. Mann*, see Thomas D. Morris, *Southern Slavery and the Law, 1619–1860* (Chapel Hill, N.C., 1996), 190–93; William Wiecek, *The Sources of Antislavery Constitutionalism in America, 1760–1848* (Ithaca, 1977), 143; Genovese, *Roll, Jordan, Roll*, 35–36; Robert Cover, *Justice Accused: Antislavery and the Judicial Process* (New Haven, Conn., 1975), 77; Brady, "Slavery, Race, and Criminal Law," 248–60; Yanuck, "Thomas Ruffin," 456–75.

54. *Caesar* was part of a liberal trend on the part of the late antebellum North Carolina Supreme Court. See Schiller, "Conflicting Obligations," 1221–22.

55. Morris, *Southern Slavery and the Law*, 291–92; *Nelson v. State*, 10 Humphrey 518 (1850). Chief Justice Joseph Henry Lumpkin of Georgia, in contrast, denied in both *Jim v. State*, 15 Ga. 535 (1854) and *John v. State*, 16 Ga. 200 (1854) that a homicide by a slave against a white man could be mitigated to manslaughter.

56. Flanigan, "Criminal Procedure," 537.

57. Andrew Fede, *People Without Rights: An Interpretation of the Fundamentals of the Law of Slavery in the U.S. South* (New York, 1992), 171, argues that such "humane" decisions were actually founded upon "principles of oppresion." "Slaves were valuable property to their owners," he later summarizes. "Consequently, procedural safeguards of some kind were appropriate when slaves were accused of one of the many serious crimes depicted in this chapter" (177). In contrast, Schiller, "Conflicting Obligations," 1227, notes that "humanizing decisions such as *State v. Caesar* . . . protect neither masters' property interests nor society's security."

Slaves and Crime: New Orleans, 1846–1862

Judith Kelleher Schafer

In the decades before the Civil War, visitors and residents of New Orleans found the Crescent City unhealthy, filthy, vice-filled, and crime-ridden. A visitor to the city claimed that its inhabitants consumed more alcoholic beverages than those in any other part of the United States. Although nuisance laws prohibited keeping houses of prostitution, "lewd and abandoned women" plied their trade openly, unmolested by the police except during an occasional burst of civic righteousness. The city had an extremely high death rate compared to the rest of the country. Yellow fever, cholera, and tuberculosis carried off thousands each year during the 1850s, more than eight thousand in 1853 alone. Crop failures and political unrest in Ireland and continental Europe caused millions to flee to the United States. Thousands entered the country at the port of New Orleans, where many fell victim to the city's most virulent diseases. The sheer number of immigrants changed the complexion of New Orleans. In 1850, the foreign-born swelled to 49 percent of the population, and even the oldest section of the city, the Vieux Carré (now called the French Quarter), contained 54 percent foreign-born, 14 percent Americans not born in Louisiana, and only 32 percent native-born. The free population of New Orleans rose from 99,071 in 1850 to 155,290 in 1860, almost all a result of foreign immigration. Although the *Daily Creole*'s xenophobic assessment of the Irish as "criminals and political prostitutes" and the Germans as "anarchists" was exaggerated, the city did have one of the highest crime rates in the United States. Few statistics exist, but the arrest rate in New Orleans seems to have been higher than in other cities. Large numbers of impoverished Irish immigrants filled the courts, charged with assault and battery, mayhem, maiming, riot, larceny, breach of the peace, and more serious crimes such as assault with a dangerous weapon, assault with intent to kill, and murder. A traveler to the city observed: "Human life [in New Orleans] is a cheap commodity."[1]

Neither free whites nor recent immigrants held a monopoly on crime in New Orleans. Slaves and free people of color also committed crimes, although far below their proportion in the city's population. In 1850 just over 17,000 slaves lived in the city. Although the majority labored in the city's households, as cooks, laundresses, nannies, valets, gardeners, and butlers, many slaves worked as draymen, shoemakers, stevedores, waiters, cigar makers, coopers, and barbers. The complexities of urban life made the strict supervision required by law impossible. Owners sent domestics to market; stevedores worked on the levees, far away from their owners' watchful eyes, and the practice of slaves hiring their own time, that is, making their own work arrangements and paying weekly wages to their owner, and living away from the master, made constant supervision impracticable. Slaves working as street vendors or flower sellers escaped constant watching by the very nature of their work. A few slaveowners allowed their slave women to serve as prostitutes, another occupation impossible to monitor closely. The New Orleans newspapers complained constantly about slaves drinking, fighting, and gambling, all of which were contrary to law. A substantial number of fugitive slaves, who attempted to pass as free, also lived in New Orleans. Subject to no regulation except that which fear of discovery and recapture engendered, they tried to blend in with the approximately 10,000 free creoles of color living in the city. Although most people of color were mulattoes, so were most of the fugitives, and although most of the Crescent City's slaves were darker skinned, even a sharp observer could not always distinguish free from slave. Although they made up only 8 percent of the city's population in 1850, free people of color were some of the most industrious and skilled citizens of the Crescent City. They monopolized certain trades—such as ironworking and plastering—and were acknowledged as some of the most skilled masons, tailors, carpenters, and merchants.[2]

Louisiana law required that whites and free persons of color accused of crimes receive the protection of the common law, but the law gave slaves accused of crimes a different standard of justice. Louisiana had no criminal code until the twentieth century, but the state legislature passed two major laws concerning criminal procedure for free people in 1805 and 1855. The Crimes Act of 1805 introduced common law principles in criminal prosecutions for white defendants and free persons of color. The Crimes Act mandated only one capital crime, that of "wilful [*sic*] murder." Imprisonment at hard labor, paying a fine, or both were the penalty for conviction for all other crimes and misdemeanors. Procedural requirements in the Crimes Act called for defendants to have a copy of the indictment in advance of trial, a list of jurors, the right to counsel, the right to present witnesses in behalf of the accused, peremptory challenges, and the right to trial by jury. According to Section 33, criminal trials were to be "according to and in conformity with the common law of England." The 1855 revision increased the number of capital crimes for free people by making execution or life imprisonment the punishment not only for murder, but for rape, administering poison, shooting, stabbing with intent to murder, or "lying in wait" to attempt to perpetrate an arson, rape, robbery, or burglary. This increase in the number of crimes meriting death or incarceration for life came at a time when many other states had abolished or were in the process of abolishing capital punishment altogether.[3]

For Louisiana slaves the law required a much less structured form of criminal procedure. From the beginning of the American period, Louisiana lawmakers provided that slaves would not be tried under the same rules and procedural protections as were whites and free persons of color. Under Louisiana law, criminal procedure for slaves acted primarily as a mechanism for determining whether property should be condemned, much as in real-property law when private property is taken for public use without the owner's consent—a forced sale with compensation to the property owner. Slave trials, then, had the same effect as a procedure for eminent domain, a taking of property by the state in the public interest. Although slaves accused of crimes in Louisiana proved vulnerable to criminal prosecutions as persons, the legal procedure to determine their fate operated strikingly like compensated property condemnations.[4]

Exempting slaves from common law safeguards underscored the special nature of slave property. The exquisite dilemma of the peculiar institution was that although slaves were property, they were also humans who could be held accountable for their misdeeds as could no horse, cow, or chicken. But to try them in the same courts under the same rules as free persons elevated them to a status that no slaveholder would or could admit. Hence the need for a separate system in which the concern was not, as with free people, procedural guarantees, but a mechanism for visiting swift, brutal, exemplary punishment on persons who had to be always reminded of their subordinate status. Louisiana's criminal law for slaves contrasted sharply with that of many of her sister slave states, most of which had abolished special slave courts and tried slaves in the same courts and under the same rules as whites. Scholars studying slave trials at the appellate level in other states have found state supreme courts surprisingly protective of slaves' rights. Louisiana's separate system prevented this from happening.[5]

In 1806 the territorial legislature passed a comprehensive law to govern the slave population that included a specific criminal code. In contrast to the Crimes Act, in which only one crime, that of "wilful [sic] murder," was a crime that merited death for free people, the "Crimes and Offences [sic]" section of the *Black Code* mandated execution for a number of crimes, including the burning of "any sacks of rice, corn, or other grain, or produce, raw or manufactured . . . maliciously burn[ing] or destroy[ing] any building or house," administering poison to anyone, slave or free, "rape upon the body of any white woman or girl."[6] Although a conviction of a "free negro, mulatto, Indian, or mustee" for these offenses also merited execution, Section 6 of "Crimes and Offences" specifically guaranteed those persons "a right to a trial by jury before the ordinary tribunal." The *Black Code* also limited certain capital crimes to slave perpetrators, including striking the master, mistress, or their children "so as to cause a contusion, or effusion or shedding of blood." Section 11 mandated execution for a slave who killed any person except by accident or in the act of defending his owner. Death by execution was also required for any slave convicted of fomenting or participating in an insurrection. Section 15 made the third conviction of striking a white person a capital offense as well as the first offense of willfully wounding or mutilating any white person.[7]

The *Black Code* provided detailed instructions for slave trials that created a mechanism quite different from "a right to a trial by jury before the ordinary tribunal" guaranteed to free persons of color and Indians. A special tribunal assembled for the occasion tried slaves accused of capital crimes, rather than a jury of their peers. The judge of the parish where the alleged crime occurred or two justices of the peace from the parish and from three to five "freeholders" of the vicinity made up the panel to try slave cases. The *Black Code* did not allow peremptory challenges, or challenges for cause, although members of the special tribunal were forbidden a relationship to the owner of the slave within "four degrees of consanguinity." The law required the special tribunals to assemble and try the case within three days of the arrest of the accused and arrive at a verdict "in the most accurate and expeditious manner." Judgments of the special tribunals were "decisive and final in all capital offences." Panels consisting of a justice of the peace and two freeholders tried slaves accused of noncapital crimes and meted out corporal punishment to those convicted at the discretion of the tribunal, although the physical punishment could not result in loss of life or limb. This system of trying slaves accused of criminal acts persisted throughout the antebellum period with only a few modifications. From the beginning of the American possession of Louisiana to the Civil War, the law denied slaves one of the most fundamental rights under American law—the right to trial by a jury of one's peers. Although free persons of color did not have a jury of their peers—the jury pool was drawn from the voting rolls, which restricted the vote to adult white males—the law mandated trials by the same jurors drawn from the same pool as whites. Slave trials in Louisiana really operated as trials of those with inferior rights by their superiors.[8]

Little evidence of procedural restraints or common law safeguards appeared in the *Black Code* requirements for the trials of slaves, but it is clear that these trials closely resembled property condemnations, which called for special juries. Section 1 required only that the panel assembled to try a slave read the accused the charge, listen to the slave's defense, and examine any witnesses to the alleged crime. Members of the special tribunal swore an oath that they would "faithfully carry into execution the act entitled 'an act for the rules and conduct to be observed toward negroes and other slaves of this territory,' according to the best of my knowledge and abilities—so help me God." This oath says nothing about seeking the truth or administering justice; the jurors swore only that they would decide the matter at hand according to the *Black Code*.[9]

The law required that those who served on each special tribunal be freeholders. Theoretically a freeholder owned real estate—and although slaves were considered immovable property as was real estate in Louisiana—the term freeholders may have been interpreted loosely to mean free white adult males. There is evidence that actually being a slaveholder was a requirement for serving on a special tribunal.[10] In contrast, the Crimes Act required that jurors in the trials of whites and free persons of color be "free white male inhabitants," residents of the state for at least one year, and "housekeepers." Furthermore, under the Crimes Act jurors were summoned to serve for a specific period of time, not for one special trial: "It is not usual to summon a petty jury for the trial of any particular case; but to issue a precept, as has already been directed in the case of a grand jury, to summon commonly forty-eight citizens to serve as petty jurors generally at each term."[11] Each slave trial necessitated the creation of a new panel, underlying the special nature of slave trials.

If a jury convicted a free person, black or white, of murder, the Crimes Act mandated execution by hanging "by the neck until dead." However, executions of slaves found guilty of several capital crimes by a special tribunal could be conducted in a manner that the panel believed "will prove the most effectual means of deterring other slaves from committing the like crimes."[12] Slave tribunals, then, had the choice of the form of execution to suit the needs of the special case before them.

The notion that trials of slaves in Louisiana resembled property condemnations is reflected in the consequences of convictions of free persons and slaves. The Crimes Act required that free persons convicted of crimes pay for the costs of prosecution and make reparation to the person or persons injured by the criminal act. The law specifically prohibited all other forfeitures or penalties, including "corruption of blood," or attainder. In slave tribunals, however, the judge or justices of the peace had the additional duty to appraise the convicted slave at a value not to exceed $500 with the "advice and consent" of two of the members of the special tribunal. The state paid the owner of the slave half of the appraised value of the slave and "the person who may have suffered from the commission of the crime," the other half. The *Black Code* excepted only slaves "taken in actual rebellion" from being appraised and their owners reimbursed for their loss.[13]

Finally, the Crimes Act guaranteed free persons accused of crimes a trial "in conformity with the common law of England," specifically trial by jury, right to counsel, a hearing before a grand jury, a copy of the indictment, a list of witnesses, jury challenges for cause, and peremptory challenges. In contrast, the *Black Code* specifically discounted any importance that may have been given to procedure: "No proceedings had by competent judges in consequence of this act shall be, annulled, avoided, or in any way impeded by any error of form." [14]

The first legislature elected under the new Louisiana Constitution of 1845 passed an act revising and expanding the *Black Code* in regard to the criminal trials of slaves. This act specifically stated that members of special tribunals had to be "owners of slaves" rather than "freeholders" of the parish in which the alleged crime occurred. The rationale for the slaveholding requirement may have been that slaveowners feared that those who did not own slaves might have been hostile to slave property. One historian suggests that the slaveholding requirement was actually a form of disenfranchisement directed at those who did not own slaves. Special tribunals trying capital crimes were now composed of ten slaveowners and two justices of the peace. In Orleans Parish, the law required that the judge of the First District Court preside over the capital trials of slaves. It was the responsibility of this judge, or in other parishes, a justice of the peace, to assemble the panel of ten slaveowners, who were to report within three days of receiving a summons. The 1846 law required each slaveowner on the panel to swear an oath to hear and judge the accused "impartially" and "carry into effect the laws of this State concerning slaves." Once more, the word "justice" did not appear in the oath, but simply a promise to conduct the trial according to the *Black Code*. The 1846 act required the district attorney of the parish to prosecute slaves accused of crimes. And although the special tribunal had to be unanimously in favor of acquittal or conviction for capital crimes, the tribunal could order "such corporal punishment as it may consider deserved by the prisoner." This freed the tribunal to order a slave found not guilty of a capital crime to be whipped anyway. If a special tribunal found a slave guilty of a capital crime and sentenced the accused to death, the panel had the responsibility to appraise the slave and order compensation to the owner of no more than $300, to be paid by the state treasurer. The act excepted owners of slaves convicted of insurrection from receiving compensation. The 1846 revision moved the execution of convicted slaves behind prison walls, except in the case of slaves convicted of insurrection. Furthermore, Section 13 of the 1846 act made legal what had been common practice from the beginning of the American period: trials of slaves accused of crimes were brought by information, not by grand jury indictment. Although the legislature had passed a law in 1841 allowing the use of informations for minor crimes and misdemeanors for free persons, black and white, a grand jury routinely brought indictments of all capital crimes and noncapital crimes with a possible sentence of more than two years at hard labor. Bringing a case by information was a time-saving procedure for lesser crimes of free persons and in capital crimes for slaves. Using informations in this way specifically devalued procedure because Louisiana law regarded slaves as property. Even if the crime were willful murder, slaves did not have the right to have the evidence assessed and the validity of the accusation judged by a grand jury as did free persons, white and black. The absence of a grand jury indictment in the trials of slaves resulted in cases going to the special tribunals in which the evidence was totally inconclusive and/or the slave was obviously innocent. Finally, Section 14 echoed the 1806 *Black Code* by denying that procedure had any importance: "That no proceedings had in accordance with this act, shall be annulled or impeded by any error of form thereon." [15]

During the 1850s, Louisiana lawmakers considered several changes in the criminal law concerning slaves. In 1852 the Louisiana House of Representatives debated whether to reinstate the practice of public executions for slaves and free persons of color convicted of capital crimes. The representative from Rapides Parish, Michael Ryan, spoke against public punishment: "The more secret the execution the more solemn. No good effect could result from the public execution of a slave, as they would frequently seize the opportunity to make confessions on the scaffold detrimental to the character of white persons, and wholly devoid of truth." C. C. Lathrop of Orleans Parish also opposed public executions: "In passing the bill we would be moving a step backwards. It was notorious that public executions have not answered the ends desired by their advocates, instead of inspiring terror, they had tended to render those criminally disposed more hardened and callous." J. G. Sever, also of Orleans, agreed, stating he was "entirely opposed to this morbid and sickly sensibility." However, Donatien Augustin of Orleans said that the rapid increase in crime demanded the public execution of all felons. Eventually the House referred the act to its Judiciary Committee, which recommended a change in the act to mandate public executions for slaves, but not for free persons of color. In a compromise, the legislature passed an act that allowed public executions for slaves at the discretion of the special tribunals. [16]

Less than two months after the adjournment of the legislature, the public execution of two white men in New Orleans produced so horrible a spectacle that the policy of having public executions for anyone, white or black, slave or free, came into question once more. A New Orleans jury convicted Jean Adam and Anthony Delisle of killing the slave Mary during the burglary of her master's home and sentenced them to hang in front of the parish prison. Testimony indicated that the two men had planned the burglary in advance, and intended to kill the slave woman if she discovered them in the act. The coroner's jury reported that the brutal killing laid open her cheek and severed her trachea and her carotid artery to a depth of three inches. Six thousand people turned out to see the execution. Mothers held small children aloft in order that they might get a better view. As rain began to fall, the spectators watched in horror as the hangman sprang the trap doors and the two men plunged to the stone pavement below. The hangman had bungled, and the nooses had slipped from their necks. The police carried the two men into the prison, where they were bled by the prison physician to restore them to consciousness, and about ten minutes later, carried back to the gallows to hang once more. Although by this time the rain fell in torrents, the crowd in the streets held their places. According to an eyewitness, the second hanging caused their injuries from the fall to bleed freely, and the drenching rain turned their white garments to crimson. The following day, the *Daily Picayune* called for an end to such spectacles:

> If capital punishment be defensible, and public executions retained, it is indispensable for all the moral effect they are supposed to have . . . that the penalties of the law should be inflicted with due order and decorum . . . to give them the desired effect on the public mind. The whole argument for public executions . . . is destroyed by such scenes . . . it was only a spectacle for the gratification of the morbid appetite for excitement, the encouragement of which is a great social fault . . . The current of opinion is setting directly against these displays . . . we trust . . . that the law will soon be changed; and if capital punishment must still be retained in our codes, that the execution be directed to take place in private, without parade or ostentation.[17]

In 1854 the Louisiana legislature passed a law requiring all executions in Orleans Parish to take place within the walls of the parish prison. However, this law did not apply to the executions of slaves. In a revision of the

Black Code in 1855, the legislature retained the special tribunal's discretion to choose whether the execution of convicted slaves should be public or private.[18]

In 1855 the Louisiana legislature passed an extensive revision of the *Black Code*, including changes in procedure for the trials of slaves. The 1855 act did not reduce the number of capital crimes for slaves. Capital crimes that merited execution for slaves still included "wilful [*sic*] murder," assault with a dangerous weapon with intent to kill, drowning, strangling, poisoning, rape of a white woman or girl, fomenting insurrection, and arson. Other crimes punishable with death or life in prison included: striking the master, mistress, their children, or a white overseer, theft, and breaking and entering. Under this act the special tribunals now had the authority to sentence slaves convicted of threatening or insulting white overseers, disobeying the overseer, insulting or assaulting a white person, and committing larceny. The 1855 revision made justices of the peace or other committing magistrates responsible for arresting and jailing a slave accused of any crime to await a trial by a special tribunal. District attorneys or "some licensed Attorney" now served as the prosecutor. Finally, the legislature extended two requirements in the 1846 act for Orleans Parish to all slave trials in the state. The slave-owners' oath put greater emphasis on securing a fair trial than did previous oaths that required only that those on the panels followed the laws for the trials of slaves; the 1855 act mandated that the participants in the special tribunal "impartially examine and judge the prisoner . . . according to law, and the evidence, to the best of my knowledge and ability, so help me God." This was the first time any emphasis on evidence or impartiality appeared in the oath.[19]

The second extension of the 1846 act for Orleans Parish to slave trials in the whole state concerned the requirement that verdicts to convict or acquit had to be unanimous. If a tribunal failed to agree on a verdict, the panel could still order corporal punishment "as it may consider deserved," although the wording of the act is not clear as to whether the decision to impose capital punishment had to be unanimous. However, this provision allowed members of what was, in effect, a hung jury, to order the accused to be whipped even though they failed to convict. As in the 1852 law, the 1855 act authorized special tribunals to determine the place of execution for slaves sentenced to death, either inside or outside of prison walls. Compensation to owners of slaves sentenced to death or life in prison continued to be for two–thirds of the value of the slave, not to exceed $750; the state paid the owner of the slave after he or she transferred title to the slave to the state, similar to a taking of any kind of property by the state.[20]

The 1855 act contained two new safeguards for slaves accused of crimes. The act guaranteed that the tribunals allow the testimony of slaves under oath as evidence. And for the first time, the act entitled a slave standing trial for a capital offense to have six peremptory challenges and "any further number" for cause. Although whites and free persons of color had twelve peremptory challenges, the 1855 act was a significant improvement. These changes ameliorated criminal procedure for slaves, but the act included the same phrase that had devalued procedure in slave trials since the 1806 *Black Code*: "That no proceedings shall be annulled or impeded by any error of form."[21]

The same legislature passed a separate act concerning the trials of slaves accused of capital crimes in Orleans Parish. The judge of the First Judicial District Court of New Orleans, which had a preference docket for criminal cases, and six "citizens, slave holders in said parish," constituted special slave tribunals in New Orleans. This act forbade the judge to take part in the deliberations of the jury; the judge was required to "exercise such powers and perform such acts as are now exercised and performed by other Judges of the State presiding on the trial of criminal cases." Lawmakers also tried to solve the burgeoning costs of criminal trials in Orleans Parish; owners of slaves convicted of any crime could not obtain release for a slave who had served the sentence until he or she paid the costs of the prosecution.[22]

In December 1856 the Supreme Court of Louisiana found the 1855 revision of the *Black Code* unconstitutional on a legal technicality. This decision meant that the 1846 act remained in force. The court's ruling destroyed the two new procedural rights in slave trials created by the 1855 act: peremptory challenges and the admissibility of slave testimony in slave trials.[23]

In 1857 the Louisiana legislature considered a bill that would have mandated sweeping changes in criminal procedure in the trials of slaves by allowing slaves standing trial to have several common law safeguards. One of the bill's supporters, arguing for its approval, stated: "[the act] prescribes the mode of trial of slaves, and is loudly called for. Under the present mode of trial, improper verdicts are very often given. This gives the negro a fair trial with the same formalities and advantages of indictment by Grand Jury, trial by Petit Jury, and right of challenge, as a white man has. It is but just, and required by the dignity of the state." Representative Hamilton of Natchitoches

Parish agreed that the act was "a good and humane law . . . [that] should have been enacted years ago. I have seen improper verdicts rendered . . . in passion and excitement, which were not just." But opposition to the bill was strong. Senator Downes of Iberville Parish spoke against the introduction of common law rights in the trial of slaves. Terming the bill "monstrous," Downes argued: "Under its [the bill's] operation no example would ever be made of slaves. Sir, my colleague but a short time since sat on a jury for the trial of a slave, and the slave was convicted. Slaveholders know how to protect their rights, and they will do so. I hope this bill will be put away in the tomb of the Capulets. I trust that so monstrous a bill will be killed summarily . . . the speedy trial of slaves when accused is absolutely necessary." In the end the legislature passed an act for the trial of slaves in the 1857 session that was nearly identical with the unconstitutional act of 1855, reestablishing the right of six peremptory challenges and the admissibility of slave testimony under oath. This act also contained the disclaimer present in all acts concerning procedure in slave trials, "That no proceedings shall be annulled or impeded by any error of form."[24]

Louisiana lawmakers passed yet another modification of the *Black Code* in 1858, one that applied only to the trials of slaves accused of capital crimes in Orleans Parish. For the first time, slaves in capital trials in Orleans Parish were guaranteed the right of counsel; if the owner of the slave refused to hire an attorney to defend the accused, the act required the judge to appoint an attorney and set the attorney's fee, not to exceed $50. However, the state Senate tabled indefinitely another proposed reform—allowing a change of venue in the trials of slaves accused of capital crimes.[25]

The 1858 legislature received a remarkable letter from Robert C. Wycliffe, the governor of Louisiana, asking the Senate to concur in the commutation of a sentence of death to life imprisonment for the slave Henry Hoops. According to Wycliffe's message to the Senate, a special tribunal in Madison Parish had convicted Hoops of the murder of a fellow slave. Hoops broke jail before the sentence could be executed. Although parish authorities recaptured Hoops, the date for his execution had passed, and the sheriff was reluctant to carry out the sentence. In the meantime, some persons in Madison Parish told the governor of mitigating circumstances and recommended a full pardon; Hoops's master requested that Hoops be transferred from the parish prison, where he awaited execution, to the penitentiary for life, which the master believed would be a just sentence. The Senate unanimously concurred with Wycliffe's request that Hoops's sentence be commuted to life in prison.[26]

In his opening address to the legislature in 1859, Wycliffe expressed his concern over cases such as that of Hoops:

> Several instances have occurred, since the passage of this Act [the act of 1846, parts of which were still in effect] when slaves convicted of the crime of murder have never paid the penalty the law demands. The special tribunal which tried them has the power to fix the time for the execution of the sentence; an appeal is taken, or a condemned slave escaped from jail; the day appointed for carrying into effect the sentence once passed, there is no provision of law authorizing the designation of another.

The 1859 legislature ignored Wycliffe's recommendation. He tried again in 1860. In his opening address he admonished members of the House and Senate:

> I have heretofore called the attention of the Legislature to the law in relation to the trial of slaves charged with capital offenses. This subject, which I deem of great importance, has failed to attract the attention of your predecessors. It now earnestly demands and should receive your attention. The manner in which slaves are now tried, by a special tribunal established for that purpose, results in sending many of them to the State Prison for offenses slight and trivial, whereas if the administration of justice in these cases, confined to the District Courts and juries, punishment would be as certain. I would recommend the repeal of the Law which inflicts upon a slave the punishment of confinement in the State Penitentiary.

Legislators at the 1860 session ignored Wycliffe's pleas, and no further revision of criminal procedure or sentencing occurred before the emancipation of slaves following the end of the Civil War.[27]

Understanding the intricacies of criminal law for slaves only gives the researcher half of the picture. How did criminal law affect slaves' day-to-day lives in New Orleans? It is important to remember that most criminal acts of slaves received punishment from their owners, especially minor crimes— being out without a pass, petty theft, being out after curfew. If punished officially, most nonviolent crimes and almost all property crime came before committing magistrates known in Louisiana as Recorders. Records of Recorder's Courts have not survived, but the New Orleans newspapers show that Recorders summarily dispensed justice in minor matters involving slaves and turned slaves accused of violent capital crimes over to the criminal court. Few records of the New Orleans criminal courts before 1846 have survived. The creation of the First District Court of New Orleans in 1846, a court with a preference docket for criminal cases and a responsibility to assemble special tribunals for the trials of slaves in Orleans Parish, may have been responsible for the clerk of court keeping more complete records of slave trials; most of the minute books, docket books, and actual case records of this court have survived. Finding the records of the special tribunals heard in this court is still a daunting task, as they are not indexed by crime or by proper name, and are only retrievable by docket number. One must therefore scan the docket and minute books page by page to find instances of special tribunals trying slaves. Fortunately, many of the records are intact; docket numbers 1–10,000 of the records, from 1846 to 1855, are on film; numbers higher than 10,000 are available in the original, usually tied up in the same red tape (now faded to brown) with which the clerk bundled them nearly 140 years ago. An examination of the trial transcripts reveals that the special tribunals tried slaves accused of crimes as the law required, while free persons of color and whites enjoyed the protection of the common law. Although free persons of color may have been accused of actions that would not have been considered crimes for whites, such as "insulting a white person," and although no free person of color could serve on a jury, they were tried with the rights guaranteed by the common law, as were whites. The records also confirm that free persons of color could testify against white persons in criminal trials, and could even have a white person arrested on their complaint. For example, Clairville Porché, a free man of color, had William Swanton, a white man, arrested on a charge of larceny because he stole an umbrella and a hunting shirt (valued at $7.00), from Porché's stand in the market. The records of the First Judicial District Court of New Orleans also reveal dozens of civil suits in which free persons of color sued whites, as often successfully as not.[28]

New Orleans was a dangerous place in the 1850s. Even a casual reading of New Orleans newspapers leaves the reader with the impression that living in the Crescent City resulted in constant exposure to crime and violence, major and minor. Slaves, as victims or perpetrators, often made their appearance on the police blotter along with free people. On one day in 1852, the *Daily Picayune* reported the arrest of a runaway slave, the appearance of a slave at the police station to protect himself from ill treatment by his master, a knife attack on a police officer by a white man, an arrest for indecent exposure, the arraignment of a slave for "cutting and wounding white persons . . . in a desperate fight on Common street," and a widow's complaint that several men "maliciously and feloniously broke the furniture of deponent's bar-room, assaulted and battered her bar-keeper, threw bottles at her and robbed her money drawer" at two o'clock the previous afternoon.[29] Some even more spectacular instances of newspaper reports of criminal action include a report of one man biting another man's cheek,[30] an attempt by one man to cut another down with an axe,[31] and a woman severely wounding another woman by cutting her with a broken bottle. The city's inhabitants were so accustomed to incidents of crimes and violence that the newspapers noted a peaceful day and night as an unusual occurrence: "The arrests yesterday and last night show either an unusual degree of somnolency on the part of the scoundrels, vagabonds and blackguards of the city, or a great want of vigilance on the part of the police. No arrests made yesterday or last night, in the whole compass of the city, rises in importance and dignity above an assault and battery, or the entering of a room with intent to rob."[32]

Police control of the city during the antebellum period was tenuous at best. From 1836 to 1852, tensions between creoles, Anglo-Americans and recent immigrants caused the legislature to divide the city into three municipalities, each with its own police force and jail; little cooperation existed between them. After the legislature reunited the Crescent City in 1852, control of the city's police went to the mayor, who had the power to hire and fire the police chief and individual police officers; political squabbles over the police department disrupted police supervision, lowered morale, and lessened police effectiveness. The firing of the police chief in 1854 caused such controversy and confusion that the governor sent the militia to patrol the city until the police resumed their duties. The appointment of the police chief and regular officers often depended solely on political factors. Naturalized citizens, appointed to the force when a mayor of the Democratic party held office, found themselves unemployed when an American (Know-Nothing) party mayor took office. The New Orleans police were not a highly visible presence during the late antebellum period. They wore no uniforms, other than blue caps, until 1855, when the city issued blue jackets with brass buttons as uniforms. Policemen received only $45 a month and worked long hours, usually twelve-hour shifts. The city often did not pay them regularly, making them highly susceptible to taking bribes to ignore violations of ordinances against prostitution, gambling, and selling liquor without a license, or actually collaborating in such crimes. Thus, the high crime rate was exacerbated by a corrupt and poorly trained and equipped police force.[33]

Slaves contributed to the high crime rate in New Orleans most often by committing minor breaches of discipline, and it fell to the city's magistrates and justices of the peace to hear citizens' complaints against slaves and dispense justice summarily. Most of the trial records of special tribunals and of free persons accused of crimes began in a Recorder's Court. Recorders in New Orleans were committing magistrates, similar to justices of the peace, and were usually the ones to whom the police or other witnesses initially reported criminal acts. By 1846 there were also five justices of the peace in Orleans Parish who decided civil matters involving less than $100 and dispatched misdemeanor trials summarily. Crimes too serious for the recorders or justices of the peace to decide summarily went to the First District Court, where the judge ordered the sheriff to arrest the accused. If the crime was a felony, the Grand Jury deliberated on whether to bring an indictment if the accused was free, but for slaves the procedure was simplified: after the judge organized the special tribunal, the district attorney brought the case as an information, that is, he "informed" the court of the accusation, even if a conviction for the alleged crime could result in execution or life in prison for the slave. For free persons, cases were brought by information only if the crime was a lesser one, such as assault and battery or larceny; free persons also had the benefit of a petit jury drawn from the regular jury pool, whereas slaves did not.

The courts of the city of New Orleans were housed in the Presbytère, a building located adjacent to the St. Louis Cathedral on the Place d'Armes (now known as Jackson Square). The Presbytère was built in the Spanish colonial period to house the leaders of the colonial Catholic church. The churchwardens of the St. Louis Cathedral rented the building to the city until 1853, when the city purchased both the Presbytère and the Cabildo— the building on the other side of the cathedral and the former seat of Spanish civil government—but the district courts, including the First District Court, remained in the Presbytère. A visitor to New Orleans described the interior of the building that housed the courts in 1847:

I cannot forget the curious scenes I occasionally saw when in the New Orleans courthouse. . . . Applewomen take possession of its lobbies. Beggars besiege its vault like offices. The rains from heaven sport among its rafters. It has everywhere a fatty, ancient smell, which speaks disparagingly of the odor in which justice is held. And yet in this building . . . are held from November until July, six courts whose officers brave damp and steam enthusiastically and perseveringly. . . . You turn . . . into a narrow alley, and brushing past a greasy crowd are soon within the criminal court, where a judge, perched in a high box, wrangles hourly with half-crazed witnesses; here you behold jurymen, who of themselves constitute a congress of nations; zealous, full-lunged lawyers; and audacious criminals ranged in boxes, very much to the satisfaction of a mustached district attorney and the merry-looking keeper of the Parish jail.[34]

The Minute Books of the First District Court of New Orleans present a vivid tableau of the city of New Orleans as a place of violence and vice. It was not uncommon for the district attorney to bring several new cases to court each day to be set for trial. For example, on January 10, 1848, the clerk of court recorded the names of nine people charged with selling lottery tickets, twenty-two accused of assault and battery, nine for larceny, and one for receiving stolen property. During the next session of the court, the district attorney charged one person with "negro stealing," and the court heard two civil suits by free men of color against a white man. Other matters handled by the court in January 1848 included several petitions for citizenship from recent immigrants, a suit by a slave woman for freedom, the trial of a free man of color accused of failing to record himself in the mayor's office as required by law, men accused of aiding a slave to escape, inveigling a slave, selling liquor to slaves, embezzlement, and robbery. In addition, the court issued a ruling allowing a free man of color to serve as an administrator of the succession (estate) of a white woman.[35]

The Minute Books reveal the arrest and arraignment of Josephine Stewart in 1853 for "keeping a disorderly brothel." According to the complaint, Stewart ran a brothel of ten prostitutes. Her house, located on Dryades Street near Gravier, served as "The resort of the abandoned of both sexes . . . said house is an annoyance to the neighborhood, when obscene and indecent language is constant . . . in said house for lucre and gain of her the said

Josephine Stewart, certain persons, as well men of evil name and fame . . . there to be and remain tippling to the evil example of all others." A jury found Stewart not guilty in May, 1854, but "keeping a brothel" continued to be a frequent item on the court's docket.[36]

Even common civility between the races seems to have been lacking in the 1840s and 1850s. "Insulting a white person" was a crime that by law only free people of color could commit, and the First District Court regularly heard these kinds of cases. In 1847 Julia Black, f.w.c., stood accused of calling a white woman "a Huzzey [sic] an old whore & bitch." A jury found her guilty and ordered her to pay a fine of $30 and court costs of $9. The accusers of other free people of color charged with insulting a white person claimed to have been called "a black guard [sic] and a thief," a "maquerelle" (a French slang word for a pimp or a procurer), a "fils de putain" (son of a whore), and "meaner than a negro."[37]

The presence of slavery increased the level of violence in the city. Although few prosecutions for cruelty to slaves exist, there were a few. One Fanny Smith stood accused of "beating, biting and burning said slaves upon the legs, body, back, face, and hands." A Grand Jury report of January 22, 1850, noted the presence of a slave girl, age eight or nine years, who had suffered abuse by her mistress and was confined in parish prison for her own safety. According to the report, her mistress had burned her all over her body and "fiendishly tortured her . . . she had been beaten and stabbed, her thumbs mashed to jelly." Most often cases in which slaveholders stood accused of mistreating their slaves were dropped before they came to trial.[38]

According to the minute books, the First District Court of New Orleans organized sixty-eight special tribunals for the trial of slaves in Orleans Parish between 1846–1862. Of these, the trial transcripts of twenty-one have vanished; the only evidence of these missing records is the clerk's entry in the minute book and references to the cases in local newspapers. We have no way of knowing whether the district attorney decided not to prosecute for lack of evidence or whether the transcripts have simply disappeared. But the existing records of the special tribunals give clear evidence of the nature of slave trials and invite comparison with trials of free persons in the same court; comparisons of slave trials with trials of free persons prove that procedural niceties were almost totally lacking in slave trials, whereas free persons of color received procedural protections as did whites accused of crimes.

For example, in 1850 the court heard a case concerning four free men of color, *State v. Célèstin Léonard, Louis Pecher, Charles Tailor, and Vignaud Toregane, f.p.c.* One of the defendants, Célèstin Léonard, stood accused of the murder of another free man of color, Edlard Maturin, alias Rivaro; the others were accused of aiding and abetting Léonard. The case began in one of the city's four Recorder's Courts, which sent it to the First District Court on September 6, 1850. The alleged murder had taken place on August 26, 1850. On November 22, the Grand Jury returned "a true bill" of indictment for murder for Léonard and for aiding and abetting for the other three; the accused were arraigned and pleaded not guilty on December 3. On December 24, attorneys for the defendant, which included Cyprien Dufour, one of the most prominent attorneys of New Orleans, and Henry C. Castellanos, a young attorney just beginning his practice, filed a bill of exceptions on the grounds that a free man of color, Sécretan, who had shared a prison cell with the deceased, claimed that the alleged victim threatened to kill Léonard. Judge John C. Larue refused the bill of exceptions, ruling that such evidence did not reduce the crime to manslaughter or make the killing of Maturin "a justifiable or excusable homicide." The jury found Léonard guilty of murder, and the others not guilty of aiding and abetting on January 11, 1851. The jury based its verdict on the eyewitness testimony of free persons of color and whites. Testimony indicated that Léonard had "sought, pursued and killed the deceased." Apparently Léonard and Maturin had agreed to fight a duel, but when Léonard glimpsed his adversary, he fell upon him and slew him. Witnesses observed that Léonard was "laboring under the influence of liquor and anger combined." The judge sentenced Léonard to death and released the other three. On January 16, Dufour and Castellanos asked for and received a suspensive appeal to the Supreme Court of Louisiana.

Dufour based his argument on two grounds. He claimed that the judge of the trial court erred by not allowing the defendants to be tried separately. Dufour and Castellanos had wanted Pecher, Tailor, and Toregane tried before Léonard, and if found not guilty, to use their testimony to exonerate Léonard. The attorney general, Isaac Johnson, cited a number of common law precedents, including *U.S. v. Gribert*, which held that the trial judge had discretion to try persons accused of a common crime separately or together. Johnson quoted Justice Joseph Story in *Gribert*: "that he had never known a case in which the sole ground for a separate trial had been to make the witnesses competent for each other." Johnson also cited several common law treatises, including *Roscoe's Criminal Evidence*. In rebuttal, Dufour also cited *Roscoe's Criminal Evidence* as well as *Phillip's Evidence*, *McNully's Evidence*, and *Chitty's Criminal Law*, and argued that Larue's refusal to allow the defendants to be tried separately was "against universal practice and is destructive of the enlightened tenderness of the law." The Louisiana Supreme Court disregarded this argument, ruling that the trial judge had used discretion properly.

Dufour's second argument concerned the trial court's refusal to admit the testimony of Secrétan, to the effect that Maturin had threatened to kill Léonard, arguing that "It is always improper and against the humane policy the of [*sic*] law, in a case of life and liberty, to shut out evidence which may attenuate the charge. . . . A man may certainly run mad from fear; and such a case may exhibit the frenzy, the *furor brevis*, which renders man deaf to the voice of reason, makes him a fit subject for the indulgence shown by the law to human frailty."

Justice Isaac Preston, writing for the court, held that even if Léonard had heard the threats, he had "time for his passion to cool and reason to resume her sway." Citing a number of precedents and common law treatises, Preston then affirmed the judgment of the lower court, citing Blackstone to justify his opinion: "No affront by words or gestures only is sufficient provocation so as to excuse or extenuate such acts of violence as manifestly endangers the life of another." Thus, even having common law safeguards denied to slaves did not protect Léonard from a sentence of death. Léonard had violated the southern concept of honor, which restricted affairs of honor to white men, and for this he had to suffer the ultimate punishment.[39]

Léonard's story does not end here. Years later, Henry Castellanos wrote about the case in his memoirs. He described Léonard as "a favorite of the Seventh Ward." Castellanos visited Léonard several times between his conviction and the date scheduled for his execution. He reported that Léonard, the son of a white man, was despondent after his conviction. His statement to the young attorney demonstrated his sense of responsibility as the girl's *parain* (godfather), a duty taken quite seriously by Catholic creoles of color and by whites, as well as his internalization of the southern white concept of honor, which held that unlike slaves, white men of honor did not fear death. An important element in this credo involved an admiration of a death that showed personal control rather than an acceptance of the inevitable.[40] "I am not afraid to die," he would frequently say, for I have already faced death without a quiver. But under circumstances so full of shame as these, I confess that I tremble. Let me confide to you a secret. It is this. I have no children, but, when I am gone away, I shall leave behind me a child, a young girl, whose godfather I am, and whom I love with passionate tenderness. Now, to think as she grows up to womanhood, she will be pointed at in the streets as the goddaughter of Célèstin Léonard, *le pendu* [the one hanged], the man that was hanged for murder, and will be made the target for every enemy's sarcasm and raillery, is more torture than I can endure. I pray God every night to deliver me from this world, and should He deny me this boon, well—here he hysterically grasped my arm,—"well I shall never die by the hangman's hand."

Castellanos described how Léonard kept his promise:

One morning, just as dawn was breaking upon the yawning and sleepy city, one of the wardens of the jail . . . was astounded at the sight of a pool of coagulated blood on the flagging of the court-yard, just immediately under the eaves of the condemned cells. Astounded at this ghastly find, the officials were soon scurrying through the hall in the direction of the convict's room. There the inanimate, nude and bloodless corpse of poor Léonard was seen stretched out upon a mattress on the floor, with arms and thighs firmly compressed with thongs, and long gashes across the brachial and femoral arteries. He had bled himself to death. It must have come as a relief to him, for a sweet smile was still playing upon his lips.

The First District Court of New Orleans organized five special tribunals for slaves accused of murdering fellow slaves between 1846 and 1862. In these cases the emphasis on the protection of slave property and the special nature of slave trials is quite evident. For example, in 1846 a special tribunal heard *State v. James, Slave of Widow Bouny*. This case also began in a Recorder's Court. According to the testimony of fellow slave Eugène, also owned by Bouny, James and the deceased slave, Victor, quarreled over five cents, which James alleged Victor owed him. After James called Victor a "son of a bitch," the two began to fight, and James struck Victor in the head with a bottle, which broke. James then shoved the broken bottle into Victor's chest. The mortally wounded slave took a few steps and fell to the ground, dead. The Recorder sent the case to the First District Court. After Judge Isaac Preston (who had risen to the supreme court by the time of the *Léonard* decision) organized the special tribunal, the district attorney brought the case by information. The special tribunal unanimously found James guilty, sentencing him to 100 lashes, twenty-five lashes every fifteen days. Once the sheriff had administered all of the lashes, the sentence allowed James to return to his mistress's service, but required him to wear an iron collar "with three branches" for five years after his release. Sentencing slaves who killed other slaves to wear shackles or iron collars allowed the convicted slaves' owners to continue to use their labor while the convicted slaves endured their punishment. In this case, Bouny owned James and the victim, both of whom worked at her bakery. To sentence James to death or life in prison would have deprived Bouny of both James and Victor, and would have caused the state to pay compensation to Bouny for the value of James (up to $500). It is clear that the tribunal did not consider killing a fellow slave as serious as killing a free person. In a bizarre way, the devaluation of slaves as persons and their value as property saved James from death or life imprisonment. The same day another special tribunal found the slave Henry Payton guilty of the murder of the slave Danwood. The special tribunal sentenced Payton to 125 lashes, twenty-five each month for five months. After his owner paid the court costs, Payton was returned to his master's service, but also had to wear an iron collar with three branches for five years.[41]

Two years later a special tribunal organized by the First District Court heard the case of the slave Cuffy, the property of the New Orleans and Carrollton Railroad, who stood trial for murder of another slave. An eyewitness testified that the incident, which occurred in a stable on Nyades Street, resulted from a quarrel between Cuffy and another slave, Miles, also owned by the railroad. Apparently Miles hit Cuffy on the head with a horseshoe and Cuffy retaliated by stabbing Miles with a large knife. A witness testified that Cuffy had exclaimed, "God damn son of a beach [*sic*]"; the wound caused Miles's death. The special tribunal reduced the charge from murder to manslaughter and sentenced Cuffy to ten years in the penitentiary at hard labor. Although the crime was clearly manslaughter rather than murder, the special tribunal had no authority to find the slave guilty of a lesser charge; the *Black Code* made no provision for a slave's conviction for manslaughter either as an original charge or as a reduction of a charge for murder to manslaughter. Slaves who killed others, free or slave, could only be charged with murder, as manslaughter did not exist as a crime for slaves. But the fact that the tribunal did this underscores the informal nature of the proceedings.[42]

In 1856 the slave George, the property of James Hopkins Jr., brutally murdered the slave Josephine, the property of Nelson Durand. George referred to Josephine as his wife, although the *Civil Code* prohibited slave marriages from having civil effects. George testified before the special tribunal organized to try him for murder to the effect that Josephine had come to Hopkins's house, and the couple had quarreled. George "told her to go away he did not want to have nothing to do with her, she struck him and told him that she was going to have him whipped." A scuffle ensued, and George picked up a dagger and stabbed Josephine "he does not remember how many times." Two other slaves owned by Hopkins testified that they saw Josephine's body lying on the kitchen floor with the knife sticking out of it. The coroner testified that when he arrived at the scene, George told him that he had killed Josephine: "that he had been out of this city and the woman was his wife and that she had slept with another man . . . he did not want to have anything to do with her . . . he did not want no woman to conquer him." When the coroner asked George what he thought would happen to him, George replied, "Yes I will be hung but I cannot help it." The coroner reported that nineteen stab wounds to the chest, four of which penetrated the heart, caused Josephine's death. The special tribunal convicted George of murder and sentenced him to hang, but the governor commuted the sentence to life in the penitentiary at hard labor. There is no record of the amount of compensation the state paid to George's master.[43]

The last case heard by a special slave tribunal organized by the First Judicial Court of New Orleans to try a slave accused of killing another slave was *State v. Jack, Slave of A. Blass* (1858). Unlike *James*, *Henry Payton*, *Cuffy*, and *George*, the Supreme Court of Louisiana heard an appeal of the verdict in this case, but for an extraordinary reason. The special tribunal found Jack guilty of killing the slave Joe, the property of J. B. Maille. Although charged with willful murder, the tribunal had found Jack guilty of manslaughter and sentenced him to five years hard labor in the penitentiary and ten lashes every sixty days during his prison term. Jack had admitted to the arresting officer that he had stabbed Joe "and intended to kill him and was damn glad he had done it." Jack's attorneys argued that the sentence was not authorized by law. The judge of the First District Court (the presiding judge of the tribunal), Theodore G. Hunt, set aside the verdict and arrested the judgment on the grounds that the sentence, a combination of whipping and imprisonment, was unfounded in law; the law stipulated imprisonment *or* whipping, not incarceration *and* corporal punishment. The attorney general appealed to the supreme court. In his reasons for issuing the arrest of judgment, Judge Hunt had argued that the sentence was "cruel, unusual & revolting to humanity & not warranted by law." The slave, he said, "would live in a state of continuous torture for Five Years with a lacerated body, suffering great pain and anguish—a condition to which death itself would be a relief. Such a punishment is abhorrent to law and humanity and cannot receive the sanction of this Court." Judge Hunt then made a remarkable statement: "The statutes of this State relative to the offences [*sic*] of slaves and the punishments for those offences, are of a defective and confused character. It is to be hoped that they will be revised and reformed—that omissions will be supplied and other defects remedied, and that the whole criminal code relative to slaves will be systematized & rendered clear and certain."[44]

Justice Cornelius Voorhies wrote the decision of the supreme court. He ruled that Judge Hunt had erred in arresting the judgment of the special tribunal. Unlike the supreme court briefs and the opinion in *Léonard*, the only cases cited were the court's own precedents in previous appeals from special slave tribunals. Neither the attorney general, the attorneys for the slave, nor Justice Voorhies cited any common law precedents or treatises. Voorhies held that the penalty decreed by the special tribunal, that of whipping and incarceration, was surely a lesser penalty than death, and that the district judge should have passed sentence accordingly, once more underscoring the informal nature of slave trials. Hunt's call for the reform of the criminal code for slaves did not appear in the published supreme court decision.[45]

Between 1846 and 1862, the First Judicial District Court organized several special tribunals to try slaves accused of the murder of free persons; three trial records have survived. The first, *State v. Adeline, Slave of James Forsyth* (1855), involved the slave woman Adeline, who confessed to killing one James Blakely, a white man. Her confession seemed to have been freely given; when Adeline saw the arresting officers, she admitted without being asked that she had stabbed the victim with a sword-cane. She said that she knew why the officers had come: to take her to the "calaboose." The special tribunal found her guilty and sentenced her to twenty-five years at hard labor in the penitentiary. Forsyth had hired an attorney, Franklin Clack, who appealed on the grounds that the court erred in allowing her confession to go to the panel, and that the length of the sentence was unreasonable. Clack argued that a twenty-five-year sentence would use her labor for the most productive years of her life, but as the sentence was not for life or for execution, the master could not claim compensation.

Chief Justice Edwin Merrick wrote the opinion for the supreme court. Merrick ruled that the confession seemed to have been freely given. In affirming the sentence of the special tribunal, Merrick accurately assessed the issue of the master's deprivation of property without compensation for twenty-five years of his slave's labor and saw whose interest was really at stake: "As the punishment of imprisonment is more merciful, perhaps, than any corporal punishment which the jury could inflict commensurate with the offence [sic] committed, the argument appears to be more in the interest of the master than the accused, and one which could be addressed to the Legislature with more hopes of success than to this tribunal."[46]

The second surviving case record, in which a slave stood trial for the murder of a free person, has survived only in fragments. *State v. Henry, Slave of W. C. C. Claiborne* (1856) involved a slave who murdered a free woman of color, Adelaide Laurent Tabony. The special tribunal found Henry guilty and sentenced him to life in the penitentiary at hard labor. The panel valued Henry at $1,100. Unfortunately, we have no further details, but the case is significant in that it shows that the murder of a free person of color merited the same penalty as if Henry had taken the life of a white.[47]

The third surviving record of a slave accused of murdering a free person is that of *State v. Kitty, Slave of Smelser* (1857). The chief witness for the prosecution, Joseph Morehouse, claimed that Kitty had come to him in a great state of agitation: "The accused came to my yard where my shop is, she said she came voluntarily of her own accord; she said that she came to me because she knew I was the friend of her master; she said that she had been hand-cuffed; she had the manacles on her hands; that she was afraid that she was going to be carried out of the state to Texas. I did not know who *Kitty* was . . . she said "I am *Kitty*, the slave of *Mr. Smelser*; I have something to reveal to you about *Mr. Smelser's* death. He was a poisoned man" (italics in original).

Her confession surprised Morehouse; the coroner had believed that Smelser had died of natural causes and had held no inquest. Morehouse told

Kitty that "she must now tell all about it, that it would be better for her to do so, that it would be better for her to tell the whole truth about the matter." Kitty's attorney, R. H. Browne, objected to the confession being admitted as evidence; he argued that it was not voluntary, as Morehouse had held out inducements to her to make her confess by telling her it would be better if she did. Judge Hunt refused to instruct the special tribunal to disregard the confession, and the panel convicted her of murder, sentencing her to life in the penitentiary at hard labor and valuing her at $800. Her attorney appealed. *Kitty* is unusual because both the attorney general and the defendant's counsel cited a number of common law precedents on the subject of the admissibility of confessions in their briefs. Justice Henry Spofford wrote the decision of the supreme court affirming the judgment of the special tribunal on the grounds that, in his opinion, Kitty had voluntarily told Morehouse the circumstances of Smelser's death at a time when she was not under any suspicion.[48]

The First District Court of New Orleans organized only one special slave tribunal that heard a case involving a slave accused of insurrection. The trial record of *State v. Albert, Slave of Dr. Rushton* began in 1853. The arresting officer testified that he had found Albert with "a cutlass, a Spanish knife, a revolver pistol, a canister, & a horn of powder, a quantity of percussion caps, and a lot of balls, moulds, [*sic*] etc." When the officer tried to arrest the slave, Albert drew his knife and said that with others, "bound & free, white & black . . . [he was] in the act of rising against the citizens of New Orleans, and creating an insurrection." The special tribunal found him guilty, sentenced him to life in the penitentiary at hard labor, and valued him for purposes of compensation at $300. James Dyson, a white man, was also implicated in this plot, and he stood trial before the First District Court. The principal witness against Dyson was a free man of color, George White. White testified that Dyson told him that he had a plan to free the slaves, a plan that included freeing those in parish prison, seizing weapons from the city arsenal and powder magazine, inciting slaves on plantations near the city to rise and come to New Orleans with cane knives and hatchets, to set fires within the city, and rob its banks. Dyson's attorney claimed that White was incompetent as a witness because he was a slave, and therefore could not testify against a white person. White called a character witness, his former master, Duncan Kenner, who testified that he had freed White for "faithful service rendered to my family in times of health or sickness . . . always been honest, faithful, and dutiful." Dyson also claimed that White was an incompetent as a witness because he had a financial interest in the case, as if Dyson were convicted, White could collect a fee as an informer. Despite these objections, the Grand Jury indicted Dyson for "using language to incite insurrection." The district attorney later changed the charge to "harboring a slave." Dyson died in jail of typhoid fever before he could stand trial. However, although Dyson clearly seemed to be the mastermind of the insurrection plot, he would have been tried for a lesser crime than insurrection with the presumption of innocence and a trial by jury; Albert had no such luck.[49]

The First District Court of New Orleans organized several special tribunals to try slaves accused of rape or attempted rape. *State v. Michel, Slave of J. B. Folse* (1852) involved a slave charged with assault with intent to commit a rape upon a white person. Under Louisiana law, rape was a crime that by definition could be committed only against white women. The alleged victim, a white woman named Jane Herbert, claimed that the slave Michel pursued her and threw her to the ground three times in attempting to rape her. "Seeing that he could not succeed," the slave ran away. Herbert went home and told her husband of the incident, and he and several of his friends left the house, caught Michel, and brought him to Herbert to identify. Herbert said that she could not positively identify Michel as her assailant, but on the following day, Mr. Herbert brought the same slave to her, and she stated that she felt sure it was Michel who had attempted to rape her. There is no explanation in the record as to why she fingered Michel as the person who had attacked her when she could not on the day of the alleged attack. Perhaps the light was better, perhaps she was less upset, or perhaps her husband pressed her to name an assailant. The special tribunal found Michel guilty, sentenced him to fifty lashes and life in the penitentiary, and valued him at $300 for purposes of compensation.[50]

Three years later, the court organized a special tribunal to try the slave William Green for the rape of a white girl, Melvinia Ellett, aged seven. The special tribunal found Green guilty and sentenced him to hard labor for life in the penitentiary. Green's attorney succeeded in getting a new trial on the basis that the court only summoned six slaveholders to serve on the special tribunal, which allowed no challenges to the jurors as no alternates could replace excused jurors. Also, Green's attorney argued, the panel had failed to make an assessment of the value of the slave. A new trial, however, produced the same verdict and sentence. The record does not include an assessment of the value of the slave. The trial record contains a request for an appeal to the Supreme Court of Louisiana, but no evidence exists that the Court ever received the appeal.[51]

The most remarkable case heard by a special tribunal involving a slave accused of attempted rape is *State v. Sam Scott, Slave of Samuel Stewart* (1856). The special tribunal tried Scott for assault to commit a rape, but found him guilty of assault and battery and sentenced him to one year at hard labor and fifty lashes. His attorney, Franklin H. Clack, argued that the special tribunal had allowed "illegal and improper testimony" to go to the jury, and that the verdict of the jury was contrary to law—that the jury had no right to convict a slave of assault and battery when the charge was assault with attempt to commit a rape. He also argued that a sentence involving hard labor was inappropriate for a conviction of assault. Clack requested an appeal to the Supreme Court of Louisiana, but on the same day, Scott withdrew the request, asking instead that the sentence be carried out: "submitting himself to the sentence of the Court." Whether Scott's owner decided to override his attorney's request for an appeal because he did not wish to take the time and expense of appealing what was a relatively light sentence for the slave, or whether he feared that a reverse and remand decision by the supreme court might have resulted in a more severe sentence, we cannot know. The alleged victim, Euphremia Willis, testified that Scott had entered her house and assaulted her as she was sitting on the sofa. He pushed her over on the sofa, and in the ensuing struggle both Willis and Scott fell on the floor. Another woman, Cornelia Charles, testified that Scott had entered her bedroom while she was asleep, raised the mosquito bar, "caught her by the wrists, held her down in the bed, forcibly kissed her on the side of the neck . . . previous to and since that time he has taken improper liberties with her and her sister, such as passing his hands over their persons, feeling them, etc., etc." On the day of trial, the two alleged victims were themselves charged with keeping a disorderly brothel, "the resort of slaves and idle persons" and selling liquor to slaves. The lesser charge and the light sentence for the slave Sam indicated that the jurors felt the women were not hostile to Sam's advances, and attempted violation of women of their reputation did not constitute a crime serious enough to condemn a slave to death or the penitentiary. In fact, as one historian has observed, white women caught in the act of having an intimate relationship with a black man often leveled accusations of rape to salvage their self-respect.[52]

Slaves who assaulted whites with intent to kill were subject to prosecution and execution or incarceration for life. In *State v. Ralph, Slave of Mrs. Louisa Gordon* (1846) a special tribunal tried the slave Ralph for "assault and stabbing with a knife with intent to kill." Ralph's owner sent him to the city early one morning on an errand, telling him to return soon. Ralph disappeared for more than three hours; when he returned Gordon questioned him about the delay. Gordon testified that Ralph was "in a great state of excitement." He spoke to his master in a "loud, insolent and insulting manner." Gordon immediately tried to chastise him, but the slave resisted. Ralph broke loose, ran for the street, and shouted at Gordon "threatening me, that he would take my Life, and shaking his fist at me, at the same time using the most insulting language." Gordon claimed that the slave drew a knife and tried to stab him; only a crowd of onlookers prevented him from doing so. Although Ralph had not wounded Gordon, the special tribunal found Ralph guilty and sentenced him to perpetual imprisonment at hard labor in the penitentiary.[53]

Another accusation of "assaulting and threatening a white man with intent to kill" resulted in a conviction for a slave. A special tribunal found the slave James guilty of assault on one Patrick Maher and sentenced him to 100 lashes, twenty-five every twenty-two days, to remain in the custody of the sheriff until all of the lashes were administered, and then to be released to his master wearing an iron collar with three branches that he would have to wear for five years. James's master had hired an attorney for his slave. After the verdict, the attorney filed a motion for a new trial on the grounds that "improper and illegal testimony was introduced on the part of the state." It seemed that one month before the trial, James had fought with the district attorney himself and had knocked him down. The district attorney dwelt upon this unrelated incident in his closing argument to the special tribunal "forcibly to the great prejudice of the accused." James's attorney alleged that the members of the panel had questioned the district attorney about the incident following his closing argument; the slave's attorney claimed that the special tribunal took the incident into consideration in determining the guilt of the slave and "greatly augmenting his punishment." Moreover, James's attorney alleged that the alleged victim of the assault, Patrick Maher, was "morally infamous and unworthy of belief," that Maher was drunk at the time of the alleged assault, and that he had expressed great vindictiveness against James and declared his determination to correct him. Furthermore, James's attorney alleged, the evidence at trial was given in a "careless, loose and contradictory manner." Despite the several irregularities in the trial, there is no record of a new trial or a lessening of the sentence.[54]

In 1850 a special tribunal convicted the slave Magdelaine of "striking and cutting a white person with intent to kill" by stabbing a member of the night watch trying to arrest her. Magdelaine, "a notorious prostitute and vagabond," was fighting in the street with what the record referred to as a "young man." Officer Brady asked Magdelaine to retire, and when he attempted to escort her to the guardhouse, she cut his right arm with a knife. Brady's wounds were not serious. The special tribunal found her guilty and sentenced her to thirty lashes in Orleans Street opposite the police jail, ten lashes each eight days, a public punishment designed to humiliate the slave and set an example for others.[55]

The last special tribunal organized by the First District Court of New Orleans to try a slave for assault with intent to murder was *State v. Bill, Slave of John Erman* (1862). The slave Bill had run away from his master until the sheriff caught him and held him in the city jail for safekeeping. According to Erman, he had gone to the jail to chastise Bill for running away. The slave had begged Erman not to whip him, and before Erman could act, Bill picked up an axe in the prison courtyard and hit Erman in the head. Erman then caught hold of Bill and threw him down. Erman testified that he was "passative" [*sic*] that Bill meant to murder him.

Two other witnesses told somewhat different stories. T. W. Roberts testified that he heard the slave "hollering as though he was being whipped. . . . Erman was now and then giving the slave a lick with the cowhide—the slave told Roberts to take him in the Cell and Kill him or do something with him." Erman replied, "God damned you I will kill you," at the same time striking him with a cowhide. Bill grabbed an axe lying at his master's feet and struck him. Roberts wrenched the axe out of the slave's hands, whereupon he grabbed for a brick, which Roberts also took away from the slave. Another witness verified that Erman was in the act of whipping Bill when the slave picked up the axe. Valuing Bill at $1,000, the special tribunal found Bill guilty and sentenced him to be hung outside the prison walls on April 25, 1862.[56]

A reading of the docket of the First District Court of New Orleans between 1846 and 1862 shows a pattern of violent personal crime that neither the police, nor city officials, nor courts, nor the law could effectively suppress. Slave crime, especially violent crime directed against whites, seemed especially threatening to the stability of a port city in which law and order often appeared tentative at best. White society at all levels and free people of color demanded that slaves remain under tight control, although the very nature of city life worked constantly against systematic supervision and consistent discipline. The system of special tribunals by its very harshness and lack of concern with procedural niceties may have given New Orleanians an illusion of control by keeping slaves' rights to the barest minimum. This system arose and continued because white society believed that swift and harsh punishment for slaves who committed crimes, especially violent crimes against whites, would serve as a terrifying example to other slaves contemplating such actions.

The records of the special tribunals organized by the First District Court of New Orleans provide ample evidence of the somewhat precarious status of Louisiana slaves accused and convicted of crimes. Although special courts were created ostensibly to protect slaves and mete out justice, their real purpose was more to maintain the subordinate status of slaves and condemn slave property, as the special nature of slave trials and the tribunals' freedom from procedural due process demonstrates. The law handicapped slave defendants by not demanding a careful observance of procedural rules. Free defendants, white and black, had at least the guarantee of trial by jury, presumption of innocence, and many other common law safeguards when they stood trial for criminal offenses, whereas slaves by law had few procedural rights. Furthermore, more of their actions were considered crimes under Louisiana law than were those for free people. These disabilities reinforced the lowly status of slaves in New Orleans and could have made the law operate on them more harshly than on free people, black and white. But conditions in the city did not result in a reign of terror over slaves. The abolition of slavery in Louisiana and the Union occupation of New Orleans during Reconstruction ended the sharply divided system of criminal law for free and unfree Louisianians and brought the newly freed African Americans into the same system under which free Louisianians had stood trial since 1805. The freedmen would find, however, that the new system offered no guarantees either. In fact, whites instituted new practices to make the law operate more harshly on the newly freed slaves and keep them "in their place."

NOTES

1. Robert C. Reinders, *End of an Era: New Orleans, 1850–1860* (New Orleans, 1964), 166–68; 102, 65–66. The number of arrests in New Orleans between September 1, 1857, and August 31, 1858, totaled 25,417; arrests in Philadelphia, a larger city, in 1858 were 21,537. Reinders, *End of an Era*, 65; Allen Steinberg, *The Transformation of Criminal Justice: Philadelphia, 1800–1880* (Chapel Hill, N.C., 1989), 235. Joseph G. Tregle Jr., "Creoles and Americans," in *Creole New Orleans: Race and Americanization*, ed. Arnold R. Hirsch and Joseph Logsdon (Baton Rouge, 1992), 164–67.

2. Richard Wade, *Slavery in the Cities: The South, 1820–1860* (New York, 1964), 329–39; Judith Kelleher Schafer, "New Orleans Slavery as Seen in Advertisements," *Journal of Southern History* 47 (February 1981): 33, 53–54; Robert C. Reinders, "Slavery in New Orleans in the Decade Before the Civil War, *Mid-America* 44 (1962): 215–16, 219.

3. "An Act for the Punishment of Crimes and Misdemeanors," Act of May 4, 1805, *Orleans Territory Acts, 1805*, Sec. 33, p. 440; Sec. 48, pp. 450–51, hereinafter referred to as the Crimes Act; Warren M. Billings, "Origins of Criminal Law in Louisiana," 32 *Louisiana History* (Winter, 1991), 63–76. "An Act Relative to Crimes and Offences," Act of March 14, 1855, *Louisiana Acts, 1855*, Sec. 1,4,7, p. 130. Louis P. Masur, *Rites of Execution: Capital Punishment and the Transformation of American Culture, 1776–1865* (New York, 1989), 118–19.

4. Crimes Act, Sec. 47, p. 450. The Louisiana *Civil Code* provided for property condemnations of nonslave property. Chapter II of the code states that persons owning property must yield it up "wherever it becomes necessary for the general use." If the owner refused, "the property may be divested from him by the authority of law." Article 2606 required a fair price to be paid in compensation to the owner, and a jury of twelve "freeholders" assessed the value of the property. *Civil Code of the State of Louisiana* (New Orleans, 1825), Chapter 2, Articles 2604–11, pp. 402–3; *Projet of the Civil Code of the State of Louisiana* (New Orleans, 1937), 317–18. In *State v. Amy*, 24 F. Cas. 792 (C.C.D. Va. 1859) (No. 14, 445), Chief Justice Roger B. Taney discussed takings of slave labor to protect society from slave criminals. See also *State v. Jim*, 48 N.C. (3 Jones) 348 (1856) and Andrew Fede, *People Without Rights; An Interpretation of the Fundamentals of the Law of Slavery in the U.S. South* (New York, 1992), 183–89.

5. A. E. Keir Nash, "Fairness and Formalism in the Trials of Blacks in the State

Supreme Courts of the Old South," *Virginia Law Review* 56 (February, 1970): 64–99; Nash, "A More Equitable Past? Southern Supreme Courts and the Protection of the Antebellum Negro," *North Carolina Law Review* 48 (February, 1970): 197–242; Arthur F. Howington, "Not in the Condition of a Horse or an Ox," *Tennessee Historical Quarterly* 34 (Fall, 1975): 249–63. However, Virginia maintained separate slave courts that resulted in a very harsh system throughout the antebellum period. Philip Schwarz, *Twice Condemned: Slaves and the Criminal Laws of Virginia, 1705–1865* (Baton Rouge, La., 1988).

6. "An Act Prescribing the Rules and Conduct to Be Observed with Respect to Negroes and Other Slaves of This Territory," Act of June 7, 1806. *Orleans Territory Acts, 1806*, "Crimes and Offences," Sec. 7, p. 198. Hereinafter called the *Black Code*.

7. *Black Code*, "Crimes and Offences," Sec. 6–7, 9, 11, 15, pp. 198–206. A "mustee" was a term meaning a person of mixed American Indian and African ancestry.

8. Ibid., Sec. 1–3, pp. 190–96. June Purcell Guild, *Black Laws of Virginia: A Summary of the Legislative Acts of Virginia concerning Negroes from Earliest Times to the Present* (Richmond, Va., 1936), 157–58. Philip J. Schwarz, *Twice Condemned*, 26–27. Daniel J. Flanigan, "Criminal Procedure in Slave Trials in the Antebellum South," *Journal of Southern History* 40 (1974): 546–47. H. M. Henry, *The Police Control of Slaves in South Carolina* (Ph.D. diss., Vanderbilt University, 1914), 58. See also Kenneth Stampp, *The Peculiar Institution: Slavery in the Antebellum South* (New York, 1956), 224–27. The 1812 Louisiana Constitution and subsequent antebellum constitutions required voters to be free white male citizens of the United States. Constitution of 1812, Article II, Sec. 6; Constitution of 1845, Title 2, Art. 10; Constitution of 1852, Title 2, Art. 10.

9. Ibid., Sec. 1, 4–6, pp. 190–98.

10. Ibid., Sec. 1, pp. 190–92. "An Act Relative to the Trials of Slaves," Act of June 1, 1846, *Louisiana Acts, 1846*, Sec. 1, p. 114. The *Black Code*, Sec. 10, p. 154, stated specifically that slaves were real estate.

11. Crimes Act, Sec. 51, p. 452; Lewis Kerr, *An Exposition of the Criminal Laws of the Territory of Orleans* (New Orleans, 1806), 160–62, 204. Louisiana lawmakers established a commercial court for Orleans Parish in 1839 that required special juries of merchants limited to settling commercial disputes involving conventional obligations (the civil law term for contracts) and sales, although an 1807 act had authorized the civil courts to call special juries in commercial matters. When, in the judge's opinion, the matter to be settled by a jury was "of such a nature as to require certain information peculiar to certain occupations or professions," the act empowered the judge to call jurors of that occupation or profession. "An Act to Create a Commercial Court in the Parish of New Orleans,

and Other Purposes," Act of March 14, 1839, *Louisiana Acts, 1839*, pp. 42–50. "An Act to Authorize a Special Jury in Certain Cases, and for Other Purposes," Act of March 9, 1807, *Orleans Territorial Acts, 1807*, p. 168. The continued reliance on special juries in Louisiana was not reflected in common law states, where it had mostly died out by the antebellum period. Richard H. Kilbourne Jr., *Louisiana Commercial Law* (Baton Rouge, La., 1980), 88, 101.

12. Crimes Act, Sec. 38, p. 444; *Black Code*, "Crimes and Offences," Sec. 1, pp. 192–94.

13. Crimes Act, Sec. 39–40, pp. 444–46. *Black Code*, "Crimes and Offences," Sec. 12, p. 202–4.

14. Crimes Act, Sec. 33–36, pp. 440–44. *Black Code*, "Crimes and Offences," Sec. 20, 22, pp. 210–12.

15. "An Act Relative to the Trial of Slaves," Act of June 1, 1846, *Louisiana Acts, 1846*, Sec. 1–15, p. 114–16; Daniel J. Flanigan, "Criminal Procedure in Slave Trials," 551. The Louisiana legislature reorganized and expanded the courts of New Orleans in 1846. The First District Court was given jurisdiction over all criminal proceedings, and criminal cases were given precedence in the docket over civil cases. "An Act to Organize District Courts in the Parish and City of New Orleans," Act of April 30, 1845, *Louisiana Acts, 1846*, Sec. 8, p. 33; "An Act Relative to Criminal Prosecutions in the First Judicial District," Act of March 8, 1841, *Louisiana Acts, 1841*, p. 59. The legislature made minor revisions and clarifications in the 1846 act the following year. Under the 1846 act it had been the parish sheriff's duty to summon the slaveholders to serve on the special tribunals. The 1847 revision gave that duty to other officials if the office of parish sheriff became vacant; the responsibility to issue summonses fell successively to the parish coroner, constable, or whomever the judge appointed. In addition, the compliance with a summons to serve on a slave tribunal was to be enforced in the same manner as for jury duty in the trials of free persons. The 1847 act also specified the procedure for slaveowners' compensation for slaves executed or condemned to the penitentiary for life: the auditor of public accounts issued a warrant to the owner of the condemned slave to receive the value of the slave determined by the special tribunal, after receiving proof of execution or delivery to the penitentiary. "An Act to Amend 'An Act Relative to the Trial of Slaves' Approved on the first of June One Thousand Eight Hundred and Forty-Six," Act of May 4, 1847, *Louisiana Acts, 1847*, Sec. 1–2, pp. 216–17.

16. *Journal of the House of Representatives, 1852*, pp. 71, 133. In 1854, the legislature once again tinkered with the provisions concerning compensation for owners of slaves executed or sentenced to life in prison. This act raised the award to two-thirds of the convicted slave's value, the amount not to exceed $750, a more realistic compensation. Lawmakers did not address the issue of whether a felony

conviction reduced the value of a slave. Once more, the special tribunal had the responsibility to assess the value of convicted slaves for purposes of compensation. "An Act to Provide Compensation to Owners of Slaves Condemned to Death or the Penitentiary, by the State," Act of March 16, 1854, *Louisiana Acts, 1854,* Sec. 1, p. 149. Public executions of slaves in New Orleans drew thousands of spectators. See, for example, "The Execution of Pauline," *New Orleans Daily Picayune*, March 28, 1846. The execution of the slave Pauline was the first public execution of a woman in New Orleans. Pauline had beaten and terrorized her mistress and confined her in a small room at the back of her house. A spectator estimated that four to five thousand people watched the execution. Henry C. Castellanos, *New Orleans as It Was: Episodes of Louisiana Life* (New Orleans, 1895), 104, 167–76. "An Act to Provide for the Execution of Slaves," Act of March 16, 1852, *Louisiana Acts, 1852,* 148.

17. *State v. Adam and Delisle*, First District Court of New Orleans, No. 7481 (April 30, 1852). All cases hereinafter cited are cases of the First District Court unless otherwise stated. *New Orleans Daily Picayune*, July 3, 1852. Castellanos, *New Orleans as It Was*, 104–11. Castellanos stated that the execution "was a sight, once seen, never to be forgotten."

18. "An Act to Provide for the Execution of Sentences to Death in the Parish of New Orleans," Act of March 1, 1854, *Louisiana Acts, 1854,* 20. Castellanos states that this act was the result of the execution of Adam and Delisle. Castellanos, *New Orleans as It Was*, 110. "An Act Relative to Slaves and Free Colored Persons," Act of March 15, 1855, *Louisiana Acts, 1855,* Sec. 51, p. 384.

19. "An Act Relative to Slaves and Free Colored Persons," Sec. 1–17, 39–47, pp. 377–79, 383–84.

20. Ibid., Sec. 49–53, pp. 384–85.

21. Ibid., Sec. 55–56, 59–60, p. 385. "An Act Relative to Criminal Proceedings," Act of March 14, 1855, *Louisiana Acts, 1855,* Sec. 22, p. 153.

22. "An Act to Provide for the Trial of Slaves Accused of Capital Crimes in the Parish of Orleans," Act of March 9, 1855, *Louisiana Acts, 1855,* Sec. 1, 4, 6, pp. 37–38.

23. *State v. Harrison, a Slave*, No. 4464, 10 La. Ann. 722 (1856); Constitution of 1845, Article 118; Constitution of 1852, Article 115. "An Act Relative to the Trials of Slaves," Sec. 14, 116; "An Act Relative to Slaves and Free Colored Persons," Sec. 1–17, 39–47, pp. 377–79, 383–84. "An Act to Provide for the Trials of Slaves in the Parish of Orleans," Sec. 1, 4, 6, pp. 37–38.

24. *Official Journal of the House of Representatives of the State of Louisiana: Session of 1857,* pp. 43–44. "An Act Relative to Slaves," Act of March 19, 1857, *Louisiana Acts, 1857,* Sec. 34, 38–39, p. 233.

25. "An Act for the Trial of Slaves Accused of Capital Crimes in the Parish of Or-

leans," Act of March 15, 1858, *Louisiana Acts, 1858*, Sec. 6–7, p. 59; *Official Journal of the Senate of Louisiana: Session of 1858*, p. 128.

26. *Executive Journal of the Senate of Louisiana: Session of 1858*, p. 12.

27. *Official Journal of the House of Representatives of the State of Louisiana: Session of 1859*, p. 6. *Official Journal of the House of Representatives: Fifth Legislature, 1860*, pp. 7–8.

28. Two of the very few reported slave tribunals in the minute books of the Criminal Court of the First District, City of New Orleans, include: *State v. Victoire, slave of Hazeur*, No. 8690, August 5, 1842; *State v. Adeline, slave of Philip Marsondet*, No. 8874, November 10, 1842. The Records of the City Court during the territorial period, the Parish Court records, and the Decisions of the Mayor in Criminal Cases, 1823–1844, are in the City Archives at the New Orleans Public Library. *State v. William Swanton*, No. 183, August 14, 1846. For a sample of trials for crimes specific to free persons of color before the First District Court see *State v. Julia Evans, f.w.c.*, No. 5410, November 23, 1850 (insulting a white person); *State v. Adele Catherine alias Victoire Pellebon, f.w.c.*, No. 5314, July 22, 1850 (insulting and assaulting a white person); *State v. Mary Ann Martin, f.w.c.*, No. 299, September 30, 1846 (being in the state in violation of the law); *State v. Lafayette Coffee, f.m.c.*, No. 4244, October 20, 1849 (failure to record himself in register of free persons of color). Louisiana law required free persons of color to have the words "free man or woman of color" after their name in any legal proceeding. Notaries and clerks of court ordinarily abbreviated this requirement by inserting f.m.c. or f.w.c. after the names of free blacks. "An Act to Prescribe Certain Formalities Respecting Free Persons of Color," Act of March 31, 1808, *Orleans Territory Acts, 1808*, pp. 138–40.

29. *New Orleans Daily Picayune*, September 20, 1852.

30. *New Orleans Daily Picayune*, September 20, 1852.

31. *New Orleans Daily Picayune*, September 21, 1852.

32. *New Orleans Daily Picayune*, September 21, 1852, October 1, 1852.

33. Tregle, "Creoles and Americans," 156–67; Reinders, *End of an Era*, 63–65. See also Dennis Rousey, *Policing the Southern City: New Orleans, 1805–1889* (Baton Rouge, La., 1996).

34. A. Oakley Hall, quoted in Leonard V. Huber, *The Presbytere on Jackson Square: The American Period, 1803 to the Present* (New Orleans, 1970), 40–41, 43–44. There were complaints that juries of the First District Court were not properly supervised. In *State v. Brunetto*, a trial for wilful murder, the sheriff took the jury to a restaurant for dinner during the jury deliberations. During the course of the dinner, which lasted for two hours, the jurors consumed cocktails of both absinthe and anisette, six bottles of claret, half a bottle of brandy, and a bottle of champagne. The jury returned to the jury room after dinner and resumed de-

liberations, finding Brunetto guilty. The defendant's attorney won on appeal to the Supreme Court of Louisiana. In a classic understatement, Justice Cornelius Voorhies declared "one or more of the jurors were not in possession of that un-clouded intellect which the accused had a right to demand." *State v. Brunetto*, No. 5376, 13 La. Ann. 45 (1858); Reinders, *End of an Era*, 73–74.

35. Minute book, First District Court of New Orleans, January 10, 1848, January 14, 1848.

36. *State v. Stewart*, No. 9351, May 11, 1854.

37. *State v. Julia Black, f.w.c.*, No. 1095 (July 3, 1847); *State v. Joseph Aguilard, f.m.c.*, No. 1159 (October 13, 1848), *State v. Louise Florian, f.w.c.*, No. 1301 (November 19, 1847); *State v. Maurice Charles, f.w.c.* (June 28, 1847); *State v. Mary Davis, f.w.c.*, No. 3542 (May 14, 1849).

38. *State v. Fanny Smith*, No. 9935 (February 23, 1855); Report of the Grand Jury, Minute Book of the First District Court of New Orleans, January 22, 1850; Judith K. Schafer, "'Details Are of the Most Revolting Character': Cruelty to Slaves as Seen in Appeals to the Supreme Court of Louisiana," 68 *Chicago-Kent Law Review* (1993): 1283–1311.

39. *State v. Léonard, Pecher, Tailor, and Toregane, f.p.c.*, No. 5602 (January 11, 1851). A "suspensive" appeal in Louisiana is one in which the effect of the judgment of the trial court is suspended pending the appeal. A "devolutive" appeal is one in which the judgment goes into effect immediately despite the appeal. In capital cases, appeals were always suspensive, for obvious reasons. In the Supreme Court of Louisiana the case was known as *State v. Célèstin Léonard et al.*, 6 La. Ann. 420 (1851). Castellanos, *New Orleans as It Was*, 114–16. Kenneth S. Greenberg, *Honor and Slavery* (Princeton, N.J., 1996), 34. See also Bertram Wyatt-Brown, *Honor and Violence in the Old South* (New York, 1986).

40. Greenberg, *Honor and Slavery*, 89–93.

41. *State v. James, Slave of Widow Bouny*, No. 181 (August 15, 1846); *State v. Henry Payton, Slave of John Eaton*, No. 186 (August 15, 1846).

42. *State v. Cuffy, Property of the New Orleans and Carrollton Railroad*, No. 3016 (November 18, 1848); *Louisiana Acts, 1823*, Sec. 1–2, p. 16.

43. *Civil Code*, Art. 182, p. 28; *State v. George, Slave of James Hopkins, Jr.*, No. 12,585 (December 26, 1856).

44. *State v. Jack, Slave of A. Blass*, No. 13,653 (July 12, 1858). In *State v. Sanité, Slave of Alexis Faurie*, No. 9934 (February 19, 1855), a special tribunal convicted the slave Sanité of assault and battery with intent to maim after she scalded the slave Auguste by throwing a pot of boiling water at his face. The special tribunal sentenced her to twenty-five lashes and six months in the parish prison. Her owner brought a writ of *habeas corpus* on the grounds that the special tribunal had no right to sentence a slave to more than eight days in prison for a noncapi-

tal crime. The judge of the First Judicial District Court released Sanité after she had been lashed and had served eight days.

45. *State v. Jack*, No. 5926, 14 La. Ann 385 (1859). See also *State v. Slave Flemming, Slave of Casimire Lacoste*, No. 1945 (March 9, 1848); *State v. Dabney Green, Slave of Capt. Thomas J. Casey*, No. 8608 (March 11, 1853); *State v. Henry, Slave of Mr. Jennings*, No. 9144 (December 9, 1853); *State v. Tom Evans, Slave of George Parker*, No. 10,487 (June 30, 1855); *State v. Cornelius, Slave of A. H. Justamond*, No. 15,361 (November 7, 1861). The penalty was lessened for slaves who wounded but did not kill other slaves. The slave Frederick stood trial for "cutting with a dangerous weapon with intent to kill" when he entered the plantation of Pierre Lacoste and stabbed the slave Charles. A special tribunal found Frederick guilty and sentenced him to twenty-five lashes and to wear an iron collar for six months at the service of his master. *State v. Frederick, Slave of P. R. Puissan*, No. 13,652 (May 15, 1858).

46. *State v. Adeline, Slave of James Forsyth*, No. 10,917 (January 29, 1856); *State v. Adeline, a Slave*, No. 4503, 11 La. Ann. 736 (1856).

47. *State v. Henry, Slave of W. C. C. Claiborne*, No. 12,586 (December 23, 1856).

48. *State v. Kitty, Slave of Smelser*, No. 12,799 (March 14, 1857). *State v. Slave Kitty*, No. 5154, 12 La. Ann. 805 (1857). Several cases in which slaves stood trial for murder seem to have been accidental deaths. In five separate incidents slaves stood trial for murder when the carts or carriages they were driving ran over a white child. Four of the special tribunals returned verdicts of not guilty: *State v. Jerry, Slave of William Massey*, No. 4648 (January 25, 1850); *State v. David, Slave of Robert F. Ferguson*, No. 9357 (February 11, 1854); *State v. Bill Mullen, Slave of the New Orleans Cotton Press*, No. 9356 (February 11, 1854); *State v. Tom Green, Slave of Mr. Stewart*, No. 15,034 (February 19, 1861). In *State v. Pompey, Slave of Mrs. Callander*, No. 6694 (July 9, 1851), a special tribunal found Pompey guilty of killing a child by driving over him with a cart and sentenced him to fifty lashes in two installments. A special tribunal found the slave Edouard not guilty of maiming a white person after he was accused of blinding a white child in one eye by throwing a brickbat during a street fight. *State v. Edouard, Slave of Mlle. Cabaret*, No. 6693 (July 9, 1851).

49. *State v. Albert, Slave of Dr. Rushton*, No. 9157 (June 27, 1853); *State v. James Dyson*, No. 9159 (June 22, 1853).

50. *State v. Michel, Slave of J. B. Folse*, No. 7755 (June 8, 1852). See also *State v. Rodney, Slave of Emanuel Prados*, No. 1987 (March 10, 1848).

51. *State v. William Green, Slave of Mrs. N. B. Hale*, No. 10,494 (July 10, 1855; May 29, 1856).

52. *State v. Sam Scott, Slave of Samuel Stewart*, No. 10,830 (February 4, 1856). *New Orleans Daily Picayune*, July 27, August 4, 16, 1855. Martha Hodes, *White*

Women, Black Men: Illicit Sex in the Nineteenth-Century South (New Haven, Conn., 1997), 61–62; Wyatt-Brown, *Honor and Violence*, 109–10.

53. *State v. Ralph, Slave of Mrs. Louisa Gordon*, No. 180 (August 15, 1846).

54. *State v. James, Slave of Davis*, No. 188 (September 18, 1846).

55. *State v. Magdelaine, Slave of Dr. Bennett*, No. 4647 (January 25, 1850).

56. *State v. Bill, Slave of John Erman*, No. 15,779 (April 14, 1862). See also *State v. Alfred, Slave of John K. Collens*, No. 9143 (December 9, 1853); *State v. Dick, Slave of William Gerard*, No. 12,228 (July 8, 1856); *State v. Jack, Slave of John Armstrong, Esq.*, No. 15,691 (February 25, 1862). For trials of slaves accused of arson and burglary, see *State v. Sam, Slave of Hardenbrook*, No. 4045 (July 20, 1849); *State v. Patrick, Slave of William Rise*, No. 4046 (July 2, 1849); *State v. Crispin, James and Edward*, No. 5253, 5254 (July 5, 1850); *State v. Jane, Slave of Mary Ellen Williams, f.w.c.*, No. 12,289 (July 8, 1856); *State v. Edward Thomas, Slave of Samuel Jerdleman*, No. 14,480 (April 21, 1860); *State v. Vincent, Slave of Ann Harty, f.w.c.*, No. 15,856 (May 26, 1862). One slave stood trial and was acquitted of the charge of giving false and illegal passes to slaves, *State v. Jim, Slave of Reynolds*, No. 11,332 (August 28, 1856).

The Law and the Culture of Slavery: Natchez, Mississippi

Ariela Gross

Traveling to Natchez, Mississippi, from the east by horse-drawn carriage in 1830, as did the "Yankee" Joseph Ingraham, one's first sight would have been "a cluster of rough wooden buildings, in the angle of two roads, in front of which several saddle-horses, either tied or held by servants, indicated a place of popular resort." This was the slave market, known as "Forks-of-the-Road" or "niggerville," the busiest slave market in the South after Algiers, in New Orleans.[1] Slave buyers entered a gate into a courtyard, where "a line of negroes, commencing at the entrance with the tallest . . . down to a little fellow about ten years of age, extended in a semicircle around the right side of the yard."[2]

The journey to Forks-of-the-Road seemed different to one who approached the pen from the other entrance. William Wells Brown remembered arriving at Natchez as the hired slave of a "soul-driver," probably Isaac Franklin, who had built the marketplace there. The slaves landed at night and were driven to the pen in the morning; as soon as they arrived in the pen, "swarms of planters [were] seen in and about them." Brown wrote about the ordeal of sale from the perspective of the trader's helper, dressing the slaves and driving them into the yard. "Some were set to dancing, some to jumping, some to singing, and some to playing cards. . . . I have often set them to dancing when their cheeks were wet with tears."[3] Isaac Stier, an Adams County slave whose father had been sold at Forks-of-the-Road, remembered his father's stories of being "fed an' washed an' rubbed down lak race horses," then "dressed up an' put through de paces that would show off dey muscles." Stier's father "was sol' as a twelve year old, but he always said he was nigher twenty."[4]

The traveler continuing along St. Catherine's Road would soon have reached the town of Natchez. Towering above the town, on a hill overlooking the Mississippi River, loomed the Adams County Courthouse.[5] Like most antebellum courthouses, it was built in the Greek Revival style, with Ionic columns in front and a tall clock tower. Its imposing architecture and its centrality in the town made it not only the primary meeting place but also the chief symbol of government authority in the environs. If the traveler had arrived at Natchez in May or November, he would have found crowds of people gathered in the courthouse square for Court Week. People came to court for many reasons, but often, what brought them there began at Forks-of-the-Road. At the courthouse, neighbors and strangers came together to work out the disputes that arose in the daily business of the slave and cotton economy. The market for slaves, land, and cotton spilled over into the courtroom in battles about unpaid debts, failed crops, and sick and recalcitrant slaves.

These two institutions, the courthouse and the slave market, were central to southern culture, but they have often been seen as quite separate and distant from one another. Cultural historians of the nineteenth-century South have not paused long on the courthouse steps. Most have assumed that for whites, rituals of honor, and for slaves, plantation discipline, replaced law as the mechanisms for resolving conflict and punishing wrongdoers.[6] Legal historians have paid attention to pressing constitutional questions, dramatic criminal cases, or broad questions of the relations between legal and economic development in the South, far from the circuit trials that mattered so much in local culture.[7] This essay will travel from the county courthouse to the slave market, drawing the connections between the two.

Much of the daily business of southern courts involved the commercial law of slavery—about half of the trials in the Adams County Circuit Court. Civil trials involving slaves were the routine events bringing townsfolk and planters together to fight over their human property, far more common than criminal trials with slave defendants. For example, during the years 1829–41, fewer than 600 criminal cases came before the Adams Circuit Court, whereas there were about 3,200 civil actions.[8] Thus, many of the functions one might have expected the southern criminal justice system to perform, such as disciplining black men, or settling affairs of honor among white men, were also handled by the civil system. While white men rarely faced criminal prosecution for striking out at slaves, they quite often found themselves in court for civil suits regarding property damage to the slave of another. This essay draws on a database of 177 slave-related civil trials litigated in Adams County, Mississippi, between 1798 and 1861, as well as a variety of local records including manuscript census schedules, tax rolls, personal papers and newspapers.[9] By looking at county trials rather than appellate opinions in state court, it is possible to see the law in action at the everyday level.

The county to which our traveler made his journey, Adams County, Mississippi, was in some ways unique and in some ways representative of the Deep South. Adams County held within its boundaries a large population of slaves, some of the richest planters in the South (the "nabobs") living in suburban estates, a free black community numbering about two hundred, and a town of white working people living on the bluff overlooking the Mississippi River. Below the bluff, "Under-the-Hill" was a raucous port known for gambling, drinking, and brawling with the famous "Bowie" knives first used in its barrooms. Natchez and its environs contained most of the wealth and population of rural Mississippi, and in the early years of statehood, in the 1820s, Natchez was a political center as well. Although the presence of a very wealthy planter class made Adams County unusual, over one-third of the county's white households contained no slaves at all.[10] In fact, the very wide range of wealth and slaveholding among the whites of Adams County, together with its large slave population, active slave market, and excellent surviving records, combine to make it a revealing point of entry into the courtrooms of the plantation South.

Court Week was a social event in Natchez, as in small towns across the South.[11] Beginning in 1832, circuit courts were held at the Adams County Courthouse every May and November.[12] Men attended court because they were litigants, jurors, or witnesses, or because their interests might be affected by a case in other ways, as creditor, debtor, or guarantor of a note. Whether or not they had business at court, "a large number" of women and children as well as men "went for the recreation and excitement attendant upon such occasions; many more went to get 'something to drink,' as it was always very plentiful on those occasions."[13] On the courthouse steps, citizens

gambled, drank, brawled, listened to oratorical flights of rhetoric, and debated politics.[14]

In attendance at courts were men, women, and children from all walks
of life. The traveler arriving at the courthouse on a spring day in 1830, for
example, might first have met some of the wealthy planters, known as
"nabobs," arriving by liveried carriage from the suburban estates that skirted
the town.[15] Gathering at the courthouse he would also have found a raucous
collection of working men, many foreign-born, especially British and Irish,
with a smattering of Germans and French, and others who haled originally
from Virginia and Maryland. Most of these town-dwellers were middle-class
and owned few slaves or none at all.[16]

The traveler would not have seen only white faces. Slaves made up about
three-fourths of the population of Adams County in 1830; most of the slaves
of Mississippi lived in Adams County and the neighboring counties. The enslaved population, however, was largely dispersed in the rural plantations,
with only 15 percent of slaves living in Natchez, whereas whites and the small
population of free blacks were concentrated in town.[17] Thus, the view from
the courthouse square would have been different from the view along the
route. The slaves who came to town for Court Week were probably body servants, carriage drivers, market people, and slaves directly involved in litigation; field hands stayed behind. The few town slaves, who would likely have
crowded the courthouse square, were probably employed primarily as domestic servants and in retail establishments; others were dockhands, draymen, brickmakers, and lumber hands.[18] They would have been joined by
the members of a small free black "aristocracy" of Natchez, which included
six families owning five to twenty slaves and some real estate.[19] Other, much
poorer free blacks might also have joined the crowd milling about in the
square—peddlers, prostitutes, and day laborers.[20]

William Johnson was a leader of the free black community, a barber and
independent businessman, protected by wealthy white patrons, who also kept
a diary for which he has become justly famous. Johnson's journal entries il-
lustrate the place Court Week commanded in the local culture. Almost every
time circuit court was in session, Johnson noted that business was doing better because of it—because more people were in town to attend—or noted
his surprise that business had not improved despite the court's being in session. For example, in May 1850, he wrote, "Buisness not very Brish for Court
times," and "Buisness rarther dull for Court to be in Cession yet," while in

November Term of that year, business was much better during Court Week, "Greate many Persons in town." During one court session in 1844, Johnson noted that a bipartisan dinner for the governor was not well attended, because the circuit judge refused to adjourn court.[21]

Johnson's diary entries also suggest that civil disputes involving slaves commanded local attention along with criminal cases. Many times he mentions legal proceedings involving slave stealing, slave beating, or other issues involving slaves.[22]

Circuit courts were an arena not only for local culture, a meeting place and focal point for the neighborhood, but also for a broader legal culture. That is, the lawyers and judges who rode circuit from county to county developed their own cohesive camaraderie, a romance and lore of the circuit, which instructed their membership in a distinctive sense of their profession, of what it meant to be a man of law. Many were convinced that it was the experience of circuit-riding that forged the legal fraternity and was the single source of legal culture in the Old South. According to Charles Warren, "many older lawyers have been of the opinion that the largest and best part of the legal education of the past was this mingling of the whole Bar together in traveling from county to county, and from court to court, the enforced personal relations which were brought about, and the presence of the younger members of the Bar during the trials of cases by their seniors."[23] Circuit riding also gave lawyers an important role in cultural transmission, transporting ideas from town to town, and linking far-flung rural areas.[24] Whereas a relatively large, wealthy town like Natchez supported its own bar, many areas relied on the lawyers who rode into town with the judge for the circuit court.

As a group, lawyers and judges were the wealthiest participants in civil trials involving slaves, and most closely identified with the planter class. Young men came to Natchez to practice law, but nearly always turned into planters over the course of their careers. The high level of slaveholding among lawyers, their close connections to the nabobs, and the fact that their practices depended heavily on the slave economy suggests the degree to which slavery helped to shape both legal culture and legal practice in the Deep South.

In many parts of the South, lawyers aimed to be statesmen. Lawyers who had built up lucrative practices had the choice to rise to the bench, to try their hand at politics, or to become planters. In Adams County, however, the well-trod path from lawyer into statesman and politician was largely closed off in the years following the Panic of 1837, when Adams County's wealthy Whigs lost political power to the Democrats of the new piney-woods counties of eastern and northern Mississippi. Natchez lawyers also disappeared from the state supreme court after 1832, when it became an elective office.[25]

Nevertheless, Natchez was known as "a mecca for lawyers." As Joseph Baldwin explained in a sketch of lawyers during the "flush times of Alabama and Mississippi," lawyers moved to the Southwest because "it was extolled as a legal Utopia, peopled by a race of eager litigants, only waiting for the lawyers to come on and divide out to them the shells of a bountiful system of squabbling."[26] When John A. Quitman, who went on to be a general in the Mexican-American War and governor of Mississippi, first arrived in Natchez to practice law, he wrote to his father, "No part of the United States holds out better prospects for a young lawyer." The reasons Quitman gave had less to do with lawyering than with cotton planting. "[The planters] live profusely, drink costly Port, Madeira, and sherry, after the English fashion, and are exceedingly hospitable. Cotton planting is the most lucrative business that can be followed. Some of the planters net $50,000 from a single crop." Quitman left no doubt that his goal as a lawyer would be to achieve planter status.[27] Joseph Ingraham, the "Yankee" who traveled the old Southwest, found a connection between the vibrancy of the slave market and the relative paucity of politically active and well-known lawyers making their home in Natchez, observing, "A plantation well stocked with hands, is the *ne plus ultra* of every man's ambition who resides at the south." Whatever their ambitions when they came to Adams County, they "soon catch the mania, and nothing less than a broad plantation, waving with the snow white cotton bolls, can fill their mental vision."[28]

This transition from lawyer to planter, and sometimes to planter-judge, was an important one among the lawyers who made their business representing parties to civil disputes involving slaves. One major dynasty of lawyer-planters began with Judge Edward Turner. Turner was born in Virginia, studied law in Kentucky, and came to Natchez in 1802, at the age of twenty-four. By 1815, he had built up a small legal practice and owned three slaves and twelve acres of land. In the 1820s he began to climb the ranks of the judiciary, first as a judge of the Adams County criminal court, then as a supreme court judge, and finally as chief justice of the High Court of Errors and Appeals. He also became a major planter and married into a nabob family, beginning a tradition followed by many young lawyers who came to

Natchez from parts north. Both John A. Quitman and William B. Griffith, his law partner, married into Turner's family; Griffith married Turner's daughter and Quitman his niece.

The tradition continued with John T. McMurran, whose career highlights the influence of slavery in tracing this path from lawyer to planter. A native of Pennsylvania, McMurran read law in Ohio with an uncle, and received no formal schooling. He came to Natchez with a letter of introduction to Quitman, and then succeeded Griffith as Quitman's law partner in 1828. By 1835, McMurran was responsible for the largest practice in Southwest Mississippi, as Quitman quit the regular practice of law when he became a state senator. McMurran married another of Edward Turner's daughters, Mary Louise. McMurran handled about a quarter of the court's business during the 1840s. Most of his legal practice, like that of most antebellum lawyers, involved debt collection, particularly on behalf of the Commercial Bank of Natchez. McMurran was the lawyer for the plaintiff in fourteen civil trials involving slaves during the 1830s, and defendant's counsel in three. This made him one of the most frequent repeat players in slave-related trials.[29] McMurran put the money from his law practice into the accumulation of land and slaves. By the 1850s, McMurran owned four plantations in Mississippi, Louisiana, and Arkansas, and together with his law partner James Carson owned hundreds of slaves and thousands of acres in Adams County alone. From his humble beginnings as a migrant with only his legal apprenticeship to recommend him, McMurran had become a wealthy planter and major slaveholder.[30]

Judges reflected the social background and politics of the bar as a whole. Before the new state constitution of 1832 introduced judiciary elections, judges were appointed by the governor. After 1832, although judges were elected, nearly all of the candidates were lawyers, and campaigns were more dignified than elections for other positions. In the first decades of the nineteenth century, a number of states had their supreme court judges ride circuit as well, which meant that they sometimes reviewed their own decisions on appeal, but by the 1830s most states had established separate systems. Even in the earliest times, when judges were less likely to have formal legal training, those who did not come from "gentlemanly" backgrounds met a backlash against their authority. Seth Lewis, the first chief justice of the Territorial Court in 1802, suffered such great scorn at Natchez as "an ignorant shoemaker" that he quit his position and went into private practice.[31]

Lawyers in Natchez, many of whom had been born or studied in the North, aspired to join the ranks of planters and to take part in planter society. The bulk of their business was commercial litigation, which in Natchez meant slave-related trials. The great majority of these lawyers made no distinction between traders and others as clients, and there was no plaintiffs' bar or defense bar. While lawyers who did banking litigation might have particular banks as steady clients and might primarily process land claims, they represented buyers, sellers, hirers, and owners in disputes involving slaves. The typical lawyer turned his legal fees into slaves as soon as he possibly could. Often, these same lawyer-planters became the local judges. Simply put, their practices rested on slavery. In this way, slavery shaped legal practice and lawyers and judges became invested in the institution of slavery.

The slave markets that provided so many lawyers with their livelihoods—both as litigators and as slaveholding planters—did a vigorous business in the antebellum Deep South. Although foreign importation of slaves ended in 1808 due to constitutional prohibition, the Deep Southern states continued to import slaves from the Upper South in ever greater numbers during the antebellum period.[32] Slave traders brought slaves from Virginia, Kentucky, and Tennessee to sell at the markets in Charleston, Natchez, and New Orleans. Overall, more than a quarter of a million slaves came into the Deep South from the Upper South each decade from the 1830s on. Local sales also accounted for a substantial part of the trade, probably more than half.[33] Individual slaveholders sold slaves to one another directly, or used local traders as intermediaries. And slaves were sold by the sheriff at public auction when a slaveholder or his estate became insolvent. In South Carolina, the one state for which we have solid numbers, these sales amounted to one-third of all slave sales.[34]

The slave trade in Natchez spilled beyond the boundaries of Forks-of-the-Road. Before 1833, slaves were sold everywhere—off boats that docked at the landing Under-the-Hill, at shops on Main Street in upper Natchez, on the steps of the county courthouse in court-ordered sales, as well as at Forks-of-the-Road. To prevent what many viewed as an unseemly display, the town in 1833 passed an ordinance to prevent public sales by slave traders. This rule was stiffened in 1835 by a second ordinance prohibiting the exhibition of slaves as merchandise on street corners and in front of stores within the city limits by anyone.[35] By the 1830s, two-thirds of the slaves in the state had originally come from Virginia, with the remainder coming from Kentucky and other states. Most slaves sent to the Southwest arrived at New Orleans by ship, and continued up the river to Natchez between October and May; the firm of Franklin and Armfield sent an additional overland coffle each summer to Natchez. Altogether, in addition to many local sales, about 1,300 slaves a year came into the Natchez market from the upper South by the 1830s; this number may have doubled by 1860.[36] In 1902, General William T. Martin, who had been a lawyer in many slave cases, remembered that "[i]n some years there were three or four thousand slaves here [at Natchez]. I think that I have seen as many as 600 or 800 in the market at one time."[37]

Slaves were also the cornerstone of the southern credit economy. An exhaustive study of credit relations in one Louisiana parish outside New Orleans has shown that slaves, because they were readily convertible into cash, were "especially desirable for collateralizing debt arrangements." In the 1850s, four out of five sales of slaves were paid in cash, and credit sales rarely had terms longer than twelve months, whereas land mortgages lasted two to five years.[38] Thus, slaves were the ideal collateral for debts. The complex web of notes traded on slaves could, and often did, fall through in years of financial panic and high land speculation. Other segments of the economy depended on slaves as well. Hiring or leasing provided an important way for both individuals and corporate entities, especially towns and cities, to obtain labor without making the major capital investment in slaves. Slave hiring may have involved as much as 15 percent of the total slave population.[39]

Market transactions, credit relations, and hires all led to disputes that had the potential to land the parties in court. If they did not succeed in settling a dispute out of court, many dissatisfied buyers and lessees turned to the law. They had to be able to afford court costs and attorney's fees that ranged from about thirty dollars to several hundred dollars.[40] Nevertheless, the people who brought their suits to county court were not the biggest planters in the Cotton Kingdom; they reflected the local population in miniature. In Adams County, about one-third owned between one and five slaves. For these plaintiffs, the illness, injury, or loss of just one slave could be devastating. Fewer than one-third were planters owning twenty slaves or more, and a much smaller number were extremely wealthy planters with hundreds of slaves and large plantations. The median plaintiff owned ten slaves and 280 acres and probably made his living through farming.[41] By contrast, de-

Table 1 Slaveholding of Parties in Court
Number of Slaves Held (%)

Party	0	1–5	6–10	11–20	21–50	50+
Plaintiffs (N = 61)	0	34	18	18	16	13
Defendants (N = 60)	10	27	18	18	5	22
Jurors (N = 124)	23	48	10	10	6	2
Witnesses (N = 107)	25	43	12	7	9	4
Adams County* (N = 1083 families)	36	28	11 (6–9 sl.)	8 (10–19)	8 (20–49)	8 (50+)

*1860 Census

fendants were the wealthiest parties appearing in circuit court. A full 22 percent were the greatest planters in Adams County, owning over fifty slaves within the county itself, not counting nonlocal holdings (such planters made up just 12 percent of the total population). Sellers were the greatest slaveholders, with the median owning sixteen slaves; the median buyer-defendant (sued for nonpayment of a note) owned only six slaves.[42] Relatively few sellers, whether appearing as plaintiff or defendant in Adams Circuit Court, were professional traders; only 24 out of 177 cases involved traders, and the majority of them were local traders who lived and worked in Natchez.

The average civil case involving slaves in Adams Circuit Court called at least five or six witnesses, judging only from the subpoenas that remain in the records.[43] Many cases whose records survive intact involved twenty or more witnesses, a few as many as fifty. Witnesses were paid one dollar for each day they appeared in court, and four cents per mile traveled, until the pay increased by half in the 1830s.[44] Witnesses' costs could make a trial quite expensive. Most witnesses appeared in court on the day of the trial. Out of 434 Adams County witnesses, 112 were identified as nonlocal and had their depositions read into testimony.[45] Of these, 42 were from Kentucky, 32 from Louisiana, and 23 from Tennessee. The large numbers from Kentucky and Tennessee reflect the slave trade through these border states to Mississippi; Louisiana witnesses were most often from directly across the river, where many Natchezians owned plantations and may also have conducted sales during the years of restricted trade in Mississippi. Even if a witness lived in Natchez, she might not appear in court. Women, in particular, often gave depositions in private to both attorneys in order to avoid a court appearance.

Nearly all witnesses in court were white. By law, dating back to 1807, no person of color, free or slave, could appear as a witness in any case "except for and against each other"; nevertheless, the Adams County Circuit Court accepted the deposition of a free man of color in at least one case, despite the objections of the other party.[46] In Adams County, two-thirds of witnesses owned five slaves or less; however, some of the remaining third owned substantial numbers.[47] Defense witnesses were much more likely to be slaveholders or even planters than plaintiff's witnesses.[48] These statistics suggest two points. First, wealthier planters defending lawsuits called their wealthier friends and neighbors to testify for them. Conversely, however, those same wealthy planters could well have their names dragged through the mud by witnesses much lower in social rank than themselves.

Most civil cases in Adams Circuit Court were decided by a jury.[49] The jurors were chosen randomly from among the white men who were "freeholders or householders" in the county.[50] Freeholders were defined in 1811 as those "persons who have made the first payment or purchase of lands from the United States."[51] However, the tax rolls included not only property owners but all of those who paid a poll tax of fifty cents, and some of the jurors appear to have been such taxpayers. Furthermore, in Mississippi as in other Deep Southern states, it was permissible to allow bystander juries, calling on qualified men who happened to be at court that day to sit on the jury, or even to form a complete jury if there were not enough jurors from the regular venire.[52] Bystander juries were the most likely to be people of the lower and middling classes. In order to qualify, jurors had to be male; between the ages of 21 and 60; citizens; and they could not be convicts for "felony, perjury, forgery, or other offence punishable with stripes, pillory, or burning in the hand." Both parties had four peremptory challenges for jurors in civil cases.[53] Overall, the composition of the petit jury stands in contrast to the grand jury, whose members, in the last decades of the antebellum period, were not chosen at random, and thus were substantially more likely to be planters.[54]

Because the parties' attorneys suggested the jury instructions, the judge's role was rather limited. He gave or refused the instructions, but added none

Table 2 Verdict by Plaintiff's Slaveholding (Percentage of All Cases)
Number of Slaves Held by Plaintiff (N = 50 Plaintiffs)

Verdict	1–5	6–10	11–50	51+	Total
For P	20	12	14	0	46
Against P	16	6	20	12	54
Total	36	18	34	12	100

Note: The Fisher's Exact (2-Tail) Test for independence gave a result of 0.052, which shows an inverse correlation between verdict for plaintiff and plaintiff's slaveholding.

A logistic regression analysis of verdict for plaintiff by plaintiff's slaveholding used the category RICH = 51+ slaves, or landholding >400 acres or >4 town lots. The regression found RICH P to be highly associated with verdict. The odds for the plaintiff to win were 2.5 times better if the plaintiff was not in the category RICH than if he was. P-value = 0.1261 because of the small sample size of plaintiffs with wealth information available.

Table 3 Verdict by Amount in Controversy (Percentage of All Cases)
Amount in Controversy (N = 111 cases)

Verdict	<$200	$200–$600	$600–$1,000	$1,000–$1,400	Total
For P	17	19	10	9	55
Against P	6	14	9	15	44
Total	23	33	19	24	99

Note: The Fisher's Exact (2-Tail) Test for independence gave a result of 0.072, showing a strong association between verdict and amount in controversy.

A logistic regression analysis of VERDICT—P with AMTGRP (amount in controversy grouped into the above categories) showed verdict to be highly associated with the amount in controversy. The odds for P decreased by 1.001 per $400 increase in the amount (P-value = 0.01).

Other variables (decade, slave gender, slave age, jurors' slaveholding, witnesses' slaveholding, and defendant's slaveholding) were not found to be significant factors in explaining odds for success of plaintiff v. defendant. The only significant factors affecting the odds of a verdict for the plaintiff were plaintiff's slaveholding\wealth and amount in controversy, which were both inversely related.

of his own.[55] This was a great limitation on the judge's power. It left room for the jury to decide many questions of law on which the parties did not propose precise instructions, or on which both sides proposed instructions, and the judge gave both. Jurors during the antebellum period "were frequently told they had the right and power to reject the judge's view of the law."[56] At the same time, judges could set aside jury verdicts. Most commonly, in Adams County, as in other trial courts in this period, judges exercised their power by ordering a new trial, thereby sending the case to a second jury, and sometimes even a third. When a motion for a new trial was refused, the only option for a dissatisfied litigant was to appeal to the High Court of Errors and Appeals in Jackson.[57]

Overall, plaintiffs and defendants did equally well in Adams Circuit Court: 44 percent of cases ended in a victory for the plaintiff; 45 percent were dismissed or ended in a victory for the defendant; 8 percent were settled; and the remainder were nonsuited or abated.[58] None of the known characteristics of slaves at issue could predict outcome (age, sex, color, or skill), and neither could the wealth of the defendant or of jurors. In warranty suits, buyers and sellers did equally well before juries—winning equally often in Adams County. The aggregate data suggest that despite variations in appellate doctrine from strong consumer protection to *caveat emptor* (buyer beware), juries largely decided cases based on the stories, or "facts," presented to them in testimony, without great regional variation or bias toward one side or the other.

The best quantifiable predictors for a plaintiff to win a civil dispute involving slaves were the amount in controversy and the wealth of the plaintiff: plaintiffs were significantly more likely to win when smaller amounts of money were at stake, and when they were less wealthy overall. Juries were probably more reluctant to cause money to change hands when the sums were greater, and juries exercised class sympathy, finding more easily for farmers with a few slaves rather than planters.[59]

The most silent participants in circuit court trials were the subjects of the disputes: the slaves themselves. There is little evidence in trial records or other historical documents about slaves' presence in the courtroom. The central subject of a dispute, graphically brought to life in testimony, embodied in words, may not have actually appeared in person very often in the courtroom. I found only one example of a court order to bring a woman slave before the jury to display her physical "defectiveness." In many cases, of course, the slave was escaped or dead, and no legal power could bring the slave to the courtroom. In other cases, slaves were unavailable because they had been resold, or simply because trials that went on for many days would take a slave away from work.

Those slaves who were living and had not successfully escaped may not have been present in the courtroom, but they were probably aware of the legal proceedings. It would not have been surprising if some of them tried to influence the legal process. Such attempts would simply have been an extension of slaves' efforts to manipulate their own sales in various ways—to be bought by an owner who seemed promising, to remain with a family member or loved one, or to avoid sale out of the neighborhood. Although conscious manipulation in all likelihood played a far smaller role in the courtroom than did the indirect influence of slaves' agency, it is likely that some slaves, for example, recognized the possibility of being returned to a former owner soon after sale if they demonstrated some "defect."

While legal records are silent on slaves' legal consciousness, other sources suggest that slaves were keenly aware of the law's influence on their lives. African Americans who fled slavery and went on to write or narrate their stories of bondage and escape often commented on the injustice of the white man's law—"*their* judges, *their* courts of law, *their* representatives and legislators."[60] Many, if not most, fugitive slave narratives listed the variety of ways that law made blacks into property and deprived them of rights, sometimes quoting statute books by section number and page.[61] As Frederick Douglass explained, "By the laws of the country from whence I came, I was deprived of myself—of my own body, soul, and spirit."[62] Most prominent in this "litany of rights denied" for most ex-slaves was the ban on slave testimony in the courtroom.[63] Because of this ban, "The temple of justice is barred against [the colored race]."[64] Jon-Christian Suggs, in a marvelous study of law and African American narrative, found that "African-American attitudes toward the law emerge as a complex welter of hope, cynicism, trust, and clear-eyed, even ironic, understanding."[65] He quotes Reverend G. W. Offley's argument "to his fellow men and women of color that the law is arbitrary and a man-made instrument that they should ignore when determining their own worth in the world."[66] Suggs points out that Harriet Jacobs's *Incidents in the Life of a Slave Girl* is "a template for the centrality of law in the slave narrative" and argues persuasively that writing by ex-slaves is obsessed with the law and with legal status.[67] Often former slaves wrote and spoke with a great deal of bitterness, with the understanding that courts were for the white man. As one ex-slave explained to an interviewer, "de only law mongst us niggers wuz de word uv ole Massa."[68] Harriet Jacobs noted that the slave girl or woman has "no shadow of law to protect her from insult, from violence, or even from death."[69]

Slaves were also acutely aware of themselves as objects of property relations and commercial transactions. As James Lucas, an ex-slave from Adams

County who once belonged to Jefferson Davis, explained to a WPA interviewer, "When Marse Davis got nominated fur something, he either had to sell or mortgage us. Anyhow us went back down de country. . . . I bleeves a bank sold us next to Marse L. G. Chambers."[70] Richard Mack noted that when he was ten years old he was "not really sold, but sold on a paper that said if he didn't take care of me, I would come back—a paper on me—a kind of mortgage."[71] Slaves were aware of their status as divisible property: they could be mortgaged, put up as collateral in credit transactions, split between life estates and remaindermen, or just plain sold down the river. Yet slaves could also be woefully ignorant of who had control of the interests in them at any given time; William and Ellen Craft only discovered that they had been mortgaged when they were sold to pay a debt.[72]

Solomon Northup told a tale of his divisible status saving his life. When his cruel master, Tibeats, was about to hang him in a rage, Northup was saved by the overseer, Chapin. Chapin gave two explanations for his action on Northup's behalf: first and foremost, he explained that his "duty is to protect [William Ford's] interests. . . . Ford holds a mortgage on [Northup] of four hundred dollars. If you hang him he loses his debt. Until that is canceled you have no right to take his life." Only as an afterthought did Chapin add, "You have no right to take it anyway. There is a law for the slave as well as for the white man." Solomon Northup owed his life to the overseer protecting the mortgage interest against the owner of the slave.[73] This anecdote, too, brought home the pressing significance of the slave testimony ban: Chapin allowed Northup to sleep in the "great house"—"the first and the last time such a sumptuous resting place was granted me during my twelve years of bondage"—because he feared that Tibeats would return to kill Northup, and he wanted white witnesses. "Had he stabbled [sic] me to the heart in the presence of a hundred slaves, not one of them, by the laws of Louisiana, could have given evidence against him."[74]

Given slaves' awareness of the importance of law in their lives, it would not be surprising if some slaves realized in some instances that running away or illness could lead to a legal suit that might result in rescission of their sale. Yet it is likely that conscious manipulation was not the norm. Just as slaves realized the dangers inherent in influencing their sales, they recognized the dominance of white men in the legal arena. What the cases reveal instead is the indirect influence of slaves on legal proceedings, both as a result of the white participants' fears of slaves' manipulation and as a by-product of slaves' efforts to resist their masters in other domains.

The slaves over whom white men took one another to court were most often young men, their average age twenty-three years. Yet the aggregate statistics on age and gender cannot tell the full story. Buyers were equally as likely to bring suit for breach of warranty regarding an enslaved woman as a man, and disputes over title involved women as often as men. Tort suits, efforts by owners to recover from other white men for damage to their slave property, account for the greater number of men who appeared as the subject of civil suit in Adams County courts. This may have been because men were more likely to be hired out, as well as more likely to rebel or run away when hired out or left with some other supervisor. Nearly every runaway slave in the sample was male.[75] The slaves at issue in civil disputes were skilled craftspeople and domestic workers as well as field hands. In litigation, female skilled slaves were usually house servants, especially washers and cooks; male slaves were most likely to be carpenters or blacksmiths.

How did the outcome of these trials affect enslaved African Americans? The most serious effect on a slave still living would be a transfer from one owner's possession to another. In a suit for possession of a slave (an action for detinue or replevin), the remedy was usually to return the slave. However, the remedy in many warranty cases as well as suits for damage to a slave was monetary damages, which might mean that money would change hands between white people without any change to the slave's situation. Yet even when a slave remained with the same owner, one should not suppose that the slave's life was not altered by the lawsuit. An owner angered by a loss in court, especially a loss in face that he might trace to a slave's misbehavior, might take out his frustration on the body of the slave. Thus, efforts to be returned to a former owner or otherwise to influence one's own disposition would have been as fraught with danger as attempts to manipulate one's original sale. Always the slave would have to walk the line between working toward the desired outcome and planning for the opposite contingency.

The road to the slave market in southern towns inexorably led to the courthouse. Along the road traveled dissatisfied buyers and sellers, owners and hirers; their neighbors coming to bear witness, weigh their case as jurors, or simply to observe; lawyers who made their living in the slave economy; and the slaves whose lives hung in the balance. On Court Day, these players participated in one of Natchez's major social rituals, invested with all of the manifestations of state authority. When they entered the courtroom, these men and women did not leave the marketplace behind. They argued for financial advantage in cases with high stakes. But they did so in the context of a culture in which not only profit but honor mattered, in the market and in the courtroom. Trials taught important lessons to participants and spectators about white honor and black dishonor, and about the character of masters and slaves, and these lessons resonated in their daily lives.

Just as the courtroom became the forum for white men's affairs of honor, they also provided an opportunity for whites to exercise honor through the dishonor of slaves. Slaves were dishonored in the courtroom both by the baring of their bodies and by the law's disrespect for their words. When ex-slaves discussed in their narratives the way the law touched their lives, inevitably they returned to the ban on slave testimony as the crowning injustice, as did Solomon Northup in his story about the evil owner, Tibeats, whose crimes went unpunished because the witnesses could not speak in court. It was the silence law imposed upon slaves that they felt most guaranteed their disempowerment. Treating the slave's word as a lie, and shutting it out of the courtroom, was the best way for white men to deny slaves access to honor as well as justice before the law. This distrust of the word of "servants," racialized in the American South, had its origins in the general English "association between mendacity and servility," and the "wide agreement that the servant's word was *not* his bond." [76] A culture that made a man's word his badge of honor stripped people of honor by denying them words.

A notorious murder case from Natchez brings home the power of the slave testimony ban. Baylor Winn was reputed in Natchez to be a man of color, a member of the same free black community as the diarist William Johnson. He and Johnson had exchanged friendly visits and had ridden and hunted together until Winn began cutting timber on land Johnson claimed, and Johnson declared Winn to be "not an Honerable Man." In 1851, in the midst of the dispute, Winn shot Johnson in ambush, in the presence of one enslaved and two free African Americans. Before he died, Johnson named Winn as his murderer. Winn was jailed, and the coroner's jury "returned a verdict that Johnson came to his death by a wound or wounds inflicted by Baylor Wynn [*sic*]." The prominent lawyer and later Civil War general William T. Martin acted as the special prosecutor to bring Winn to justice for Johnson's murder. Martin was hamstrung, however, by the slave testimony ban. His only hope to prove Winn the murderer was to demonstrate to the court Winn's "negro blood"; only if Winn were of color could the eyewitness testimony of blacks be admitted against him. Two juries deadlocked over this question, and the state gave up its efforts to convict Winn when a jury voted that he had not been proven to be a "negro." Johnson's murder went unpunished. It is not surprising that blacks, free and enslaved, saw the testimony ban as a license to kill blacks with impunity.[77]

Sometimes this silencing literally erased slaves' stories from the historical record. Less dramatic than a murder trial, *Forniquet v. Lynch* was a little replevin case that appears from the trial record to be a boring ownership dispute, with little testimony, small amounts of money in controversy, and no interesting legal issues.[78] On the face of it, Charles Lynch, the governor of Mississippi from 1836 to 1838, sued Edward P. Forniquet in 1834 over possession of the slave Ellen. Only one deposition remains in the record, that of planter Richard Terrell. The case was dismissed. However, the correspondence between Governor Lynch and his lawyer, George Winchester, reveals a vivid human story behind the scenes and demonstrates the myriad ways in which the law dishonored and erased the agency of both slaves and free blacks.

The story begins in 1803. In that year, Charles Lynch bought a slave, Bob Leiper, in Kentucky, and moved with him to Natchez. Lynch must have been Bob's third owner at least, as he had taken the last name Leiper from one owner, and a second, Meriwether, sold him to Lynch. Lynch explained that he then "permitted Bob and his family to reside in Natchez, and under the control of Micajah Terrell, Judge [Edward] Turner, and others, to hire himself out." To the community, Leiper was known as a free black. He lived with his wife, Rhoda, and started a large family, many of whom lived as free or hired themselves out. In 1826, Lynch officially freed Bob Leiper, his wife, and daughter Charlotte, and recorded the deed with the judge of Concordia Parish. Apparently there were conflicts between Lynch and Leiper over the emancipation, because Lynch later claimed to his lawyer George Winchester that the emancipation never formally took place. In his claim in the replevin case, Lynch stated, "About 1826 or 7 [he] agreed to emancipate Bob and some of his children upon certain terms, with which Bob and his family have not complied. None of them have ever been legally emancipated, but several of them are permitted to have their freedom and are considered as free by the

Governor." The record does show, however, that subsequent to the disputed emancipation, Lynch sold to Bob Leiper his son Robert, Jr., and a Natchez lot; Bob bought his granddaughter Matilda from someone else, and then freed his son, granddaughter, and another daughter. In 1838, Robert Leiper, Sr., his daughter-in-law, and two grandchildren sailed for Liberia; local historians suggest that "[in 1841] former Governor Lynch must have been still selling Leiper children to the free Leipers remaining in Natchez."[79]

At all events, it is undisputed that before 1826, Bob Leiper was not free but quasi-free. He lived apart from his master, raised his family, and hired out his own time. In May 1822, Leiper purchased a slave for his own use, Ellen, at a sheriff's sale. According to Lynch, Leiper paid for Ellen himself, but the bill of sale was given to Christopher Kyle, a white Natchez merchant, who assigned her to Bob in May 1825 "to keep as his own until called for by him."[80] Ellen lived most of the time with the Leipers at Natchez, but Lynch "had the girl in his possession at Monticello in 1827 or 8," at which point, Lynch explained to Winchester that he "let her go back to Natchez with old Rhoda and to remain with her, as she was old and in bad health, the girl might render her some service."[81]

When Ellen turned sixteen in 1829, a slave belonging to Edward P. Forniquet applied to Bob Leiper to marry Ellen. Leiper made it a condition of his consent to the marriage that Forniquet should buy Ellen "until she was of age when she would become free." Forniquet's slave, Ellen's husband, paid Leiper's note himself, perhaps from wages earned working overtime, and only "under these representations" was Forniquet "induced to purchase." As Governor Lynch's lawyer, George Winchester, observed, Ellen's husband was "much attached to the girl."[82]

At this point, however, Lynch decided to exercise his rights of ownership, informing Leiper in essence that any slave who belonged to his slave was his slave too. Of course, by 1830 Bob Leiper no longer belonged to Lynch. But whatever had passed between Lynch and Leiper during the controversy over Leiper's emancipation had obviously stayed with Lynch. Lynch sent an emissary to Forniquet to demand Ellen, "but Forniquet refused to give her up." Some time passed before Lynch took legal action. He wrote to his lawyer, George Winchester, in February 1837, that he would pay Forniquet about $100 (the $200 Forniquet paid Bob Leiper for Ellen, minus $100 for her hire) in order to have Ellen back. Forniquet replied that he was willing to rescind the sale if Lynch would submit the matter to arbitration under John T. McMurran.[83] The fact that Ellen's husband had put up the money for her sale was irrelevant to the negotiation between her white buyer and seller.

Despite Edward Forniquet's willingness to settle, the matter dragged out for several more years. One letter from Lynch to Winchester concerns legal action against the estate of Meriwether, the Kentuckian from whom Lynch first acquired Bob Leiper.[84] The letter mentions at least four depositions already taken in that suit; it also refers to a deposition of Anselm Lynch, to prove Ellen's residence with Governor Lynch during the year 1826, before he let her return to Leiper's wife Rhoda. There is no other record of this case, nor of its outcome.

On March 21, 1839, Charles Lynch filed a complaint against Forniquet in Adams Circuit Court. Lynch's complaint alleged that Ellen and her two children were worth $2,500, and demanded the money or the slaves, plus payment for hire. Forniquet retained Montgomery and Boyd, prominent Natchez lawyers, to represent him in the matter. The trial record contains only one set of interrogatories, served on a neighbor planter by Winchester's associate, asking him whether he was acquainted with Lynch's father and with Robert Leiper, and whether he had ever heard either Lynch or his father speak about the freedom or ownership of Leiper. The case was dismissed two terms later, in November 1840, but it appears to have been dismissed by the judge, and Charles Lynch paid the costs, so there may have been some kind of settlement.

Forniquet v. Lynch reveals that a case that appears from the legal record to have been a dispute between two white men was in fact about a black man's dishonor. This case was only incidentally between Governor Lynch and Edward P. Forniquet. It was really about Lynch putting Robert Leiper in his place: a subordinate place. Lynch gave Leiper quasi-freedom—but he was only "free" so long as he observed unspoken boundaries. When he reached for the prerogatives of the master class—the prerogatives of *whiteness*—he had to be disciplined. First, he bought a slave; at this juncture, Lynch simply reminded him of who owned whom by beckoning Ellen to live with him for part of a year before sending her back to old Rhoda. But when Leiper tried to *sell* a slave for profit, Lynch took legal action.

Power relations among whites, free blacks, and enslaved blacks come into relief in this dispute. First, there is the fact of freed slaves owning their own slaves. Some free blacks bought family members in order to give them freedom. In one sad South Carolina case, a free man of color, Lyles, bought his sick wife from a former master, Bass, just months before she died. Feeling no pity, the master gouged his former slave for $600, despite the fact that he would have gotten almost nothing for a sick woman on the open market. When Lyles sued Bass for breach of warranty after her death, the trial judge opined that "we cannot deprive [Bass] of his good bargain." However, in Natchez as elsewhere, many slaveholding blacks were masters like others; William Johnson fills his pages with his troubles over his unruly slave Stephen and the necessity for frequent whippings. Here, Robert Leiper bought a girl slave for his own use as a domestic servant until she turned twenty-one, when he agreed to set her free. Perhaps he saw this as a type of apprenticeship for her; perhaps he hoped that a young woman house servant would allow his wife to enjoy certain luxuries or freedoms; or perhaps he hoped for some kind of intimacy with this young woman. Unfortunately, the records remain silent on the relationship between Robert Leiper and Ellen.

The case highlights the precarious position of free blacks—above slaves but below whites in the southern hierarchy. In the 1830s, the South was moving swiftly to assert the color line rather than the slave/free line as the boundary that mattered. *Forniquet v. Lynch* illuminates the role of law in ordering relations among the three groups and maintaining the hierarchy. In the correspondence, there is evidence of slaves as moral agents, trying to live honorably within the constraints of slave society. A nameless male slave tried to marry Ellen, approaching Leiper first. He then worked to raise the money to buy Ellen from Leiper, although in practice this meant his owner had to buy her. All of these transactions centrally involved people of color: the main players were Leiper, Ellen, and Ellen's husband. But "the law" here is nearly synonymous with "the white man." The law not only helped the whites to assert their ownership of Ellen's body, but it silenced Ellen, her husband, and even the free Robert Leiper, removing them from the dispute as parties and even as witnesses. In *Forniquet v. Lynch*, the law literally erased the black principals in the dispute, and all evidence of black moral agency, remaking a legal conflict as between two white men. Charles Lynch dishonored Bob Leiper, and the legal process confirmed his dishonor. Just as slavery and race helped to shape the legal culture of Natchez, the law helped to shape the way ordinary Natchezians thought about race.

NOTES

This essay is drawn from Ariela Gross, *Double Character: Slavery and Mastery in the Antebellum Southern Courtroom*, copyright © 2000 Princeton University Press.

1. Michael Tadman, *Speculators and Slaves: Masters, Traders, and Slaves in the Old South* (Madison: University of Wisconsin Press, 1996), 96; D. Clayton James, *Antebellum Natchez* (Baton Rouge: Lousiana State University Press, 1968), 197.

2. Joseph Ingraham, *The South-West by a Yankee* (New York: Harper and Brothers, 1835), vol. 2, 192–93.

3. William W. Brown, "Narrative of William Wells Brown, A Fugitive Slave," in *Puttin' On Ole Massa*, ed. Gilbert Osofsky (New York: Harper and Row, 1969), 193–94. See also Henry Bibb, *Narrative of the Life and Adventures of Henry Bibb, an American Slave*, in Osofsky, 113–15.

4. Isaac Stier autobiography, in *The American Slave: A Composite Autobiography*, ed. George P. Rawick (Westport., Conn.: Greenwood, 1977), vol. 10: *Mississippi Narratives*, part 5, supp. series 1, p. 2057.

5. The courthouse was built in 1819.

6. See, for example, Edward L. Ayers, *Vengeance and Justice: Crime and Punishment in the Nineteenth-Century American South* (New York: Oxford University Press, 1984), 18, 32 (only a "circumscribed . . . segment of life . . . was controlled by law"; "honor and legalism . . . are incompatible"); Michael Hindus, *Prison and Plantation: Crime, Justice, and Authority in Massachusetts and South Carolina, 1767–1878* (Chapel Hill: University of North Carolina Press, 1980), 42–55 (dueling as a "negation of the law," 43; weak legal authority as a function of the Code of Honor in South Carolina); Christopher Waldrep, "Substituting Law for the Lash: Emancipation and Legal Formalism in a Mississippi County Court," *Journal of American History* 82 (March 1996): 1428 ("The state only reluctantly intervened in master-slave relations, regarding law as too burdened with procedure effectively to control human chattel. Owners realized law must be kept from their slaves"); Winthrop Jordan, *Tumult and Silence at Second Creek: An Inquiry into a Slave Conspiracy* (Baton Rouge: Louisiana State University Press, 1993) (important conflicts remain outside the formal legal system); Michael Wayne, *Reshaping Plantation Society: The Natchez District, 1860–1880* (Baton Rouge: Louisiana State University Press, 1983), 16 (plantation its own law); Michael Wayne, "An Old South Morality Play: Reconsidering the Social Underpinnings of the Proslavery Ideology," *Journal of American History* 77 (December, 1990): 838–63 (important conflicts remain outside the formal legal system); Peter Kolchin, *American Slavery, 1619–1877* (New York: Hill and Wang, 1993), 127–32 (looking only at legislation, and noting that most slave discipline took place on the plantation). Bertram Wyatt-Brown, while recognizing that in

southern towns, "[t]he courthouse, more than the church, was the center for local ethical considerations," has also focused exclusively on the criminal law, and the extent to which the criminal justice system allowed extralegal sanctions to replace legal ones. Bertram Wyatt-Brown, *Southern Honor: Ethics and Behavior in the Old South* (New York: Oxford University Press, 1982), 366.

7. For studies of slavery and criminal law, see Waldrep, *Roots of Disorder*; Ayers, *Vengeance and Justice;* Philip J. Schwarz, *Twice Condemned: Slaves and the Criminal Laws of Virginia, 1705–1865* (Baton Rouge: Louisiana State University Press, 1988); Daniel J. Flanigan, "Criminal Procedure in Slave Trials in the Antebellum South," *Journal of Southern History* 40 (November 1974): 537–64; Michael Hindus, *Prison and Plantation.* The obvious exception to this generalization about historians of slave culture is Eugene Genovese, whose theory of paternalism rests on an understanding of "the hegemonic function of the law." Eugene D. Genovese, *Roll, Jordan, Roll: The World the Slaves Made* (New York: Random House, 1976), 25–49. James Oakes's fascinating discussion of slavery and law centers on the political significance of law rather than the cultural connections, and also focuses on statutory law. James Oakes, *Slavery and Freedom: An Interpretation of the Old South* (New York: Alfred A. Knopf, 1990). For an early work pointing to law's importance in the South, see Charles Sydnor, "The Southerner and the Law," *Journal of Southern History* 6 (1940).

   For studies of constitutional questions, see, for example, Robert M. Cover, *Justice Accused: Antislavery and the Judicial Process* (New Haven: Yale University Press, 1975); Paul Finkelman, *An Imperfect Union: Slavery, Federalism, and Comity* (Chapel Hill: University of North Carolina Press, 1981); James Oakes, "'The Compromising Expedient': Justifying a Proslavery Constitution," *Cardozo Law Review* 17 (1996): 2023–56; William M. Wiecek, *The Sources of Antislavery Constitutionalism in America, 1760–1848* (Ithaca, N.Y.: Cornell University Press, 1977).

8. The figure for criminal cases comes from Bertram Wyatt-Brown, "Community, Class, and Snopesian Crime," in *Class, Conflict, and Consensus: Antebellum Southern Community Studies*, ed. Orville V. Burton and Robert C. McMath (Westport, Conn.: Greenwood, 1982), 178; the number of civil actions is my own estimate. Edward Ayers estimated three or four civil cases for each criminal case in the typical southern court. Ayers, *Vengeance and Justice*, 32.

9. The cases were drawn from a sample of 10,317 out of approximately 30,000 causes of action filed between 1798 and 1860. Typically, case files included a complaint, subpoenas for witnesses, and a warrant for the defendant. Only about 4 percent of these causes of action ended in a trial; most were undefended debt actions. If the case went to trial, the file also included transcripts of testimony, depositions, attorneys' motions, jury instructions, and at times, even notes

made by the judge or by an attorney. The cases were also cross-referenced with the minute books of the circuit court, in which jury lists were kept. The hand-written documents were tied and stored in metal drawers, in approximate chronological order. Within drawers, the files were not arranged in any particular order. I sampled every third drawer for the years 1798 to 1850 and every drawer for the years 1851 to 1860.

10. In 1860, the census counted 1,083 free families in Adams County. Only 688 residents were heads of household who owned slaves within Adams County. Thus, about 36 percent of free people (of whom only a handful were people of color) belonged to households with no slaves. Census of 1860, Adams County.

11. Orville Vernon Burton's excellent county study of Edgefield, South Carolina, discusses the county courthouse as the local seat of power and symbol of both political and cultural authority. Orville Vernon Burton, *In My Father's House Are Many Mansions* (Chapel Hill: University of North Carolina Press, 1985), 28–29. For colonial antecedents, see Darrett B. Rutman and Anita H. Rutman, *A Place in Time: Middlesex County, Virginia, 1650–1850* (New York: Norton, 1984), 125. A. G. Roeber has written persuasively about the centrality of Court Day as a social ritual in colonial Virginia towns. Roeber, "Authority, Law, and Custom." See also Rhys Isaac, *The Transformation of Virginia, 1740–1790* (Chapel Hill: University of North Carolina Press, 1982).

12. By statute, circuit courts could last no more than eighteen days, but the average duration of a court term was much shorter—one week in the early decades of the nineteenth century, and two weeks between 1830 and 1860. T. J. Fox Alden and J. A. Van Hoesen, *Digest of the Laws of Mississippi* (New York: Alexander S. Gould, 1839), sec. 3, p. 115.

Most civil cases involving slaves went to the circuit court after 1832. The superior court handled cases of less than $50, and even the least expensive slave was worth several hundred dollars. There was also a chancery court, which had jurisdiction over equitable claims of $500 or less. However, most litigants in slave-related litigation were seeking monetary damages rather than a remedy in "equity," such as enjoining the parties to carry out the terms of their contract; furthermore, the circuit court could give equitable relief for claims of more than $500, which included most slaves. A sample of 179 cases before the superior court of chancery in Natchez revealed only three suits involving slaves.

13. A. J. Brown, *History of Newton County, Mississippi from 1834 to 1894* (Jackson, Miss.: Clarion-Ledger Co., 1894), 427.

14. Ibid., 428.

15. During the 1820s and 1830s, the cotton planters of the Natchez district amassed great wealth in land and slaves. Three hundred fifty Natchez nabobs owned more than 250 slaves in the 1850 or 1860 census in all fifteen states, although

only seven owned more than 250 in Adams County itself in 1850. William K. Scarborough, "Lords or Capitalists? The Natchez Nabobs in Comparative Perspective," *Journal of Mississippi History* 54, no. 3 (1992): 240–42. See also Morton Rothstein, "The Natchez Nabobs: Kinship and Friendship in an Economic Elite," in *Toward a New View of America*, ed. Hans L. Trefousse (New York: B. Franklin and Co., 1977), 97–112. D. Clayton James, *Antebellum Natchez* (Baton Rouge: Louisiana State University Press, 1968), 139, 243, 136.

16. James, *Antebellum Natchez*, 94, 177, 230, 137.

17. Even so, more than a third of the people of Natchez were black; by 1860, there were 2,131 slaves, 3,607 whites, and 225 free blacks. Population Schedules of the Eighth Census of the United States, 1830, 1860. By contrast, some of the pineywoods counties of Mississippi, Georgia, and Alabama had total populations of a few thousand with only a few hundred slaves. Adams County had the eleventh highest slave population in the Deep South in 1830. Census of 1830.

18. Ronald L. F. Davis, *The Black Experience in Natchez, 1720–1870* (Natchez, Miss.: Special History Study, Natchez National Historical Park, 1993), 51; Census of 1860.

19. They were the Johnsons, the McCarys, the Barlands, the Fitzgeralds, the Fitzhughs, and the Woods. Davis, *Black Experience*, 59–60.

20. Life grew more difficult for free blacks of all classes beginning in the 1830s. That decade saw a tightening of the legal restrictions on free blacks, and elimination of many of the legal rights that had separated them from slaves. In the summer of 1841, a campaign popularly known as the "Inquisition" was conducted against the free black community to discover violators of the strict laws of the 1830s and to deport them from the state. John Hebron Moore, *The Emergence of the Cotton Kingdom in the Old Southwest: Mississippi, 1770–1860* (Baton Rouge: Louisiana State University Press, 1988), 264–66; James, *Antebellum Natchez*, 179.

21. William Johnson, *William Johnson's Natchez: The Antebellum Diary of a Free Negro*, ed. William R. Hogan and Edwin A. Davis (Baton Rouge: Louisiana State University Press, 1951; Port Washington, N.Y.: Kennikat Press, 1968), vol. 2, 721–22, 757, 492 (May 13, 1850, May 16, 1850, November 11, 1850, May 29, 1844).

22. For example, on January 6, 1844, Johnson wrote, "A trial came of[f] before Esqr Woods to day and it was Parkhurst was tried for stealing a Darkey belonging to Fields." On May 10, 1850, Johnson mentioned a warranty suit over slaves between Rhasa Parker and William Pullam. On December 13, 1839, Johnson learned from Mr. Wales of Washington that Philo Andrews was "Still aliving and was seen some where in Mobile or in Mexico and told me He Left her in consequence of his Stealing a Negro and that he Proberly was now a Live and

the property that had was Now, He thought, owend [*sic*] by Mr Brooks." Ibid., 471, 720, vol. 1, 274. See *Parkhurst v. Field*, Drawer 317 Docket no. 142, November 1845, Adams Circuit Court Records, Historic Natchez Foundation (HNF); *Andrews v. Brooks*, Drawer 100 Folder 6, Docket no. 5, May 1820, Adams Circuit Court Records, HNF.

23. Charles Warren, *A History of the American Bar* (Boston: Little, Brown, 1911), 206.

24. Orville Vernon Burton, in his community study of Edgefield, South Carolina, found that "lawyers were . . . important in the spreading of ideas. . . . lawyers linked Edgefield with the other South Carolina districts." Burton, *In My Father's House*, 21. Lawyers were leaders of many of the social and cultural organizations in Adams County; as lawyer John Quitman boasted to his brother in 1836, "I am President of a states rights association, of an anti-Abolition society, of an anti-Gambling society, of a Mississippi cotton company, of an anti-Dueling society, of a railroad company, director of the Planters bank, grand master Mason, Captain of the Natchez Fencibles, trustee of Jefferson college and Natchez academy, besides having charge of a cotton and sugar plantation and 150 negroes." Moore, *Cotton Kingdom*, 191, John A. Quitman subject file, Mississippi Department of Archives and History (MDAH); records of the "Natchez Fencibles," John A. Quitman and Family Papers, Box 1, Folder 2, LSU; Thomas Reed Papers, Box 1, Folder 1, LSU.

25. In the 1820s, the "Natchez junto," including most of the town's leading lawyers, held sway in state politics, occupying the governor's chair as well as that of the attorney general for most of the years between 1817 and 1832. James, *Antebellum Natchez*, 97, 113–14, 119; Moore, *Cotton Kingdom*, 243. Edward Turner and J. S. B. Thacher were the only Natchezians to serve on the High Court of Errors and Appeals between 1832 and 1861.

26. James, *Antebellum Natchez*, 97; Joseph Baldwin, *The Flush Times of Alabama and Mississippi* (New York: Sagamore Press, 1957 [reprint]), 34.

27. Katharine M. Jones, *The Plantation South* (Indianapolis: Bobbs-Merrill, 1957), 235–36.

28. Joseph H. Ingraham, *The South-West by a Yankee* (New York: Harper and Brothers, 1835), vol. 2, 84–85.

29. Joyce Broussard-Hogan, "The Career of John T. McMurran: From Yankee Lawyer to Planter Elite in the Natchez District, 1823–1866" (unpublished manuscript, available at MDAH).

30. Broussard-Hogan, "McMurran," 12. For another lawyer who became a planter through speculation on slaves using his first legal fees, see biographical sketch of Lyman Harding, April 22, 1859, in the J. F. H. Claiborne Papers, Book G, Roll

9, MDAH; Lyman Harding subject file, MDAH. Edward Turner subject file, MDAH. George Poindexter, an early lawyer who went on to be governor of Mississippi, doubled his slave- and landholding between 1807 and 1815, when he paid taxes on 58 slaves and 810 acres in Adams County alone. Adams County Personal Tax Rolls, Miss. Territ., Roll no. 299. William Vannerson, who moved to Natchez from Virginia in 1823 with one slave, acquired 27 slaves during his active years in practice in Adams County in the 1830s before going on to be a Lawrence County probate judge. Adams County Personal Tax Rolls, Miss., Roll B-592.

Overall, the average lawyer in a slave-related case owned 13 or 14 slaves in Natchez; about 150 acres of land; one or two lots in town where he kept his law office, together worth nearly $9,000; a carriage; and a gold watch. However, this average reflects the period of time during which these lawyers were active in practice. Although there were certainly more "middle-class" lawyers who never succeeded on the scale of Turner or McMurran, only four lawyers of thirty-five paid no taxes on slaves during their active years of law practice.

31. Seth Lewis Memoirs, 15–16, MDAH.

32. Of the Deep Southern states, only South Carolina became a net exporting state during the 1820s. Louisiana, Mississippi, and Alabama remained net importing states through 1860, and Georgia, during the 1850s, was split between a net importing region in the west and a net exporting region in the east. Broadly speaking, the eastern seaboard, settled early like the older regions of the Upper South, became exporters over the course of the antebellum period. Tadman, *Speculators and Slaves*, 6–7, 12. All five states imported an estimated 650,000 slaves between 1800 and 1859. Ibid., 12.

33. No reliable estimates exist of the actual percentage of slave sales that can be attributed to local noncourt sales. Michael Tadman's conclusion that the rate of local sales was "at least as high and probably higher than the per capita rate of interregional sales of Upper South slaves" is almost certainly right. Ibid., 112, 118–21.

34. Thomas Russell, "South Carolina's Largest Slave Auctioneering Firm," *Chicago-Kent Law Review* 68 (1993): 1277–78.

35. *Code of the Ordinances of the City of Natchez, Now in Force* (Natchez, Miss.: Giles M. Hillyer, 1854), 151–52.

36. Davis, *Black Experience in Natchez*, 15; Wendell Stephenson and Isaac Franklin, *Slave Trader and Planter of the Old South* (Baton Rouge: Louisiana State University Press, [1938] 1968), 34–54.

37. Quoted in Frederic Bancroft, *Slave Trading in the Old South* (Baltimore, Md.: J. H. Furst Co., 1931), 304–5.

38. Richard H. Kilbourne, Jr., *Debt, Investment, Slaves: Credit Relations in East Fe-liciana Parish, Louisiana, 1825–1885* (Tuscaloosa: University of Alabama Press, 1995), 52. "In three of four years sampled in the decade of the 1850s (1850, 1853, 1856, and 1859), the slave market accounted for almost 80 percent of the total cash market for both land and slaves." Ibid., 50.

39. Morris, *Southern Slavery and the Law*, 132.

40. Court costs included the clerk's fee, daily pay to witnesses and jurors, fees to justices of the peace for taking depositions, and the sheriff's fee for serving subpoenas and warrants. See "An Act to Establish the Fees of Justices of the Peace and Constables," Docket Book no. 2 of Magistrate Edward Turner, Natchez, Miss. Territ., F. Edward Turner Papers, Kuntz Collection no. 600, Howard-Tilton Memorial Library, Tulane University; *Digest of the Laws of Mississippi* (1839), sec. 106 (witnesses' costs); *Revised Code of the Statute Laws of the State of Mississippi* (Jackson, Miss.: E. Barksdale, 1857), sec. 17, art. 205, p. 513 (witnesses' costs). A long case involving many witnesses could cost hundreds of dollars. See, for example, *Smith v. Meek*, Drawer 232, no. 76, April 1838, Adams Cir. Ct., HNF (court costs of $435.19; jury gave a verdict for $13,100.54, but this was vacated when the parties settled and the defendant paid costs).

41. These numbers derive from a sample of sixty-one plaintiffs in slave-related litigation. By comparison, there were a significant number of nonslaveholders in the town of Natchez; in 1860, there were only 12 slaveholders in town with 20 or more slaves; 113 with 6–20, and 257 with 1–5, leaving a large majority with no slaves. In agricultural households outside Natchez, there were few without slaves (11 percent) in 1860, 28 percent with less than 20, 27 percent with 20–49, and 34 percent with more than 50. Overall in the county, 38 percent of slaveholding households held 1–4 slaves; 37 percent held 5–19; 12.5 percent held 20–49, and 12 percent held more than 50. Census of 1860.

42. The median hirer owned nine, and the median defendant accused of a tort (such as beating a slave to death) owned ten. The averages were much higher, because of the unusual number of great planters included: the average defendant owned 62 slaves, 1,000 acres of land, one or two town lots, a watch, and a carriage; his land in the county alone was worth about $13,400.

43. This number is necessarily inexact but is probably an underestimate. Sometimes only a subpoena list was available, but no testimony. In these cases, it is only possible to know whether witnesses actually testified in court if receipts remain indicating how many days a witness served. On the other hand, where testimony survived but not subpoena lists, it is possible that more witnesses testified, or at least were subpoenaed, than those for whom testimony was recorded. Testimony is usually the most incomplete part of the record because it depended

on the judge or clerk of the court to record, as opposed to complaints, answers, motions, and subpoenas, which were filed by the parties. For eighty cases in which I found subpoena lists, testimony, or receipts, there were 434 witnesses; however, it is likely that evidence of many others was lost.

44. *Digest of the Laws of Mississippi* (1839), chap. 37, sec. 106, p. 142; *Revised Code of Mississippi* (1857), sec. 17, art. 205, p. 513.

45. Unlike today, there was little pretrial discovery in antebellum cases. Although litigants had a right to obtain discovery of documents by petition, usually they built their cases on witnesses' testimony as to the contents of contracts and other documents. Lawyers frequently took depositions, but these were actually received as legal testimony by the court and read into the record before the jury, rather than merely being a pretrial information-gathering mechanism. In Mississippi, this practice dated back to the first Judiciary Act of 1807 in the Territorial period. Depositions were taken either by both lawyers, if local, or by a justice of the peace in a foreign locale using written interrogatories and cross-interrogatories sent by the lawyers. Witnesses answered orally, and their answers were copied down.

Such depositions were allowed for witnesses outside the territory, or with plans to leave the territory. After statehood, more detailed reasons for witnesses to forgo court appearance were enumerated in the statutes; age, illness, residence more than sixty miles from the place of trial, and gender exempted witnesses. Female witnesses did not have to appear in court unless one of the parties filed an affidavit "that the personal attendance of such female in open court, is necessary for the ends of justice." In practice, some women did appear in court, but many took advantage of the deposition law. Depositions have survived in the legal record far more often than transcripts of testimony at trial, which were sometimes written up by the clerk of court, and sometimes by the judge himself after the fact. Laws of 1857, p. 514.

46. Act of February 10, 1807, sec. IX. People excluded from testifying "except for and against each other" included "[a]ll negroes, mulattoes, Indians, and all persons of mixed blood, descended from negro or Indian ancestors, to the third generation, inclusive, though one ancestor of each generation may have been a white person." *Digest of the Laws of Mississippi* (1839), sec. 110, pp. 143–44.

Beeler v. Leeper, Drawer 169 no. 26, May 1830, Adams Cir. Ct., Miss., and Book of Judgments NN, 382, HNF. Beeler's attorney, George Adams, objected to the testimony of Moses Wanzer, a 34-year-old "Merchant Taylor" of color, living in New York, but the judge (probably Edward Turner) overruled the objection.

47. Forty-three percent of 107 witnesses for whom I obtained information owned

between one and five slaves; and another 25 percent owned none. The average witness was a white man who owned seven slaves, about 180 acres of land, a town lot, and a carriage.

48. The average defense witness had sixteen slaves, 436 acres, and 1.5 town lots, whereas the average plaintiff's witness had nine slaves, 100 acres, and one town lot.

There were only 63 cases in which I could both identify which party called the witness and locate the witnesses in tax or census records. Therefore, we should take these results with caution.

49. Juries were listed only in the minute books of the court, and not in the trial transcript. Thus, I matched trials to juries only in those cases where the clerk noted in which minute book the trial was recorded. I was able to find jury lists for eighteen cases, one of which had two mistrials and three juries; I obtained information on an average of six jurors per jury.

50. The sheriff gave the clerk a list each year, and the clerk chose sixty of these for the venire. Before 1830, fifty-one were chosen every two years. *Digest of the Laws of Mississippi* (1839), sec. 122, p. 147.

51. Act of December 7, 1811, *Statutes of the Mississippi Territory*, sec. VIII, p. 27.

52. *Digest of the Laws of Mississippi* (1839), sec. 133, p. 150.

53. *Digest of the Laws of Mississippi* (1839), sec. 138, p. 150; sec. 142, p. 151.

54. Laws of 1848, sec. 136; Christopher Waldrep, "Black Access to Law in Reconstruction: The Case of Warren County, Mississippi," *Chicago-Kent Law Review* 70 (1994): 583–621.

55. Laws of 1848, ch. 61, art. 9, sec. 14, from Circuit Court Act, March 2, 1833.

56. Alan Scheflin and Jon Van Dyke, "Jury Nullification: The Contours of a Controversy," *Law and Contemporary Problems* 43 (Autumn 1980): 54.

57. Renee B. Lettow, "New Trial for Verdict Against Law: Judge-Jury Relations in Early Nineteenth-Century America," *Notre Dame Law Review* 71 (1996): 542–53. Whereas Lettow describes a general trend toward greater judicial control over jury behavior, in my view the Adams County trials suggest a great deal of jury power. Even granting a new trial, when it was used, only sent the case to another jury.

58. This relationship changed over time: in the 1830s and 1840s, defendants did considerably better than plaintiffs, even when settlements are considered to be favorable results for plaintiffs (on the assumption that defendants would not settle unless there was some likelihood of a plaintiff victory). This result is not statistically significant, because of the small number of cases in the sample. In the 1830s and into the 1840s, during a period of financial panic, juries were more favorably inclined toward debtors. In warranty cases where a slave seller sued on

a note, juries in the 1830s were more sympathetic to the debtor/buyer, who won in four out of five such cases, instead of one out of two in other decades. In the more common cases where a buyer sued a seller for his money back, buyers and sellers each won about half the time, in the same ratio they did over the entire period. There was no significant change over time in the wealth of the parties, jurors, or witnesses.

59. The odds for the plaintiff were 2.5 times worse if he was a great planter than if he was not. I defined great planters as owners of fifty-one or more slaves (which also encompassed all large landholders) or owners of four town lots (which included wealthy town dwellers who did not own land within the county). It is interesting that verdicts for the plaintiff correlated with plaintiff's wealth but not with defendant's wealth; because of the small number of cases in which all information was available for plaintiffs and defendants, it was impossible to compare the wealth of both in a particular case. It is also very possible that a larger sample might have allowed greater correlation with defendant's wealth.

60. Frederick Douglass, "An Account of American Slavery," *The Frederick Douglass Papers*, ed. John W. Blassingame (New Haven, Conn.: Yale University Press, 1979), vol. 1, 141. Italics added.

61. See, for example, Bibb in Osofsky, 76–77; William and Ellen Craft, *Running a Thousand Miles for Freedom* (New York: Arno Press, 1969), 13–15. Of course, the quotations from statute books may suggest coaching or editing by white abolitionists; however, the overall theme of the importance of law in maintaining slavery pervades all of the narratives.

62. Douglass, "My Experience and My Mission to Great Britain," *Douglass Papers*, vol. 1, 37.

63. Oakes, *Slavery and Freedom*, 69.

64. Douglass, *Douglass Papers*, vol. 1, 37.

65. Jon-Christian Suggs, *Whispered Consolations: Law and Narrative in African-American Life* (Ann Arbor: University of Michigan Press, 1999), 64.

66. Ibid., 65.

67. Ibid., 28 and chapter 1 passim.

68. Simon Walker autobiography, *The American Slave: A Composite Autobiography*, ed. George P. Rawick (Westport, Conn.: Greenwood, 1941, 1973), series 1, vol. 6: *Alabama and Indiana Narratives*, 404.

69. Harriet Jacobs, *Incidents in the Life of a Slave Girl* (New York: Oxford University Press, 1988), 45.

70. James Lucas autobiography, *American Slave*, supp. series 1, vol. 8: *Mississippi Narratives*, part 3, 1339.

71. Richard Mack autobiography, *American Slave*, vol. 2: *South Carolina Narratives*,

parts 1 and 2, 151. See also Jim Allen autobiography, *American Slave*, supp. series 1, vol. 6: *Mississippi Narratives*, part 1, 54 ("Mars John Bussey drunk my Mudder up. I means by dat, Lee King took her and my brudder George for a whiskey debt"); Sam McAllum autobiography, *American Slave*, supp. series 1, vol. 9: *Mississippi Narratives*, part 4, 1352 ("Mr. Stephenson were a surveyor an' he fell out wid Mr. McAllum an' had a lawsuit an' had to pay it in darkies. An' Mr. McAllum had de privilege of takin' me an' my mother, or another woman an' her two; an' he took us"); Ephraim Robinson autobiography, ibid., 1852 ("the Marster knew if he hurt you or killed you it was his loss. Once when a slave hand ran away and they were trying to catch him, another plantation owner shot his Marster's slave in the hip and magots [*sic*] got in the place. The slave died, and not only did the slave owner sue the other man but never spoke to him again"); Adline Thomas autobiography, *American Slave*, supp. series 1, vol. 10: *Mississippi Narratives*, part 5, 2094 ("She, her mother, sister, and a brother were put on the block and sold to settle the debt at Ripley, Mississippi").

72. Crafts, *A Thousand Miles for Freedom*, 11.

73. Northup, in *Puttin' On Ole Massa*, 285.

74. Ibid., 289.

75. One consequence of the fact that the sample contained many more male runaways was an age skew in the sample: Runaways tended to be older than other slaves in the civil courtroom, averaging thirty years of age, which pushed the mean age of male slaves higher than that of women.

76. Steven Shapin, *A Social History of Truth: Civility and Science in Seventeenth Century England* (Chicago: University of Chicago Press, 1994), 84, 92.

77. William R. Hogan and Edwin A. Davis, introduction to *William Johnson's Natchez*, 55–62; *Natchez Courier*, June 20, 1851.

78. Drawer 245 no. 615, April 1839 (dismissed November 1840), Adams Cir. Ct., Miss., HNF. Replevin was an equitable remedy, in which the plaintiff asked the court to return property that had been wrongfully detained by another.

79. Statement of Lynch—Claim to Ellen, Folder 6, Box 2E906, Winchester Family Papers, Center for American History, University of Texas at Austin (CAH-UTA); Adams County Land Deed Records; Hogan and Davis, *William Johnson's Natchez*, 346, n. 21.

80. Apparently, Bob had Ellen "bid off" under two separate executions—an earlier one for $50 to some unknown white man, and then for $150 to Christopher Kyle. Kyle had recently completed the manumission of two female slaves and their children—Nancy and her two sons in 1819, and Caroline and her son in 1824; he eventually left most of his property to Nancy. Deed Book R29, Adams County Land Deed Records; Davis, *The Black Experience*, 59.

81. Charles Lynch to George Winchester, April 4, 1838, Folder 2, Box 2E904, Winchester Family Papers, CAH-UTA.
82. George Winchester to Charles Lynch, March 21, 1837, Folder 1, Box 2E904, Winchester Family Papers, CAH-UTA.
83. Ibid.
84. Charles Lynch to George Winchester, April 4, 1838.

Women and the Law: Domestic Discord in North Carolina After the Civil War

Laura F. Edwards

Elizabeth Rhodes was angry. She and her neighbors in Wilkes County, North Carolina were just beginning to piece together their lives after the Civil War. Economic devastation and the violent internal conflict that had raged in the western part of the state had shattered this white yeomen community. For Elizabeth, the twenty-five-year-old wife of a landless man and mother of two young daughters, daily life must have been a struggle. On this day in 1867, however, it was her husband, Benjamin, who pushed Elizabeth to her limits. He struck her "three licks with a small size switch not as large as a man's thumb." According to one witness, she had given him no provocation "except some words uttered by her." Evidently, Benjamin found those words more provocative than the witness. But if he intended to silence Elizabeth with his blows, he failed. Instead of submitting, she filed charges against him.[1]

Benjamin Rhodes fought back, not with his fists, but through the legal system. One year later, Elizabeth's case found its way to the state supreme court, where Justice Edwin Reade sided both for and against her. While theoretically striking down the customary right of husbands to discipline their wives, he also refused to lift "the curtain" of domestic life and expose "to public curiosity and criticism the nursery and the bed chamber." Instead, he drew a firm line around the household, sharply separating private and public space. "Family government," Justice Reade declared, "being in its nature as complete in itself as the State government is in itself, the Courts will not attempt to control, or interfere with it, in favor of either party." Although rebuked, Benjamin Rhodes retained his right to govern his family as he saw fit.[2]

But this highly privatized view of domestic life clashed with that of Elizabeth Rhodes, who had tried to make her marital conflict public. She was not alone. Women in the state had been bringing domestic violence cases to the local courts for a long time. Their success in prosecuting at the local level indicates that many men shared these women's concerns. In her study of antebellum North Carolina, Victoria Bynum found that at least thirty-nine women swore out peace warrants against their husbands in three counties between 1850 and 1860. Of the forty-nine divorce petitions filed in these counties from 1830 to 1860, eleven women charged physical cruelty. After the war, freedwomen joined poor white women in court. The Freedmen's Bureau regularly dealt with family disputes, including domestic violence. So did the local courts. In the twenty-five years following the war, there are records of thirty-three domestic violence cases in Granville, Orange, and Edgecombe counties. Many more cases never made their way into the written record since minor violence lay within the jurisdiction of local magistrates, who were notoriously bad record keepers. Even if a magistrate made note of a complaint, county authorities generally saved only those cases that moved into the jurisdiction of the Superior Court.[3]

This article examines the disjuncture between popular and legal conceptions of private life in North Carolina through the lens of domestic violence against women, using local court records as well as those of the state supreme court. Like the communities of which they were a part, poor African American and white women saw domestic life as a public institution in which neighbors and kin were expected to play active roles. This construction of family relations not only explains women's willingness to file charges against their husbands but also their success at the lower levels of the judicial system, where community involvement shaped the reception and outcome of domestic violence cases. In this way, individual domestic disputes became community debates over the distribution of power between men and women within and outside their households. Speaking with distinct voices, women articulated their own ideas about their rights and pushed their neighbors, kin, and local officials to acknowledge their concerns.

Their claims resonated well beyond their communities as well. Making "private" grievances "public," poor white and African American women called into question legal precedents that subordinated wives to their husbands and left them isolated within a domestic sphere. In the process, they contributed to a larger debate over the boundary between private and public life. The placement of this line was crucial to the entire structure of southern society. Before emancipation, the private authority of white male household heads translated directly into public rights. The economic, legal, and moral responsibility they assumed gave household heads the power to represent their dependents' interests in the public arena of politics. By contrast, law and social convention denied both private and public power to those who were supposed to be subsumed within the private sphere—wives, slaves, and children. Of course, these groups occupied distinctly different positions. Equating the subordination of slaves, which was absolute, with the subordination of white women and children would constitute a serious misrepresentation of southern society. But the positions of these groups overlapped in the sense that they lived as dependents within the private sphere, sheltered from the public gaze. Subject to the governance of a household head, they could not claim the requisite civil and political rights that would allow them to move freely in the space outside the household's borders.[4] The abolition of slavery upset this delicate balance, opening up a whole series of questions about the private obligations and public privileges of all southerners—white and black, male and female, adults and children. After all, if one domestic relationship could be dissolved with the stroke of pen, then what was so inviolable about the rest? At the very least, they might be subject to some alterations. Elizabeth Rhodes thought so. Justice Reade did not.

Despite Reade's decision in *Rhodes*, poor white and African American women kept lifting "the curtain" surrounding domestic life. Ultimately, the state supreme court found it impossible to ignore their cases because questions of public power were so directly involved. The result was a significant revision of the laws, opening up the private sphere to public regulation and making it easier for women to prosecute their husbands. These changes, however, did not fundamentally change the balance of power between husbands and wives. Instead of strengthening the position of women, the court abrogated more power to the state as the arbiter of domestic life. The implications of these decisions reached into the twentieth century, where they anchored not just the principle of government intervention in family life but also the continued exclusion of poor women's voices from public debate of these very measures.

During the antebellum period, the North Carolina Supreme Court viewed marital relations through the prism of slavery. This was particularly true between 1833 and 1852, when Thomas Ruffin was chief justice. Routinely placing the sanctity of marriage above the happiness of particular individuals, Ruffin insisted that the institution grounded the entire social edifice of the slave South. His views on marriage meshed neatly with his paternalistic proslavery philosophy, which defined the household in terms of reciprocal obligations. White women, according to Ruffin, belonged within households as wives, just as African Americans belonged within households as slaves. While bound by responsibilities, wives and slaves could also demand maintenance and protection from their husbands and masters. The possibility that marriage could be severed at will introduced contingency into this web of relations. If husbands could easily shed their obligations and wives could easily remove themselves—or be removed—from the household, then there was nothing to keep men and women in their "natural" places. The same logic called the "natural" subordination of African Americans as slaves into question as well.[5]

Ruffin articulated this view with particular clarity, but North Carolina was not unusual among southern courts in emphasizing the link between marriage and slavery. In the antebellum period, southern courts generally kept their distance from domestic relations of all kinds for precisely this reason. Violence by husbands against wives was no exception. Georgia and Tennessee did pass statutes in the 1850s criminalizing wife beating. In fact, they were the first states in the nation to do so. These laws reflected widespread concern in the country as a whole about abusive husbands and battered wives. But in the context of the slave South, occasionally lifting the "veil" surrounding the domestic sphere affirmed its essential privacy. By disciplining the most violent excesses of patriarchs, the courts preserved the integrity of the system as a whole. Other southern states, moreover, did not follow the lead of Georgia and Tennessee. Most passed no new legislation and most state supreme courts refused to consider either wife- or child-beating as a criminal matter until after the Civil War.[6] The North Carolina court considered domestic violence only as a component of divorce cases, not as a crime in its own right. It did not rank high on the list of marital abuses either. Abandonment and extreme cruelty were only grounds for a divorce from bed and board during the antebellum period. The marital tie could be completely dissolved only in a few circumstances—adultery combined with abandonment on the part of either party, adultery on the part of the wife, and impotence. Even then, women had difficulty proving extreme cruelty because the court granted husbands such wide latitude in family governance and insisted that the integrity of the institution of marriage outweighed the happiness of the individual parties.[7]

This legal construction of domestic life, however, was foreign to many North Carolina residents, black and white. For slaves, marriage was a relationship governed by custom and the community, not the law. African Americans continued to determine marital status by these same standards after the war, as shown by Noralee Frankel's work on Mississippi freedwomen and the pension records of North Carolina's black Union soldiers. The community recognized a couple as husband and wife when they took on certain responsibilities for each other: the woman washed, cleaned, cooked, and tended the house, while the man contributed to her and her children's maintenance. Both men and women could sever the marital bonds if their partners abandoned their responsibilities or otherwise mistreated them. Irvin Thompson, for instance, married his first wife in a legal ceremony soon after the war and lived with her about a year. "Then she associated with other men and left me," he told a pension examiner. "No I did not get any divorce. She just went off a whoring and I lost track of her." Soon afterward, he married another woman in a legal ceremony that the community also accepted as a valid marriage. Mary J. Moore ended her marriage in a similar way. Her husband beat her and ran around with other women on the sly, but when he began to live openly with another woman, she considered the marriage over and her neighbors concurred. She went on to live with several other men in a series of monogamous relationships recognized as valid marriages by the community.[8]

Most common whites accepted the concept of legal marriage enough to formalize their unions and separations. Even so, community recognition still played a significant role in determining marital status. Although North Carolina did not allow common law marriage in the antebellum period, the absence of other forms of state supervision, such as marriage-registration laws, forced the courts to accept the word of witnesses as proof of marriages. The Pension Bureau found itself in the same dilemma when examining the claims of white Union soldiers' widows. In 1889, for instance, Adam Pate told a pension examiner that he knew Ford and Sina Howell had "lived together as man and wife and I was told that they were regularly married." Fortunately Sina could produce others who actually witnessed her wedding. But, as Adam

Pate's testimony indicates, it was not so much the legal ceremony as the community's acceptance of it that validated the Howells' union. Wealthy Braddy's experience is suggestive. As a refugee in Newbern during the war, she eloped with a Union soldier. The preacher who heard their vows made no record of their marriage. Her family and neighbors, however, required no written documentation and accepted the union. The two, according to a neighbor, "were recognized by everybody to be man and wife." Soon afterward, Wealthy's husband moved away from the area with his regiment and never returned. Wealthy then remarried. Only when she tried to claim her first husband's pension thirty years later did her marital irregularities surface. The pension examiner discovered that her first husband was still alive and that the marriage had been invalid since he had legally married another woman in Connecticut before the war. The Pension Bureau rejected her claim. When her second husband, also a Union soldier, died about ten years later, Wealthy submitted another claim. Once again, she ran into trouble. A justice of the peace had presided at this second marriage, but he also failed to record it. As he informed the examiner, "at that time the law did not require us to record the license." Instead, Wealthy turned again to her neighbors, who affirmed that the wedding had taken place and that the community recognized them as husband and wife. Although her second marriage was legal, it too existed more in the collective memory of the community than in a written record of a legal contract.[9]

In determining valid unions, common whites looked to the substance of the relationship just as African Americans did. Edward Isham, born in Georgia in the 1820s and executed for murder in North Carolina in 1860, provides a particularly graphic example. Shortly before his death, Isham's lawyer, David Schenck, recorded his life story. A heavy drinker, irrepressible brawler, and shameless womanizer, Isham seems to have embellished an already colorful tale, which was hardly typical of the lives of most common whites. Even so, the way he described his own marital relations and those of the other whites around him is telling. Isham lived with a series of women in the relationship of husband and wife, marrying the last in North Carolina right before his death. The other men and women in his story lived in similar relationships, "taking up" sometimes, marrying occasionally, and "separating" without the sanction of legal contract. Isham may have married some of his wives in legal—if not legally binding—ceremonies. Yet he ultimately defined long-term relationships by the role he and his wife assumed within the relationship—specifically his economic responsibility for her welfare and her work keeping house for him. John Bell of Granville County shared this view. According to his wife, Eliza, he left her in 1862 to "take up and cohabit with one Emily Tillotson." John eventually moved on to other women and out of the state altogether. But promiscuity was not the only way he had failed as a husband. He also made no "provision for the maintenance and support of herself or for her child." Unlike her husband, Eliza moved more clearly within the culture of legal marriage and used this evidence to establish adultery and abandonment in the formulaic language of her divorce petition. But she also understood the signs of her husband's informal separation—rejecting any responsibility for her economic support and openly "taking up" with another woman.[10]

The way common whites and African Americans emphasized the substance of the relationship rooted the legitimacy of each union deep within the dynamics of local communities where such factors as the family's reputation, the husband's and wife's standing with their neighbors, and a host of other conflicts peculiar to the locality were all important factors. By contrast, formal law created a uniform standard of marital relations that varied from state to state, giving the impression that sweeping geographic variations explain both legal differences and the social and economic relations that shaped the law. At the same time, the law treated marriage as an abstract entity, important to society as a whole, but unaffected by concrete kin and community relations. This is not to say that either regional social and economic variations or the universal standards of the law were meaningless at the local level. As we will see, the law played a powerful role in shaping the way women argued domestic violence cases and how local courts received them. Rather the intent is to situate marriages within the context that gave them meaning: a dense web of relations within specific communities where legal universals had to accommodate the particularities of everyday life.[11] Acknowledging these local particularities does not preclude generalization; but it does move our attention away from the outcome to the process—from the verdict in each domestic violence case to the dynamics that shaped those underlying conflicts.

Neighbors and kin were well positioned to judge the substance of marital relationships because the rhythms of domestic life were so public. Poor people did not think of their dwellings as private havens from the public sphere, but as functional components in an integrated world of work. It was there that women turned raw materials into usable goods: they tended the garden and preserved its bounty; they collected eggs and made butter for sale; they butchered hogs and prepared the meat for the smokehouse; and they wove cloth and sewed their families' clothes and linens. In her study of white tenant women in North Carolina during the early twentieth century, Margaret Jarmon Hagood noted that the yards of rural houses, cluttered with farm implements and tools, served less as a boundary between the house and farm than a transition between two parts of a single unit of production. The same could be said for poor women in the earlier century. Poor African American and white women worked regularly in their own families' fields and as occasional hired labor in the fields of their wealthier neighbors. Black women also worked for wages as domestic servants and washerwomen.[12] Just as poor people's work patterns defied the separation between private and public space, so did the terrain of their domestic lives. With open doors and windows, their houses mingled physically with the world outside just like the laundry that spilled out into the yard and billowed in the wind. Even inside, houses were not neatly divided into private and public living areas. Most contained only one or two rooms, where family members slept, ate, visited, and entertained. During North Carolina's sultry summer nights, poor people abandoned their stuffy interiors altogether and turned their neighborhood into parlors.[13]

Family borders were also flexible, expanding and contracting to include kin and unrelated friends who stayed and worked with the family for extended periods of time. Everyone crowded together in small, one- and two-room houses, where privacy was virtually impossible. At special events, such as births, deaths, and illnesses, the boundary between the family and the community disappeared almost entirely, as neighbors gathered to celebrate or to grieve, to offer advice and assistance, or just to observe. Privacy of any kind was virtually impossible, as the unmarried Henrietta World discovered. The neighbors all inquired when Henrietta's belly grew big, only to be told by her mother that Henrietta had a tumor. Unconvinced, their suspicions were confirmed when a dead infant was found nearby in the woods. This time, the neighbor women came to inspect Henrietta physically. Among them was one woman who walked into the World house, eyed Henrietta, then unceremoniously reached out and "felt of Dft's breast." Under the circumstances, this woman felt justified in taking the liberty. But then, walking into a relative's or neighbor's house unannounced was not that unusual anyway.[14]

In this context, domestic conflicts were rarely secret. Quarrels between husbands and wives, parents and children, sisters, brothers, cousins, and unrelated housemates all spilled out into streets, yards, and fields. In Edgecombe County, the noise of Gray and Louisa Thigpen's argument attracted two neighbors, one who was in her house and another who was working in a nearby field. Both dropped what they were doing to go to the Thigpens, and later testified to the source of the contention and the nature of the fight itself. Four people saw Mary Ward the day her husband Louis was shot dead. Passing them on the road, one heard enough of their quarrel to paraphrase it in some detail. As he testified, Louis told Mary "she had to go home and stay there that he was going to whip her after he got her there, she told him that she would not go home with him that one or the other of them would die before they got there, that if they started home she would kill him before they got there." Even when conflicts were contained within the four walls of individual houses, close living quarters drew in all the dwelling's occupants. An upstairs neighbor, for instance, knew that Granville County's David Burwell, an African American man, had been sick because she could hear his groans through the floor. She divulged this information while testifying to a fight between David and his wife Dicey, which she had monitored with great interest from her window. Usually, there was no shortage of adult witnesses in domestic violence cases. In many, at least one person had seen the fight in question, and others lined up to relate what they knew of the incident. They generally knew a great deal, offering up both information and opinions about the couple's domestic life.[15]

Public knowledge, however, did not always translate into public involvement because poor African Americans and whites respected men's authority over their households. Two instances of domestic violence that ended in murder suggest the reluctance to intervene. The first involved Eli and Elizabeth Jacobs, a white couple who lived in Orange County. Their neighbors noted Eli's abusive behavior toward Elizabeth long before she died in November 1879. Afterward, the community was awash in gossip as neighbors held forth on the incident and debated the cause of her death. A group of women who examined the body before the burial concluded that she died of natural causes. Others maintained that Eli was responsible. As Joseph Jacobs later claimed, Eli "was verry [sic] unkind to her, and he had threatened to kill her." By January Eli's detractors convinced the coroner to exhume her body and call an inquest to investigate her death. The jury, however, found the evidence against Eli inconclusive. Frances Henderson's Granville County neighbors were more united in their opinion of her husband, Robert. But they too acted only after her death. As Frances, an African American woman, lay moaning in her bed, her husband sat visiting with friends just a few yards away. When they asked what was wrong with her, he told them to ignore her, that she was sick. The next morning, Frances was dead. The entire neighborhood turned out to pay their last respects, but this was not the only reason they gathered at the Henderson household. They were also suspicious about the cause of her death. Virtually everyone who testified at the inquest knew that Robert habitually beat Frances. Based on this knowledge and what information they gathered as they prepared her badly bruised body for burial, they called in the local authorities. None of these witnesses approved of his behavior, but neither did they feel compelled to censure him before his abuse resulted in death.[16]

Doing so stretched the bonds and taxed the resources of the community. Errant husbands could threaten outsiders who challenged their domestic prerogatives with the same violence they used against household members. Robert Henderson, for instance, opposed his neighbors' call for an inquest. His position is not particularly surprising, considering the growing suspicions about his guilt. Far more striking is the way he expressed himself, asserting a proprietary right to her body with a belligerence that probably explains both Frances Henderson's bruises and the delay in her neighbors' response: "she was mine before she died and she is mine now." Samuel Lawrence understood his relationship with his wife in similar terms. Accused of beating her in 1882, he responded "that she was his wife and he would prank with her as much as he pleased." Like Robert Henderson, Samuel Lawrence drew a veil around his relationship with his wife, claiming the privilege to act "as he pleased" without interference from either the community or the court. When the justice of the peace announced his intention to protect Mrs. Lawrence "so far as the law was concerned," Samuel Lawrence flew into a rage. After showering the justice with verbal threats, he fought off the deputy charged with arresting him. Declaring that "there were not enough damned negros or poor white men on the ground to arrest him," he also denied the community's authority to act as mediator and judge.[17]

When community members did step in, it was usually to protect women's lives at moments of crisis. Two domestic disputes that ultimately made their way to the state supreme court illuminate a common pattern of intervention.

One involved a fight between Ridley and Mary Ann Mabrey, a white couple from Halifax County. A small crowd gathered to watch. But it was only after Ridley drew a knife and slashed at Mary Ann that one of the bystanders stepped in and pulled her out of harm's way. Those who witnessed the fight between Cynthia and Richard Oliver, a white couple from Alexander County, reacted similarly. They watched Richard strike Cynthia four times before they stopped him, explaining that they considered this sufficient because Richard "struck as hard as he could." Richard, however, did not. As he boasted in court, if no one else had been there, "he would have worn her out." Although they did intervene, onlookers in both cases considered the two men's authority over and right to discipline their wives to be legitimate, at least to some extent.[18]

It was the extent of that power that was in question. Communities were often divided in their response to domestic disputes. So were juries in the Superior Courts. The jury that tried Benjamin Rhodes found him guilty of striking Elizabeth "three licks with a small size switch not as large as a man's thumb without any provocation." But it was "undecided how to find as matter of law upon the guilt or innocence of the defendant" and gave the decision over to the judge. In short, the jury members either did not know or could not decide whether Benjamin Rhodes's actions were criminal. They did not, however, rule out the possibility altogether. Neither did the juries that judged Ridley Mabrey and Joseph Huntley. Because Mary Ann Mabrey had sustained no physical injuries, she could not prove excessive physical force under the traditional rule of thumb. Rachel Huntley, a white woman from Haywood County, had a better case. Her husband Joseph, who was also white, had whipped her with "such violence as to break the skin and raise whelks upon her person and to draw the blood so that . . . it came through the clothing." But, as Rachel admitted, her injuries were not so severe as to incapacitate her, a fact that could excuse her husband's actions as appropriate chastisement. Both juries claimed uncertainty as to the legal meaning of these incidents. "If upon these facts," the Superior Court jury in Joseph Huntley's case declared, "the defendant is in law guilty we find him guilty and if upon these facts the defendant is in law not guilty we find him not guilty." Ridley Mabrey's jury stated its conclusion with virtually the same words. These jury members, like those who tried Benjamin Rhodes, could not dismiss the idea that Ridley Mabrey's and Joseph Huntley's transgressions might be sufficiently serious to qualify as criminal acts.[19]

Such sustained community action in domestic violence cases was usually directed at men who were also known troublemakers. Community members and local officials, for instance, had run out of patience with Benjamin Rhodes, Richard Oliver, and Joseph Huntley long before their wives even thought of filing charges against them. All three were brawlers, drinkers, and womanizers who appeared regularly in the court records and left a trail of aggrieved victims and angry witnesses in their wake: Benjamin Rhodes had been charged with beating a neighbor woman and for fighting publicly with two other men; Richard Oliver claimed one man had assaulted him with a knife and was accused of threatening to kill another; and Joseph Huntley had been arrested four times for selling liquor without a license, twice for fornication and adultery, and once for a public fight. Not surprising, their wives had no difficulty in convincing others that these men needed disciplining.[20]

If community members sometimes needed prodding, women themselves were far less ambivalent about the extent of their husbands' prerogatives. Although infidelity figured into many domestic disputes, most also turned on questions of men's and women's responsibilities and the relative distribution of power within their households. Men claimed their wives neglected their household chores, children, and contributions to the family income. Women, in turn, charged their husbands with abandoning their economic duties and using excessive force to impose their will on other household members. Richard and Cynthia Oliver, for instance, battled over these issues. According to the trial transcript, Richard "came home intoxicated in the morning after breakfast was over, got some raw bacon, said it had skippers and his old wife . . . would not clean it, sat down [and ate] a little, threw the coffee cup and coffee pot to the corner of the house, went out [and] cut two switches." No doubt Cynthia disapproved of her husband staying out all night and coming home drunk when he should be out working in the fields. She certainly refused to accept his discipline for her alleged shortcomings as a housekeeper. When a peace warrant did nothing to alter his behavior, she left his house and filed criminal charges against him. The impasse between Sarah and David Taylor sums up the differences that plagued many couples. According to a friend who tried to bring about a reconciliation, Sarah agreed to return "if her husband would promise not to whip her again." David, however, "refused to make the promise + said he would whip her when she deserved it or when he saw fit."[21]

Poor African American and white women did not always passively accept their husbands' blows. Martha White, for instance, took offense when her husband William found it necessary to "advise" her "on her duties." As William explained, "she would get into a passion, abuse him, sometimes assault him." One witness saw them rolling around on the floor, pulling out each other's hair. Martha, this witness maintained, seemed to have the upper hand. Even Martha openly admitted to defending herself when she felt physically threatened, although she denied ever instigating an attack. Dicey Burwell reacted similarly when her husband David knocked both her and her sixteen-year-old daughter to the ground several times with a maul. Wresting the weapon from David's control, she hit him so hard that he was unconscious for almost an hour.[22]

Women might occasionally pin their husbands to the floor or even knock them out, but they lacked the social power, economic resources, and legal standing that would allow them permanent control over their households. Publicity provided a measure of protection, giving them the opportunity to mobilize the community in their behalf and to subject their husbands to the scrutiny of neighbors and kin, who could and did reprimand individual male household heads. When a fight escalated beyond their control and help was not at hand, women often left their own houses for those of neighbors and kin. In fact, when neighbors and kin did become involved in an ongoing domestic dispute, it was generally because the wife had actively enlisted their aid.

Kin usually proved the most sympathetic. Westley Rhodes, a white man from Orange County, discovered just how proactive families could be. Rhodes, who had long "indulged himself in the habits of intemperance and abuse to his wife," beat her "in a most cruel manner" one night in 1823. Mrs. Rhodes, who was also white, "fled to her father's house" for protection. After hearing the story, her mother immediately marched back to Westley, "reprimanded him for his conduct," and "struck him with a tobacco stem which she had picked up on the road." By this time, Mrs. Rhodes's grandfather had also appeared at the house, apparently to get his two cents in as well. Infuriated and outnumbered, Westley lunged at the old man with a knife. In so doing, he only widened the scope of community involvement in his domestic affairs and undermined whatever sympathy he might have claimed.[23]

Postwar parents could be equally supportive. So were brothers, sisters, grandparents, uncles, and aunts. All housed women and their children when they fled their husbands, acted as mediators, and assisted in women's legal suits when all else failed. Perhaps the most telling example of the importance of women's kin ties are their husbands' objections. Martha White's husband flew into a rage when he suspected her of using all the flour to bake for her relatives. Richard Oliver threatened to cut his wife Cynthia "to pieces" with a switch if "she talked with her people." Later, he drove her out of the house, claiming that "she and her damned mother had aggravated him near to death." Because women could summon so few resources in their own name, family ties were equally important for the wives of propertied men. David Taylor, who owned considerable land, insisted that his wife Sarah "would have been as tolerable and happy as that of other women . . . had it not been for the meddlesome interference of her mother and brothers and father." At one point, he became so angry that he got out his gun and threatened to shoot Sarah's brother.[24]

Women also drew in reluctant neighbors, as did Martha White. She described her husband as "quarrelsome" and "very frequently in the habit of applying abusive epithets to her, of threatening her with violence and of striking and attempting to strike her." Martha defended herself in kind, but when she found herself on the losing side of one particularly brutal battle, she "immediately . . . started to Mr. Grimsley's, a neighbor, for protection." One year later, after she suffered a severe blow to her head, she "immediately left his house" again and sought shelter with another neighbor. Neither neighbor was particularly inclined toward Martha. As Matthew Grimsley later testified, her husband "provided well for his family." Besides, he had never actually seen her husband abuse her. But Matthew could not deny the abuse either, because Martha had shown him her injuries. In this way, she successfully drew him to her side whether he wanted to be there or not.[25]

Matthew Grimsley sheltered Martha White a few days and testified at her divorce. The neighbors and kin of other women did not get off so easily. Some acted as mediators, shuttling back and forth between the two parties, trying to work out an agreement. There was a strong incentive for them to do so. If mediation failed, they could gain permanent additions to their households. After Cynthia Oliver left her husband, she lived with her parents for several years, an eventful time in which she prosecuted a criminal action for assault against her husband, which ultimately made its way to the state supreme court, and she filed successfully for a divorce. Cynthia probably remained with her parents afterward, considering that she had a small child, no means of support, and no property except her bedding, linens, and clothes. In Granville County, Mrs. Hedding and her children stayed with three different neighbors at various times while married to her husband, Polaseo. Others provided food and clothes, for Polaseo not only beat his wife and children but refused to support them as well. According to A. J. Yancey, "Mrs. Hedding came to my house one day and said Mr. Hedding had taken every thing from her" and left her "without anything to eat or wear." The expectation was that he and the other neighbors would provide what her husband did not. They did, although their patience ultimately wore thin. In 1883, six neighbors filed charges against Polaseo Hedding for abandonment. Admitting no wrong-doing and arguing that he had never technically left his family, Polaseo fought back and won. No doubt the neighbors soon found themselves providing for Mrs. Hedding and her children once again.[26]

When necessary, women themselves appealed to the legal system. The lower levels of the court system could function as an extension of community authority, just as church disciplinary hearings did. This was particularly true during Republican rule when local magistrates were elected by their neighbors. Inquests and trials took place on the front yards and porches of residences and country stores. They were attended by neighbors and overseen by elected officials who were known and respected in the community. Robert Henderson's formal inquest, for instance, bore a remarkable resemblance to the earlier, informal hearing conducted by the community. Neighbors gathered once again to give their recollections of the day Frances died and their impressions of her relationship with Robert. Although the coroner, an outsider, inspected the body and presided over the hearing, the jury, composed of people in the community, rendered the decision. To some extent, the coroner derived his authority from the community, which had already concluded that Robert Henderson had a hand in his wife's death. Eli Jacobs's case proceeded in a similar fashion, with the community acting as a chorus, interpreting and judging the incident from their personal knowledge of those involved.[27]

Familiar faces and surroundings, however, could be misleading. The courts were a distinct arena, with its own legal guidelines and discourse. Given the presumption of domestic privacy and male governance within the home, it was not a particularly friendly arena for any woman. It was that much less hospitable for women who were black, poor, or both. Court officials generally gave only minimal attention to women's charges of domestic abuse. Mrs. Lawrence's experience is particularly telling. After she made her complaint, public attention focused on the conflict between the magistrate and her husband. In fact, the magistrate's testimony suggests that he was not really concerned with Mrs. Lawrence's well-being at all. Earlier that day, Samuel Lawrence had disrupted the courtroom during a trial and had repeatedly ignored the magistrate's orders to settle down. By the time Mrs. Lawrence walked into his office, the magistrate was already more than willing to make life difficult for her husband and probably agreed to arrest Lawrence for this reason. Then, when Lawrence threatened him and lashed out at the deputy, even better options presented themselves. Charging Lawrence with resisting arrest, the magistrate dropped all reference to Mrs. Lawrence and her complaint. Many complaints never made it into the records at all because magistrates deemed them unworthy of legal action. Little information remains for those that they did act on. Usually, just the formal complaint survives, giving only the names of the parties involved. It provides no information on the events leading up to the charges, let alone any insight into the woman's perspective on them. Ironically, then, the legal system tended to erase women at the very moment they demanded public recognition.[28]

When court officials did take notice, they imposed legal categories on domestic violence cases that further obscured women's voices. For the court even to consider intervention, women had to cast themselves as hapless victims. This construction described few of the domestic violence cases involving poor white and African American women, as the example of Dicey Burwell suggests. Like so many other similar cases, the fight between Dicey and her husband David was not an isolated incident, but one of many in a very turbulent relationship. Dicey Burwell testified that her husband had "been kind to me since he professed religion but was cruel before." If David was "cruel," Dicey did not suffer in silence. In the fight that landed the couple in court, it was Dicey, not her husband David who was officially charged as the assailant. Her position as such was purely a matter of chance. Had it been one of David's blows that had knocked Dicey unconscious, instead of the other way around, she would have become the victim. Other poor women fought back as well—with their fists, handy kitchen utensils, community pressure, and warrants. These women also imagined a different position for themselves outside their households. Articulating a view of their rights at odds with those allowed by law, they challenged legal presumptions that their husbands could exercise broad disciplinary rights over them and that they, as wives, were without public recourse. In all these ways, poor women refused to become victims. But that is how they had to represent themselves if they hoped to gain any hearing at all.[29]

It was not an easy role for poor white and African American women to assume. The very act of filing public charges undercut their credibility in the eyes of elite white court officials. Wealthy white women measured and maintained their respectability through their distance from the immorality and violence associated with public space. Criticizing female lawyers in the North, one local North Carolina newspaper breathed a sigh of relief that "none of our Southern ladies have deemed it consistent with womanly modesty and delicacy to enter such an arena. It is bad enough to be a witness in court, without being compelled to try cases the evidence in which are not suited to 'ears polite.'" Elite white women rarely appeared in court even as witnesses, let alone as complainants.[30]

These gender conventions buttressed older assumptions that the "lower classes" were less sensitive and more prone to violent outbursts than those from the "higher ranks" of society. Such distinctions were deeply embedded into the law, as Justice Reade's decision in *Rhodes* indicates. Explaining why "[e]very household has and must have a government of its own," he wrote: "Suppose a case coming up to us from a hovel, where neither delicacy of sentiment nor refinement of manners is appreciated or known. The parties themselves would be amazed, if they were to be held responsible for rudeness or trifling violence. What do they care for insults and indignities?" Reade then contrasted the sensibilities of the poor with those of "the higher ranks, where education and culture have so refined nature, that a look cuts like a knife, and a word strikes like a hammer; where the most delicate attention gives pleasure, and the slightest neglect pain; where an indignity is disgrace and exposure is ruin." As this logic suggests, elite court officials did not consider poor white and black men's violent outbursts to be particularly unusual or egregious.[31]

Ironically, the same legal regime that privatized domestic relations also provided poor white and African American women access to the courts. While the supreme court upheld the inviolability of domestic government in *Rhodes*, it also declared that the state did "not recognize the right of the husband to whip his wife." Moreover, it reserved the right to intervene in domestic government "where permanent or malicious injury is inflicted or threatened, or the condition of the party is intolerable." Revising the older "rule of thumb" (which allowed a man to discipline his wife as long as the instrument was not larger than an average man's thumb), the court would now judge domestic conflicts by the injuries resulting from the assault, not the size of the instrument that had been used. This opening allowed poorer white and African American women to use the courts in disputes with their husbands and to place limits on men's power within their own households and communities. In this way, the courts became reluctant partners in the efforts of African American and poor white women to enforce their versions of appropriate domestic relations.[32]

The result was a transformation of the laws relating to domestic violence. Although the state supreme court upheld the principle of domestic privacy established in *Rhodes*, it increasingly lifted the veil surrounding it. By 1874, in *State v. Richard Oliver*, the Court disallowed the traditional "rule of thumb," pronouncing it inconsistent "with our present civilization." In the 1879 case of *State v. Simpson Pettie*, the court judged Pettie's abuse of his wife particularly "brutal" and gave itself the power to decide "the propriety of the punishment," "for the protection of the wife, and, through it, for the protection and good order of society." If anyone had the power to chastise, it was a judge. Five years later, in *State v. Joseph Huntley*, the supreme court lowered the evidence required to upgrade domestic violence to serious assaults that lay within the jurisdiction of Superior Courts, rather than local magistrates.[33]

Women may have forced the court's hand in these cases, but the state supreme court had its own reasons for altering the rules. After emancipation released black men from their role as dependent slaves, postwar legal and political changes set them up as household heads in their own right. Poor white men benefited as well, although to a lesser degree. Historians of Reconstruction have documented how profoundly disturbing elite white southerners found these changes and how they tried to overturn them in desperate battles over economic independence, civil rights, and universal manhood suffrage. But the legal principle of domestic privacy also buttressed poor people's independence, with its protective curtain that shielded large portions of their lives from state interference. After the war, poor African Americans and whites wielded this theoretical weapon with great success, using it to protect their families from the intrusion of meddling outsiders. Poor African Americans and whites also mobilized key components of domestic privacy to justify demands for a more equitable distribution of economic resources and political power. As they argued, women and children could not perform their role as dependents unless their menfolk could protect and provide for them, men could not meet these duties without the necessary economic and political power, and families—the cornerstone of society—would disintegrate unless men and women could fulfill their proper roles.[34]

The private autonomy of poor African Americans and whites came under attack at the same time their public rights did. As Peter Bardaglio has argued, southern courts and other state institutions increased their power to oversee and regulate the domestic sphere throughout the late nineteenth century. Even as many whites increasingly relied on vigilante violence as a way to "regulate" the behavior of African Americans, southern lawmakers began transferring other key elements of patriarchal power from the hands of individual men to the state. This process, which continued into the twentieth century, gave agents of the state the latitude to pass judgment on a wide range of family issues affecting poor white as well as black families. To this end, judges delved into the characters of litigants to ferret out the "worthy" husbands, wives, and children from the "unworthy" ones. The 1877 divorce case, *Taylor v. Taylor*, illuminates the court's role. Citing frequent evidence of abuse, Sarah Taylor maintained that her husband David's abuse had made her life intolerable and, therefore, constituted grounds for divorce. In response, Justice Bynum reiterated the court's longstanding position that no universal measure of "intolerable" conditions could ever apply in all cases: "The station in life, the temperament, state of health, habits and feelings of different persons are so unlike, that treatment which would send the broken heart of one to the grave, would make no sensible impression upon another." But instead of throwing out the case, as an earlier judge might have, Bynum insisted on the court's right to judge the matter. Frank Bumpass, an African American in Granville County, faced exactly this kind of individualized scrutiny when he tried to have his three grandchildren legally apprenticed to him in 1881. "Frank Bumpass," his white employer testified, "is a colored man, well behaved and likely to treat the children in a becoming manner and I hereby recommend him as a suitable person." Bumpass obviously thought himself suitable as well. But the right to determine suitability ultimately resided with the courts.[35]

As long as poor whites and African Americans retained their hold on public power, they could use their access to the system and their clout with Republican officials to include themselves among those considered "suitable" and "worthy." But these decisions acquired far more ominous meanings as the tide of Republican influence ebbed and conservatives flooded back into the judicial system in the mid 1870s. The curtain of domestic privacy lifted at the same time that poor whites and African Americans lost power within governmental institutions, exposing them to unprecedented state regulation at the moment of their greatest vulnerability. Justice Bynum's 1877 decision in *Taylor v. Taylor* is suggestive. Reiterating the same racial and class distinctions as Justice Reade did in *Rhodes*, he noted that "[a]mong the lower clases [*sic*], blows sometimes pass between married couples who in the main are very happy and have no desire to part; amidst very coarse habits such incidents occur almost as freely as rude or reproachful words." In this particular case, however, the court could not overlook such behavior because both the husband and wife belonged to "respectable walks of life." Although the logic of this decision would seem to remove the households of poor whites and African Americans from public scrutiny, it did not. Instead, it labeled "lower classes" as coarse, rude, violent, and uncivilized people, while also obstructing "unrespectable" women's claims to state protection.[36]

Forty-five years after Elizabeth Rhodes filed charges against her husband, Judge Walter Clark addressed the Federation of Women's Clubs in New Bern on the legal status of women. After discussing the laws relating to married women's property rights, domestic violence, and suffrage, Clark attributed the recent changes to "progress." "Among savage tribes," he argued, "the club of the husband was logical. And under the common law so was the lash, because women being kept in ignorance and deprived of property rights could be thus governed. But when they were educated and given the right to own property these things became illogical and impossible." If "progress" made such change inevitable, it was a circle of enlightened men and women who carried out its designs. This assumption, widespread among Progressive reformers in the South, positioned the poor and dispossessed as passive recipients of reforms they never could have conceived of themselves. In his talk to the New Bern Women's Clubs, for instance, Clark made no mention of the poor women who actually brought domestic violence cases. If anything, he left the impression that the lash and club were still common where ignorance and poverty reigned.[37]

Judge Clark's analysis still carries a great deal of power today. Historians look to the Progressive era, its women's club members and outspoken male advocates to find evidence of reform. Restoring the voices of poor white and

African American in the nineteenth century recasts our understanding of this later period. Judges did transform the laws governing domestic life, but they did not do so in a cultural vacuum. It was poor women who forced the court's hand, by challenging their husbands' power and insisting on making their private disputes public. As such, they claimed public space for themselves and politicized their own domestic concerns long before middle-class women reformers ever thought to do so. Of course, the results were not what the women who brought the cases had intended. The court intervened in private life to promote "good order" and to uphold the rules governing "our present civilization," expanding its own power to oversee the lives of all poor people, while also maintaining the line around private space that proved so problematic for women.[38] Poor women could only speak publicly of their domestic concerns to appeal to the patriarchal protection of male judges. These constraints effectively silenced poor women because they found it so difficult to express the complexities of their lives in these terms. The legacy of these legal decisions continues to shape scholarship today. Like reformers of the Progressive era, historians presume poor women's passivity and even assume to speak for them without ever stopping to consider the political reasons for their silence.

NOTES

Michael Bellesiles, Giovanna Benadusi, Kirsten Fischer, John McAllister, Don Nieman, and Chris Waldrep all read drafts of this essay, and their comments have improved it enormously. Helpful, too, were the thoughts of Ed Baptist, who read an early version. I also owe a great deal to the insightful questions and comments of Stephanie McCurry, Steve Hahn, Rachel Klein, and a group of wonderful graduate students at the University of California, San Diego, where I presented this work. A postdoctoral fellowship from the Smithsonian Institution at National Museum of American History provided research funds and the time to write the first draft. The Newberry Library graciously opened its doors and provided me intellectual stimulation and work space during the time I did revisions. Finally, this piece previously appeared in similar form as "Women and Domestic Violence in Nineteenth-Century North Carolina," in *Lethal Imaginations: Violence and Brutality in American History*, edited by Michael Bellesiles (New York: New York University Press, 1999), 115–36.

1. *State v. Rhodes*, no. 9368, Supreme Court Original Cases, 1800–1900, North Carolina Division of Archives and History (NCDAH).
2. *State v. Rhodes*, 61 N.C. 453 (1868).

3. For antebellum cases, see Victoria Bynum, *Unruly Women: The Politics of Social and Sexual Control in the Old South* (Chapel Hill: University of North Carolina Press, 1992), 81, 74. For postwar cases, see *State v. Jones*, 1866; *State v. Taylor*, 1867; *State v. Bryant*, 1868; *State v. Phillips*, 1868; *State v. Thigpen*, 1869; *State v. Williams*, 1869; *State v. Robbins*, 1872; *State v. Thorn*, 1874; *State v. Harrell*, 1875; *State v. Dawson*, 1877; *State v. Daniel*, 1877; *State v. Lloyd*, 1878; *State v. Sugg*, 1879; *State v. Lawrence*, 1886; all in Criminal Action Papers, Edgecombe County, NCDAH. *State v. Lyon*, 1866; *State v. Ray*, 1867[?]; *State v. Harris*, 1868[?]; *State v. Mayo*, 1869[?]; *State v. Riley*, 1875; *State v. Doherty*, 1885; all in Criminal Action Papers, Orange County, NCDAH. *State v. Estes*, 1866; *State v. Newton*, 1867; *State v. Clay*, 1869; *State v. Wortham*, 1870; *State v. Hunt*, 1871; *State v. Webb*, 1875; *State v. Snit*, 1875; *State v. Frazier*, 1875; *State v. Thorp*, 1878; *State v. Gipsom*, 1880; *State v. Lewis*, 1881; *State v. Hall*, 1882; *State v. Hedding*, 1885; all in Criminal Action Papers, Granville County, NCDAH. For family disputes in the Freedmen's Bureau, see Nancy Bercaw, "The Politics of Household: Domestic Battlegrounds in the Transition from Slavery to Freedom in the Yazoo-Mississippi Delta, 1850–1860," Ph.D. diss., University of Pennsylvania, 1996, chap. 5; Ira Berlin, Stephen F. Miller, Leslie S. Rowland, eds. "Afro-American Families in the Transition from Slavery to Freedom," *Radical History Review* 42 (1988): 89–121; Eric Foner, *Reconstruction: America's Unfinished Revolution* (New York: Harper and Row, 1988), 88; Noralee Frankel, *Freedom's Women: Black Women and Families in the Civil War Era* (Bloomington: University of Indiana Press, 1999); Leslie Ann Schwalm, *A Hard Fight for We: Women's Transition from Slavery to Freedom in South Carolina* (Urbana: University of Illinois Press, 1997). The presumption that domestic violence was always "minor," regardless of the injuries sustained, was revealed and challenged in *State v. Huntley*, 91 N.C. 617 (1884).

4. Elizabeth Fox-Genovese, *Within the Plantation Household: Women in the Old South* (Chapel Hill: University of North Carolina Press, 1988), 192–241; Stephanie McCurry, *Masters of Small Worlds: Yeoman Households, Gender Relations, and the Political Culture of the Antebellum South Carolina Low Country* (New York: Oxford University Press, 1995) and "The Two Faces of Republicanism: Gender and Proslavery Politics in Antebellum South Carolina," *Journal of American History* 78 (March 1992): 1245–64. See also Bynum, *Unruly Women*, 59–87; Bill Cecil-Fronsman, *Common Whites: Class and Culture in Antebellum North Carolina* (Lexington: University Press of Kentucky, 1992), 133–50.

5. Victoria Bynum, "Reshaping the Bonds of Womanhood: Divorce in Reconstruction North Carolina," in *Divided Houses: Gender and the Civil War*, ed. Catherine Clinton and Nina Silber (New York: Oxford University Press, 1992),

322–23; see also Bertram Wyatt-Brown, *Southern Honor: Ethics and Behavior in the Old South* (New York: Oxford University Press, 1982), 244–47, 283–91, 300–306. For the connection between the subordination of women in marriage and that of African Americans in slavery, see also Bynum, *Unruly Women*; Peter Bardaglio, *Reconstructing the Household: Families, Sex, and the Law in the Nineteenth-Century South* (Chapel Hill: University of North Carolina Press, 1995); McCurry, *Masters of Small Worlds* and "The Two Faces of Republicanism"; Fox-Genovese, *Within the Plantation Household*, 334–71. See also Eugene Genovese, *Roll, Jordan, Roll: The World the Slaves Made* (New York: Vintage Books, 1976), 3–112.

6. For developments in the legal handling of domestic violence in the North, see Cornelia Hughes Dayton, *Women Before the Bar: Gender, Law and Society in Connecticut, 1639–1789* (Chapel Hill: University of North Carolina Press, 1995). Georgia and Tennessee were actually the first states in the nation to criminalize wife beating after the Revolution. Although northern courts and legislatures were slow to deal with this particular issue, they did begin intervening in other domestic matters long before southern courts. For the North, see Michael Grossberg, *Governing the Hearth: Law and the Family in Nineteenth-Century America* (Chapel Hill: University of North Carolina Press, 1985). For the treatment of domestic violence generally in the nineteenth century, see Bardaglio, *Reconstructing the Household*, 33–34; Bynum, *Unruly Women*, 70–72; Linda Gordon, *Heroes of Their Own Lives: The Politics and History of Family Violence* (New York: Viking, 1988); McCurry, *Masters of Small Worlds*, 85–91; Pleck, "Wife Beating in Nineteenth-Century America," *Victimology* 4, no. 1 (1979): 60–74; Jerome Nadelhaft, "Wife Torture: A Known Phenomenon in Nineteenth-Century America," *Journal of American Culture* 10 (Fall 1987): 39–59; Pleck, *Domestic Tyranny: The Making of Social Policy Against Family Violence from Colonial Times to the Present* (New York: Oxford University Press, 1987); Christine Stansell, *City of Women: Sex and Class in New York, 1789–1860* (Urbana: University of Illinois Press, 1987), 78–83; Wyatt-Brown, *Southern Honor*, 281–83.

7. For the legal changes in divorce in nineteenth-century North Carolina, see Bynum, "Reshaping the Bonds of Womanhood," and *Unruly Women*, 68–77. See also Bardaglio, *Reconstructing the Household*, 32–34, 134; Jane Turner Censer, "'Smiling Through Her Tears': Ante-Bellum Southern Women and Divorce," *American Journal of Legal History* 25 (January 1982): 114–34; Catherine Clinton, *The Plantation Mistress: Woman's World in the Old South* (New York: Pantheon Books, 1982), 79–85; Wyatt-Brown, *Southern Honor*, 242–47, 283–91, 300–307.

8. Quotes from Jacob Moore, 14th Reg., Co. A, U.S. Colored Troops, Heavy Ar-

tillery; Irvin Thompson alias Cherry Thompson, 37th Reg., Co. K, U.S. Colored Troops, Infantry; both in Pension Records, RG 15, NA. My analysis is based on hundreds of Civil War pension files, which provide an excellent source for the construction of marriage among both blacks and common whites because widows had to establish the legitimacy of their relationships to claim a pension. In North Carolina, most of the testimony comes from the eastern counties, which were occupied early by Union troops and where many black and white Union veterans continued to live after the war. But pension records from other parts of the South are similar, suggesting that the basic attitudes were widespread, although the specific nuances of the community's recognition of various relationships did take different forms. Divorce cases and other local court records dealing with marital relations elsewhere in North Carolina confirm that this view of marriage was not confined to the state's eastern shore or even just to African Americans. For an expanded discussion of these issues, see Laura F. Edwards, "'The Marriage Covenant Is at the Foundation of All Our Rights': The Politics of Slave Marriage in North Carolina After Emancipation," *Law and History Review* 14 (Spring 1996): 82–124, and *Gendered Strife and Confusion: The Political Culture of Reconstruction* (Urbana: University of Illinois Press, 1997), chap. 1. My reading relies heavily on Noralee Frankel's conceptualization of African American marital relations in *Freedom's Women*. Although she does not draw the same conclusions as Frankel, Schwalm's discussion of African-American families in *A Hard Fight for We* is also suggestive on this point; see especially 87–90, 335–49. Also see Leon Litwack, *Been in the Storm So Long: The Aftermath of Slavery* (New York: Alfred A. Knopf, 1979), 243–44. For parallels between African Americans and nineteenth-century attitudes as a whole, see Hendrik Hartog, "Marital Exits and Marital Expectations in Nineteenth Century America," *Georgetown Law Journal* 80 (October 1991): 95–129.

9. Pension files of Ford Howell and Benjamin Braddy; both in Reg. 1, Co. F, North Carolina Infantry; Pension Records, RG 15. Benjamin Braddy, Wealthy's second husband, was a North Carolina native. For a discussion of state regulation of marriages in the South, see Grossberg, *Governing the Hearth*, 75–81. The court recognized common law marriages after the war, see *Jones v. Reddick* 79 N.C. 290 (1878).

10. Biography of Edward Isham alias Hardaway Bone in the notebook of David Schenck, David Schenck Papers, NCDAH; *Bell v. Bell*, 1871, Divorce Records, Granville County, NCDAH. Divorce petitions from the antebellum period confirm that poor white men and women regularly took up with and separated from each other without legal sanction; see General Assembly Records, NCDAH. Also see McCurry, *Masters of Small Worlds*, 89–90, 183; J. Wayne

Flynt, "Folks Like Us: The Southern Poor White Family, 1865–1935," in *The Web of Southern Social Relations: Women, Family and Education*, ed. Walter J. Fraser, Jr., R. Frank Saunders, Jr., and Jon L. Wakelyn (Athens: University of Georgia Press, 1985), 225–44. For the tension between legal and customary forms of marriage and separation in the nineteenth century as a whole, see Hartog, "Marital Exits and Marital Expectations." For further discussion of Edward Isham, see Charles C. Bolton, *Poor Whites of the Antebellum South: Tenants and Laborers in Central North Carolina and Northeast Mississippi* (Durham: Duke University Press, 1994), 1–10; Scott P. Culclasure, "'I Have Killed a Damned Dog': Murder by a Poor White in the Antebellum South," *North Carolina Historical Review* 70 (January 1993): 13–39; Charles C. Bolton and Scott P. Culclasure, eds., *The Confessions of Edward Isham: A Poor White Life of the Old South* (Athens: University of Georgia Press, 1998).

11. Martha Minow makes a similar critique of family law in *Making All the Difference: Inclusion, Exclusion, and American Law* (Ithaca: Cornell University Press, 1990) and "We, the Family: Constitutional Rights and American Families," *Journal of American History* 74 (December 1987): 959–83.

12. For the lack of distinction between "home" and "work" in the lives of the yeoman, poor white, and African-American women as well as the commonality of field work and wage labor for them, see Margaret Jarmon Hagood, *Mothers of the South: Portraiture of the White Tenant Farm Woman* (Chapel Hill: University of North Carolina Press, 1939; reprint, New York: Greenwood Press, 1969); Tera Hunter, *To 'Joy My Freedom: Southern Black Women's Lives and Labor After the Civil War* (Cambridge: Harvard University Press, 1997); McCurry, *Masters of Small Worlds*, especially 73–84. See also Bercaw, "The Politics of Household," chap. 5; Bolton, *Poor Whites of the Antebellum South*, 38–39; Frances Sage Bradley and Margetta A. Williamson, *Rural Children in Selected Counties of North Carolina* (U.S. Children's Bureau, 1918; reprint, New York: Negro Universities Press, 1969), 34–35, 72–73; Frankel, *Freedom's Women*; Jean Friedman, *The Enclosed Garden: Women and Community in the Evangelical South, 1830–1900* (Chapel Hill: University of North Carolina Press, 1985), 23; Dolores E. Janiewski, *Sisterhood Denied: Race, Gender, and Class in a New South Community* (Philadelphia: Temple University Press, 1985), 28–38; Jacqueline Jones, *Labor of Love, Labor of Sorrow: Black Women, Work, and the Family from Slavery to the Present* (New York: Basic Books, 1985), 58–66, 74–75, 81–99; Schwalm, *A Hard Fight for We*; Deborah Gray White, *Ar'n't I a Woman: Female Slaves in the Plantation South* (New York: Norton, 1985), 119–41.

13. In contrast to the housing of the elite, most North Carolina houses contained only a few rooms, where the residents lived without making elaborate distinc-

tions between public and private space; see Catherine W. Bishir, *North Carolina Architecture* (Chapel Hill: University of North Carolina Press, 1990), 287–99; John Michael Vlach, *Back of the Big House: The Architecture of Plantation Slavery* (Chapel Hill: University of North Carolina Press, 1993), 153–82; Michael Ann Williams, *Homeplace: The Social Use and Meaning of the Folk Dwelling in Southwestern North Carolina* (Athens: University of Georgia Press, 1991). In *To 'Joy My Freedom*, Hunter notes a lack of distinction between "family" and "community" in Atlanta's black community. Historians have made similar arguments for antebellum common whites; see Cecil-Fronsman, *Common Whites*, 150–68; Robert C. Kenzer, *Kinship and Neighborhood in a Southern Community: Orange County, North Carolina, 1849–1881* (Knoxville: University of Tennessee Press, 1987).

14. *State v. World*, 1883, Criminal Action Papers, Edgecombe County, NCDAH. For the flexibility of family structures among black southerners and the importance of extended family ties, see Berlin, Miller, and Rowland, eds., "Afro-American Families"; Orville Vernon Burton, *In My Father's House Are Many Mansions: Family and Community in Edgefield, South Carolina* (Chapel Hill: University of North Carolina Press, 1985), 237–38, 263–64, 274–79; Barbara J. Fields, *Slavery and Freedom on the Middle Ground: Maryland During the Nineteenth Century* (New Haven: Yale University Press, 1985), 156; Hunter, *To 'Joy My Freedom*; Jones, *Labor of Love, Labor of Sorrow*; Charles Joyner, *Down by the Riverside: A South Carolina Slave Community* (Urbana: University of Illinois Press, 1984); Schwalm, *A Hard Fight for We*. By contrast, studies of poor and common whites in the South have largely ignored these questions because they have generally assumed the presence of individuated nuclear families and focused on households in relative isolation from each other. Recent work, however, suggests both the importance of community ties and the fluidity of individual families; see Bolton, *Poor Whites of the Antebellum South*; Cecil-Fronsman, *Common Whites*; Kenzer, *Kinship and Neighborhood in a Southern Community*.

15. *State v. Thigpen*, 1869, Criminal Action Papers, Edgecombe County; *State v. Ward*, 1877, Criminal Action Papers, Edgecombe County; *State v. Burwell*, 1880, Criminal Action Papers, Granville County; all in NCDAH. In both poor white and African American communities, family and neighbors (who were often kin as well) and local church congregations also mediated family conflicts.

16. *State v. Jacobs*, 1880, Criminal Action Papers, Orange County; *State v. Henderson*, 1883, Criminal Action Papers, Granville County, NCDAH. For similar cases, see Cecil-Fronsman, *Common Whites*, 133; McCurry, *Masters of Small Worlds*, 130–35.

17. *State v. Henderson*, 1883; *State v. Lawrence*, 1882; Criminal Action Papers, Gran-

ville County, NCDAH. Susan A. Mann, in "Slavery, Sharecropping, and Sexual Inequality," *Signs* 14 (Summer 1989): 774–99, maintains that black men assumed patriarchal power over women after the war. So does Bynum, in "Reshaping the Bonds of Womanhood." Frankel, *Freedom's Women*, takes a more nuanced approach to black men's assertions of authority within their families, pointing out that the notion of "patriarchy" misrepresents their power in southern society. As she argues, African-American men could never be patriarchs in the same way as elite white or even poor white men because they lacked both the material resources and ideological authority, in the form of white skin, necessary to assume that role.

18. *State v. Mabrey*, 64 N.C. 592 (1870); *State v. Oliver*, 70 N.C. 60 (1874). Also see *State v. Mabrey*, no. 9,616; *State v. Oliver*, no. 10,815; both in Supreme Court Original Cases, NCDAH.

19. *State v. Rhodes*, no. 9368, Supreme Court Original Cases, 1800–1900; *State v. Mabrey*, no. 9,616, Supreme Court Original Cases, 1800–1900; *State v. Huntley*, 1884, Criminal Action Papers, Haywood County and no. 14,130, Supreme Court Original Cases, 1800–1900; all in NCDAH. In *Heroes of Their Own Lives*, Gordon comments on how domestic violence was not the result of dysfunctional households but was embedded in the power relationships of what was considered a "normal" family.

20. *State v. Rhodes*, 1864, 1867, Criminal Action Papers, Wilkes County. *State v. Teague*, 1873; *State v. Oliver*, 1874; Criminal Action Papers, Alexander County. *State v. Huntley*, 1883, 1884, Criminal Action Papers, Haywood County. All in NCDAH.

21. *State v. Oliver*, no. 10,815, Supreme Court Original Cases, 1800–1900; *State v. Oliver*, 1873, Criminal Action Papers, Alexander County. *Taylor v. Taylor*, no. 11,767, Supreme Court Original Cases, 1800–1900. All in NCDAH.

22. *State v. Burwell*, 1880, Criminal Action Papers, Granville County, NCDAH. *White v. White*, Divorce Records, Lenoir County, NCDAH. Also see Frankel, *Freedom's Women*.

23. The account of Westley Rhodes appears in Cecil-Fronsman, *Common Whites*, 133; see also 156–64. Kenzer, *Kinship and Neighborhood in a Southern Community*, 20–22, makes a similar point.

24. *White v. White*, Divorce Records, Lenoir County; *State v. Oliver*, 1873, Criminal Action Papers, Alexander County, and no. 10,815, Supreme Court Original Cases, 1800–1900; *Taylor v. Taylor*, no. 11,767, Supreme Court Original Cases, 1800–1900; all in NCDAH.

25. *White v. White*, Divorce Records, Lenoir County, NCDAH.

26. *Oliver v. Oliver*, Divorce Records, Alexander County; *State v. Oliver*, 1873,

Criminal Action Papers, Alexander County; *State v. Oliver*, no. 10,815, Supreme Court Original Cases, 1880–1900. *State v. Hedding*, 1883, Criminal Action Papers, Granville County. All in NCDAH.

27. *State v. Henderson*, 1883, Criminal Action Papers, Granville County; *State v. Jacobs*, 1880, Criminal Action Papers, Orange County; both in NCDAH.

28. *State v. Lawrence*, 1882, Criminal Action Papers, Granville County, NCDAH. For discussions of the gendered meanings embedded within the law, see Grossberg, *Governing the Hearth*; Minow, *Making All the Difference*; Carole Pateman, *The Sexual Contract* (Stanford: Stanford University Press, 1988); Wilson, *Law, Gender, and Injustice*.

29. *State v. Dicey Burwell*, 1880, Criminal Action Papers, Granville County, NCDAH. In "Smiling Through Her Tears," Censer argues that antebellum women also had to conform to the court's vision of victimized womanhood to obtain divorces. See also Bardaglio, *Reconstructing the Household*, 32–34. This gender construction hardly fit those held by poor white and African American women; see Bynum, *Unruly Women*; Edwards, *Gendered Strife and Confusion*, chap. 4; Frankel, *Freedom's Women*; Glenda Elizabeth Gilmore, *Gender and Jim Crow: Women and the Politics of White Supremacy in North Carolina, 1896–1920* (Chapel Hill: University of North Carolina Press, 1997); Martha Hodes, *White Women, Black Men: Illicit Sex in the Nineteenth Century South* (New Haven: Yale University Press, 1997); Hunter, *To 'Joy My Freedom*; Schwalm, *A Hard Fight for We*. See also Jacquelyn Hall, "Private Eyes, Public Women: Images of Class and Sex in the Urban South, Atlanta, Georgia, 1913–1915," in *Work Engendered: Toward a New History of American Labor*, ed. Ava Baron (Ithaca: Cornell University Press, 1991), 243–72, and "O. Delight Smith's Progressive Era: Labor, Feminism, and Reform in the Urban South," in *Visible Women: New Essays on American Activism*, ed. Nancy A. Hewitt and Suzanne Lebsock (Urbana: University of Illinois Press, 1993), 166–98; Nancy A. Hewitt, "In Pursuit of Power: The Political Economy of Women's Activism in Twentieth-Century Tampa," in *Visible Women*, 199–222 and "Politicizing Domesticity: Anglo, Black, and Latin Women in Tampa's Progressive Movements," in *Gender, Class, Race and Reform in the Progressive Era*, ed. Noralee Frankel and Nancy S. Dye (Lexington: University of Kentucky Press, 1991).

30. *Torchlight* (Oxford, North Carolina), Jan. 25, 1876; see also *Torchlight*, Sept. 23, 1879. See also Edwards, *Gendered Strife and Confusion*, chap. 3; Gilmore, *Gender and Jim Crow*; George C. Rable, *Civil Wars: Women and the Crisis of Southern Nationalism* (Urbana: University of Illinois Press, 1989); LeeAnn Whites, *The Civil War as a Crisis in Gender: Augusta, Georgia, 1860–1890* (Athens: University of Georgia Press, 1995). As these works point out, elite white women did take steps into the public sphere, but they were tentative ones in the late nine-

teenth century. See also Nell Irvin Painter, "The Journal of Gertrude Clanton Thomas: An Educated White Woman in the Eras of Slavery, War, and Reconstruction," introduction to *The Secret Eye: The Journal of Gertrude Clanton Thomas, 1848–1889*, Virginia Ingraham Burr, ed. (Chapel Hill: University of North Carolina Press, 1990), 1–67.

31. *State v. Rhodes*, 61 N.C. 453 (1868).

32. *State v. Rhodes*, 61 N.C. 453 (1868).

33. *State v. Oliver*, 70 N.C. 60 (1874); *State v. Pettie* 80 NC 367 (1879); *State v. Huntley* 91 N.C. 617 (1884).

34. For an expanded discussion of these issues, see Edwards, "'The Marriage Covenant is at the Foundation of all Our Rights'" and *Gendered Strife and Confusion*.

35. *Taylor v. Taylor*, 76 N.C. 433 (1877); The Matter of Frank Bumpass and Ella Lumsford, Matt Lumsford, and Rosa Lumsford, 1881, Apprentice Bonds, Granville County, NCDAH. As Grossberg has argued, northern courts during the antebellum period had taken on broad discretionary powers in issues of family law—what emerged was, in his words, a judicial patriarchy; see Grossberg, *Governing the Hearth*. While North Carolina courts continued to uphold the patriarchal power of male household heads, they also expanded their power to oversee family relations. Peter Bardaglio makes a similar argument for the South in *Reconstructing the Household*, expanding it to the state as a whole and highlighting the implications for women as well as poor white and African American men. The cases dealing with domestic issues are too lengthy to list here; for representative cases that extended the court's control over the private sphere, see for instance *John Beard v. Hudson*, 61 N.C. 180 (1867); *State v. Rhodes*, 61 N.C. 453 (1868); *State v. Harris*, 63 N.C. 1 (1868); *Stout v. Woody*, 63 N.C. 37 (1868); *State v. Hairston and Williams*, 63 N.C. 451 (1869); *State v. Reinhardt and Love*, 63 N.C. 547 (1869); *Biggs v. Harris*, 64 N.C. 413 (1870); *State v. Mabrey*, 64 N.C. 592 (1870); *State v. Adams and Reeves*, 65 N.C. 537 (1871); *State v. Brown*, 67 N.C. 470 (1872); *Mitchell v. Mitchell*, 67 N.C. 307 (1872); *State v. Alford*, 68 N.C. 322 (1873); *Horne v. Horne*, 72 N.C. 530 (1875); *Thompson v. Thompson*, 72 N.C. 32 (1874); *Long v. Long*, 77 N.C. 304 (1877); *State v. Shaft*, 78 N.C. 464 (1878); *State v. Keesler*, 78 N.C. 469 (1879); *Miller v. Miller*, 78 N.C. 102 (1878); *Webber v. Webber*, 79 N.C. 572 (1878); *Scoggins v. Scoggins*, 80 N.C. 319 (1879); *Muse v. Muse*, 84 N.C. 35 (1881); *White v. White*, 84 N.C. 340 (1881); *State v. Edens* 95 N.C. 693 (1886); *Johnson v. Allen* 100 N.C. 131 (1888). The court, however, kept itself out of the issue of child abuse: *State v. Jones* 95 N.C. 588 (1886).

36. *Taylor v. Taylor*, 76 N.C. 433 (1877).

37. Walter Clark, "The Legal Status of Women in North Carolina: Past, Present, and Prospective," address to the Federation of Women's Clubs, New Bern, North Carolina, May 8, 1913. See also "The Legal Status of Women in North

Carolina," Committee on Legislation, State Federation of Women's Clubs, 1914; "The Gospel of Progress," Elon College, North Carolina, June 6, 1911; "Equal Suffrage," Richmond, Virginia, January 30, 1914; Walter Clark, "Ballots for Both," Greenville, North Carolina, December 8, 1916. All in the North Carolina Collection, University of North Carolina, Chapel Hill.

38. Quotes from *State v. Oliver*, 70 N.C. 60 (1874); *State v. Pettie* 80 N.C. 367 (1879). For this process, see Bardaglio, *Reconstructing the Household*.

Extralegal Violence and the Planter Class: The Ku Klux Klan in the Alabama Black Belt During Reconstruction

Michael W. Fitzgerald

The Ku Klux Klan's campaign of extralegal terror figures significantly in contemporary writing on Reconstruction and the law, but in a backhand fashion. The recent literature revolves around the control of the freedpeople's labor, and night riding is often depicted in the context of this overriding issue. To cite one prominent study, Eric Foner's *Reconstruction* emphasizes labor control and the agency of the plantation elite in terrorist operations.[1] In broad terms, the fate of the plantation system was at stake in Reconstruction politics, a reality that encouraged extreme partisan strife. Still, the assumption that labor control directly motivated terrorist violence requires scrutiny, because the timing of postwar changes in cotton production suggests a more nuanced reality. A detailed examination of one wealthy black belt area reveals complex attitudes toward violence. Some planters welcomed terrorist operations, but the Klan's presence threatened agricultural production. Ambivalence, rather than overt participation, characterized this group of large landowners and their plantation managers.

Hale County, in the central Alabama cotton belt, witnessed a sanguinary outbreak of Klan activities; it also had an unusual concentration of surviving plantation records, perhaps because of its number of absentee landlords. It was one of the wealthiest areas in the state, and large plantations dominated the landscape, with African Americans numbering over three-quarters of the population.[2] Wartime destruction bypassed the area until the very end of the war, and so peace and emancipation came suddenly to the vicinity in May of 1865. Here, as elsewhere, coping with the new freedpeople was an all-absorbing concern, with familiar complaints about lax work habits, insubordination, women not working, and the like. "I cannot see any mode of making them work, so long as they have the privileges of freemen," one white observed disgustedly.[3] More optimistically, W. H. Tayloe concluded that "in time we will have order, but the Darkies won't work until compelled by want."[4] The postwar crops were awful, but as Josiah Gorgas observed, most local planters faced emancipation with surprising composure.[5]

It was only the advent of Military Reconstruction and the tumultuous events of 1867 that set the stage for the emergence of large-scale violence. The implementation of black suffrage destabilized the plantation system throughout the South, but locally the murder of a prominent black political leader in June brought turmoil. Alex Webb was appointed voter registrar by the military authorities, in part for his involvement in the Union League movement, a clandestine Republican club. He was gunned down on the streets of Greensboro by a small merchant, John Orrick, regarded as dissolute by local whites. After the shooting, armed freedmen descended on the county seat, demanding Orrick's arrest along with those they thought implicated in the escape. The streets were reportedly filled with "Negroes swearing furiously, threatening to sack & burn the town, destroy the white race."[6] Informal posses of freedmen searched the countryside for several days, eventually bearing one half-dressed suspect to Greensboro in triumph. "Our people had become exasperated up to a good healthy fighting point," one planter observed, adding that it was not easy to prevent the suspect's friends "from making war on the Negroes at once."[7] A local plantation manager agreed that "So much excitement prevailed last Saturday the whites secretly armed themselves for the fight if it did begin."[8] One white described an organized militia, complete with officers and alarm signals.[9]

Local planters along with other whites were alarmed by the turn of events. Greensboro was the social and economic center of the county, and many planters maintained residences there. The disturbances rippled through the countryside for weeks after the assassination, and secret meetings and martial drilling by the freedmen continued. A salute fired by a Union League militia inspired a rumor that a race war had broken out, and armed freedmen again descended on the town in force. Though that incident ended without bloodshed, fearful forebodings became evident in planter correspondence.

John Parrish repeatedly predicted that the freedmen would have to be "sold, sent away, or killed."[10] There were reports of disputed crop settlements, and a rural magistrate felt unable to serve legal documents without troops.[11] One landowner and factor spoke of "the whisper of apprehended trouble with the negroes," adding that "many nervous people are seriously disturbed."[12] He passed on the disquieting rumor of an insulting conversation one white woman had on the street with a black man. An absentee planter, after a visit, concluded that in some districts "the white man will come out & give it up to the Negro."[13]

Thus it is clear that planters and their plantation managers were weighing a resort to violence even before Ku Klux Klan operations began locally. As one exasperated planter observed, "I am willing to do almost anything and submit to anything in preference to nigger domination."[14] What is not so evident is how prominently labor concerns, per se, loomed in planters' thinking. To what extent should the initiation of terror be viewed as an exercise in labor control, rather than self-defense or political intimidation? All these motivations overlapped in a confusing if mutually reinforcing fashion. The political turmoil directly affected production; for example, one overseer reported that the Webb shooting had cost him a solid week of work at a crucial time. Planters widely commented that political agitation undermined plantation discipline, and so terrorist activities necessarily had a labor control dimension. According to one overseer, the freedpeople had "gotten so much politics into their heads" that it was "almost impossible to get them to do any thing."[15] Another white agreed that Radical "utopian notions" had rendered the region almost uninhabitable.[16]

The postemancipation conflict over the terms of land tenure made the plantation system highly vulnerable to political instability. Since Appomattox, cotton planters in Hale County, as elsewhere, tried to maintain production much as they had before the war, with gang labor, overseers, tight supervision, and women and children in the work force. This plan of operation proved unprofitable, and 1867 would witness the worst of several dreadful crops. In one planter's words, "I don't think there are five men in Hale Co. who have made expenses this year."[17] Republican political agitation added to the general turmoil. A plantation manager thought infernal Radical teachings made freedmen suspicious of whites, concluding that "the day is over for working large numbers together."[18] Beginning in the spring of 1868, some landowners moved to decentralize production, allowing squads of freedpeople access to acreage under their own management, or even renting to the freedpeople directly. In Hale County as across the cotton South, this was a milestone in the long-term shift toward sharecropping and other forms of decentralized tenant farming.[19]

Thus the emergence regionwide of the Ku Klux Klan in the spring of 1868 came at a curious time in agricultural terms. At this very moment, large numbers of cotton planters reorganized production in the direction of greater autonomy for ex-slaves. By all accounts the new arrangements were successful; the freedmen went back to work with some enthusiasm. Furthermore the price of cotton began to rise simultaneously, to remain high for the next few years. The planters were awash in optimism about their agricultural prospects just as the terrorist campaign began. In the words of a visiting cotton factor, his contacts were "rather cheered by the advance in cotton . . . many talked in better spirits and feel like doing something."[20] Overseer W. O'Berry commented that he himself "never was in better spirits about making a crop," because his freedpeople went to work on time and obeyed orders.[21] In May, another manager observed the "Negroes every where working better than any time since they were free."[22] The evidence would suggest that planters and their managers, like other local whites, looked with some sympathy upon the Klan's extralegal campaign of intimidation and violence. But it would seem that political outrage or a jittery desire for self-defense dictated their actions. Narrow economic self-interest would argue against such a risky undertaking, at a time of rising expectations for cotton production.

There was, however, one economic motive for rural violence that the shift to decentralized tenant farming only exacerbated. Punishment of petty theft, rather than repression of the labor force in general, motivated most extralegal agrarian violence. After the war, planters were troubled by increasing theft of livestock, particularly pigs, which roved unprotected through the woodlands of the plantation belt. Now, with guns and hunting dogs, hungry freedpeople could make short work of the stock with little risk. The shift to tenant farming and sharecropping only made matters worse, for now tenants were thrown on their own devices to feed themselves and their families, rather than being issued supplies by the employer as had previously been the case. As a result, one overseer observed, a man could not raise pigs "if he kept them in one end of his house."[23] Henry Watson complained one Christmas to his mother that "the race of *turkies* has become almost extinct in this region since the days of freedmen." [24] These losses were irritating to planters, though they were modest in relation to the improving situation in cotton production. Moreover, planters gradually reorganized stock production—enclosing their animals and granting the freedpeople more opportunity to raise livestock—so that the complaints of theft grew less urgent over time. Even so, the notion of the Klan as vigilantes fighting theft retained some attractiveness to the planters.

As the Klan notices and public operations began in March and April 1868, there are occasional indications of sympathy among those who owned and managed Hale County's great plantations. One beating in particular offers a useful gauge of public opinion; in March, a group of young men beat J. B. F. Hill, a white northern Methodist minister and Union League organizer. Though not following the Klan modus operandi, the attack was probably influenced by the flood of Ku Klux publicity, and it certainly offers a useful vehicle for examining attitudes toward lawlessness. After the beating, the participants were arrested by the army, tried, and sentenced to federal prison. Hill had been accused of theft, and planters and white opinion tended to sympathize with his assailants. John Parrish, for example, complained that nothing was done when whites were murdered, but "let a negro be killed by a white man and you never saw such a show of bayonets . . . and 20 or 30 of the best men in the country arrested." [25] Similarly the local newspaper, the *Greensboro Beacon*, voiced more outrage at such arrests than condemnation of the original assaults. The newspaper's editor, Colonel Harvey, would emerge as a forceful critic of Klan violence, but initially his paper temporized on Klan misdeeds. [26]

During the presidential election year of 1868, one can find scattered comments by planters and their managers that endorsed or sympathized with white violence. For example, plantation manager W. W. Gwaltmey had long fantasized about filling thieves with lead, and his letters hint at collusion with the Klan. [27] He was certainly partisan enough in his political sympathies, observing that the white South would be discreet and remain calm until November, but if the electorate didn't "put this matter right, *the South will*." Gwaltmey predicted a bloodbath if the Republicans won; he had heard too many men say that they preferred "to bury wife & children & go with them," rather than stand such an outrage. [28] Gwaltmey himself would clearly be an eager participant, to the point that his absentee employer urged restraint upon him. In the context of a statewide campaign of Democratic press promotion of the Klan, or denial of Klan misdeeds, these expressions of political enthusiasm were fairly typical.

The planters' partisan sympathies clearly induced some to support or excuse the Klan. But the more crucial issue here is the relative unimportance of labor control as a motive. Economic concerns seemingly propelled planters in the opposite direction. One overseer, L. L. Singleton, thought "political excitement will interfere with the laborers here so that we will not be able to save our crops as easy as we made them." [29] He noted that the freedmen were talking of emigrating to Liberia. Republican activist James K. Green was indeed holding emigrationist meetings in the countryside, an effective tactic given the increasing demand for labor. More often than not, planters expressed concern that campaign disorder would undermine production. Even some of those favorably disposed toward vigilantism feared its social impact. For example, John Parrish sympathized with captured night riders, yet even he complained that in their despair whites were becoming "careless, I might even say reckless," drinking too much and letting their children run wild. [30] He concluded that "if we can keep down political excitement, perhaps something can be done" but he feared disorder would drive freedmen out of the area.

The election of President Grant in the fall, combined with the gathering of the first profitable crop since the war, put planters in a less confrontational mood. Immediate fears of violence or insurrection became less evident. Furthermore, the overt promotion of Klan terror in extreme Democratic papers like the *Tuscaloosa Independent Monitor* had provoked a Republican backlash in the North. The editor of the local Greensboro paper noted the implications, and began quietly denouncing lawlessness, with some impact on opinion in the surrounding countryside. Practical men concluded that the political excitement of the previous year hurt business. Even before Grant's election, factor and landowner J. A. Wemyss said several Hale County contacts talked "more of their farms & labor & crops" and less about politics, which he felt was a favorable sign. [31] After election day, Wemyss found them curiously hopeful about the freedmen and the future. [32] An impatience with partisan distractions or a fatalistic acceptance of the national situation became far more evident. John Parrish, for example, found that "our people have dropped politics, and are preparing either to leave the country or go to work." [33] He heard planters talk of raising hogs again, because it seemed that freedmen were behaving better. Similarly J. A. Wemyss hoped the Klan's Nathan Bedford Forrest and other extremists would hold their peace. Now that cotton paid he wanted planters to mind their business, make good crops, and get the South back on its feet.[34]

Labor instability, and especially theft, remained concerns, but by early 1869 planters anticipated boom profits, a matter of overriding significance given widespread bankruptcy. John Parrish reported that planters expected to get a whopping thirty cents a pound: "our people are excited on the subject of cotton, if they had labor would all go to raising it."[35] The price of lands shot upward too, recovering dramatically from previous years. A rush of optimism ensued among large landowners; the wealthy John Watson knew of "no country where a young man, if willing to work, can do better than at the South."[36] The crop for 1869 turned out beautifully, and a Selma cotton factor, speaking of Hale County and its vicinity, agreed that the planters "all made money this year" and were feeling "much encouraged to try again."[37] He was satisfied that the freedmen had worked well. In this context, lack of workers became the planters' most pressing concern. The overseer George Hagins reported having four hundred uncultivated acres, which represented nearly half his improved land. "We have the teams but cannot get the labor," he wailed, adding that he could not rent the land out either.[38] The murder of one of his hands filled Hagins with despair, in part because the man could not be replaced. Such complaints could not be redressed by the Klan; terrorists might deter laborers from leaving, but they could hardly force workers into the vicinity. The wealthier the planter, the better his land; under normal circumstances wealthy planters could outbid other landowners for laborers, but not if night riders scared hands away.

Shortage of hands, rather than theft or labor instability, was the salient agricultural issue for wealthy Hale County planters after 1868. A. C. Jones, the owner of three plantations, denounced the Radicals, but he spent more energy boasting of his profits and rising land values. In January 1869 he reported excellent returns, adding that at current prices cotton was "still the best business that I know." He expressed entire satisfaction with the freedmen's labor, they having "gone to work with a *will*" for the first time since emancipation.[39] Things went equally well the following year, with the only ugly question being the labor problem; Jones feared that planters would be driven to make further concessions by the prevailing labor shortage.[40] One overseer agreed, complaining of "the greatest wireworking here to get hands you ever saw."[41] Some whites were offering most anything to get them, he complained.

In this context, planters seemed little inclined toward violence; they instead spent considerable energy in conciliating their employees. For example, P. B. Cabell defended his manager's lax discipline on the grounds that "the Negroes have to be handled *gingerly* by him & he cannot force them. . . . The labor question is so serious a one at present that by too much exactness on our part we may spoil all & lose our next year's crop."[42] Overseers and owners wrote back and forth about freedmen's desires for school buildings, new homes, or churches on plantation property, evidencing every indication of willingness to be agreeable. For example, overseer W. O'Berry recommended selling freedmen land to build a schoolhouse, in order "to keep hands in the neighborhood." Others who previously did so could "get a plenty of hands."[43] O'Berry was rehired as overseer for 1870, despite an alcohol problem, precisely because of fears the hands might leave with him.[44] These concerns were all pervasive; one overseer urged his employer to build new homes for his hands, lest they move on. The secret to retaining laborers, he concluded, was "to make them comfortable and deal fairly & impartially with them."[45]

These expressions were echoed by the *Greensboro Beacon*, which proved acutely aware of the dangers of insufficient labor. In early 1870, editorials warned that "few planters in this section" secured the number of hands they wanted.[46] The *Beacon* repeatedly denounced unscrupulous planters for decoying off labor already under contract, fearing that the shortage of hands would allow too many undercapitalized freedpeople to rent land independently.[47] The paper hoped that massive importation of coolie labor would solve the problem, and in general demonstrated substantial attention to the fears of planters regarding their work force. These concerns doubtless contributed to the increasing rigor with which the *Beacon* denounced terrorist operations, especially once the 1868 elections were over. After one Klan murder in a neighboring county, the paper observed that "our condition will certainly never be improved by acts of lawlessness—though it may, by such acts, be made worse."[48] Not a ringing denunciation of the Klan, perhaps, but the paper was outspoken enough to irritate Democratic newspapers across the region.

Other factors encouraged political moderation among the planters of Hale

County. With the inauguration of the Reconstruction state government in the summer of 1868, local administration passed into the hands of Republicans, the most prominent of whom was Probate Judge William T. Blackford. In view of the gigantic majority blacks comprised at the polls, some attempt to accommodate the local officials made sense, especially after the November elections demonstrated that Reconstruction would not be reversed any time soon. Aware of the destabilizing influence Blackford might exercise if he chose, local notables worked out a détente with the scalawag judge, who was eager to oblige them where possible. Blackford routinely gave "labor speeches," urging the freedpeople to obey their contracts and work hard.[49] These addresses were delivered in the presence of planters, the best men in the community in his description. Blackford believed that market forces encouraged planters to pay decently. The freedman was "in many instances" treated justly by landowners, though it was "as a matter of policy, in order to secure his labor from year to year."[50] Blackford reportedly blamed the "damned sand-hill-ites" for cheating the freedmen, these presumably being the smaller planters and farmers working poorer land.[51]

The initiation of Republican rule encouraged bipartisan cooperation on one crucial public issue: railroad promotion. The region's Whiggish planters had long been interested in improving the transportation infrastructure, and as Gavin Wright has argued, the emancipation of their capital in slaves left planters eager to improve their sole major asset, land.[52] The reconstruction government approved generous state subsidies for railroad construction, which set up a scramble by localities to lure railroads into their areas. This depended both on local solicitation of capital and endorsement of bonds by city and county governments along the route. The Selma, Marion, and Memphis Railroad, reorganized under the leadership of sometime Klan chieftain Nathan Bedford Forrest, projected a route through Hale County and possibly through Greensboro itself. General Forrest's drive to secure local subsidies coincided with the Klan terrorist campaign, and intersected with it in complex fashion. John Parrish observed in May 1869 that "our people are still excited on the R. Road question . . . *as usual* we are divided."[53] Parrish himself publicly promoted the proposal, but the largely geographic divisions among whites gave rise to alliances across party, racial, and class lines. The point is that subsidies were impossible without the support of the freedmen and their Republican officeholders.

Besides Parrish, several of the region's prominent planters invested in the railroad and promoted the subsidy drive. A. C. Jones, worth almost $60,000 in land alone, observed that the railroad "will be built & pass by this place," which would give stimulus to land prices.[54] He urged his business associates to invest in plantation land, describing the local mood as "buoyant."[55] In a public speech, he claimed that he and a dozen colleagues were willing to fund the county subscription privately, if the voters were unwilling to do so. Parrish and Jones were both active, partisan Democrats, but the railroad issue brought them into working alliance with Republican leaders, allegedly including financial incentives—or bribes—for their cooperation. General Forrest often shared platforms with Republican spokesmen for the measure, canvassing two counties with Judge Blackford himself. Similarly the Democratic editor of the *Greensboro Beacon*, Colonel John G. Harvey, supported the subsidy proposals. The pro-railroad forces won at the polls in mid-1869; the city approved a subsidy by a vote of 166 to 1, while the county bonds passed by a vote of 2,260 to 301.[56] The extensive collaboration of Harvey and his colleagues with the Republican officeholders, especially Judge Blackford, doubtless moderated the tone of political discourse. Even after the bonds passed, moreover, partisan rancor and social disorder might inhibit outside investment and impede actual construction. Editor Harvey continued to denounce the Klan, even praising Blackford for his fiscal prudence; while an appreciative Judge Blackford awarded the *Beacon* the public printing. Harvey may have been disposed to reject lawlessness anyway, or thought planters needed social peace, but the exigencies of the railroad campaign doubtless stiffened his resolve.

The broader point should be evident: Hale County's wealthy elite had economic reason to be wary. A campaign of agrarian violence directed at the work force made little sense in a context of rising expectations, amid aggressive efforts to conciliate scarce laborers. Furthermore, the Klan's local operations meshed badly with plantation labor needs. If planters directed the violence toward agricultural ends, one might expect targeted violence on a limited scale, whippings of suspected thieves or insubordinate freedpeople. But several accounts insist that there were few whippings, "not about here" at least.[57] One white claimed that none occurred in the county, another recalled a single one, and the *Beacon* reported few.[58] Though some such assaults occurred, deadly force instead characterized Klan operations. Klansmen killed at least three freedpeople, shot two more, and burned or fired upon several cabins and schools. Assassination and arson thus predominated, directed mostly at political leaders. This was guaranteed to scare off laborers; it also risked retaliation with unclear consequences. The unrestrained mayhem of local Klansmen would seem ill-suited to the labor needs of the plantation system.

One planter concluded that "the quiet, law abiding people" did not give Klan operations "more than passing notice."[59] An examination of planters' business and personal correspondence indeed reveals little enthusiasm. Negative evidence of this sort allows few firm conclusions, but it is suggestive that such sources yield few supportive comments about the Klan, especially after the presidential election of 1868. The references one does find are almost exclusively in a political context, describing fears of racial disorder; agricultural matters are seldom discussed in their letters as prompting vigilante activities. In public, however, one occasionally did see prominent planters defend the utility of the Klan to combat theft. This suggests that most of the favorable references were for press consumption; partisan Democrats preferred to depict the Klan as anything but political intimidation and murder. It could thus be defended or excused more easily before a skeptical national audience. In a curious way the glare of publicity led Klan apologists to highlight agricultural motives, to project a labor control agenda much less evident in the writings of the planters themselves.

The evidence suggests that the impetus for the sustained terror in Hale County came from outside the local plantation elite, both geographically and in class terms. While the identities of members of the terrorist organization are largely unknown, one of the organizers recalled that his immediate circle were "college boys" from a small institution in Greensboro, initially called in to stop the Union League meetings that were causing "farmers lots of worry and trouble."[60] If the composition of the local movement is obscure, the pattern of public support is much more evident, because the extensive collaboration between the Democratic planter elite and the Republican leadership attracted unfavorable notice. Partisan Democrats throughout the region found the moderate editorial policies of the *Greensboro Beacon* objectionable. The paper's solicitude for the planters and their labor problems was deemed excessive, and the planters themselves came in for muted criticism. In mid-1869, for instance, Judge Blackford faced a challenge to the sufficiency of his official bond, and he reportedly threatened that if disqualified he would "take two or three thousand hands off the plantations . . . and break up the planting interest in Hale County."[61] A public meeting of freedpeople gathered in Greensboro to back up his threat.[62] These efforts reportedly induced several of the "weak-kneed" sort to endorse his bond, believing that they could exercise a restraining influence on the freedpeople. According to one Democratic lawyer, these were "landowners, large planters" from the wealthy southern portion of the county.[63]

Klan operations became one venue of a larger struggle for the political direction of the conservative movement, with radical Democrats from outside the county linking up with like-minded locals. Press criticism of the *Beacon* manifested this clearly. As one Hale resident wrote, "we wish very much that we had a bold paper here—one that would express the feelings of the white people—but, alas! It is not so, and we have to appeal to Tuscaloosa."[64] Both the *Tuscaloosa Independent Monitor* and the *Eutaw Whig* exemplified Democratic extremism; both overtly promoted Klan operations in Hale County. Rival railroad ambitions probably encouraged the two papers to take the offensive, but the political differences were fairly dramatic too. Ryland Randolph's *Monitor* was particularly vitriolic, denouncing "Jack Gaseous Harvey" for "bowing and bending to Scalawags" like Judge Blackford.[65] This drew a rejoinder—ironically—from Nathan Bedford Forrest, defending cooperation with Blackford and ridiculing the war record of his critics.[66] If these expressions could not altogether arrest Klan activities, it is nonetheless true that Hale was "conspicuous" for its "law-abiding character."[67] During 1869 and much of 1870, Klan operations in Hale remained more sporadic than in the surrounding counties.[68]

The election campaign of the fall of 1870 and the election of Democratic governor Robert Lindsey set the stage for the triumph of Klan political violence. The advent of a conservative administration made expulsion of local Republican officeholders possible. Fifty Klansmen, reportedly from outside the county, descended on Greensboro in January 1871; failing to locate Judge Blackford, they liberated a sympathizer from the county jail.[69] The subsequent arson of a livery stable, reputedly by freedpeople in retaliation, brought the community to the brink of racial confrontation. The *Beacon* denounced the raid in vigorous terms, calling for a public meeting to be attended by the residents of the surrounding countryside. "*There are questions involved which are of vital moment to the planting interest*," the paper emphasized.[70] This time, however, editor Harvey had difficulty rallying sufficient planter support. A gathering of planters and political notables in Harvey's office was bitterly divided; some argued that everyone already knew how they felt, so "why array these people, whoever they are, against us as citizens?"[71] This counsel suggested some ambivalence toward the Klan campaign.

Several factors had eroded planters' support for the civil authorities, the deteriorating economic situation being most pressing. The outbreak of the Franco-Prussian war in the fall of 1870 disrupted the worldwide cotton trade. A declining cotton price just at harvest time, combined with poor weather, led to unanticipated financial reverses. Blackford's role as labor mediator with the freedpeople became less pressing given the circumstances. As one Democrat observed, the planters tolerated Blackford for a long time, but during "the latter part of his career as probate judge, they all got to regarding him as a disturber, intermeddling with contracts and the like."[72] Still more dramatic was the fate of the Selma, Marion, and Memphis railroad. General Forrest had negotiated the sale of hundreds of thousands in railroad bonds with German investors, but the war eliminated that funding source. As A. C. Jones observed, the construction money was "now nearly exhausted," and the fiscal confusion made luring other investors difficult.[73] The half-finished railroad lapsed into bankruptcy, whereupon promoters no longer needed Blackford.

Despite vigorous efforts by editor Harvey, the situation remained volatile for weeks; it was obvious that if anything happened Greensboro "might be burned at any time."[74] The *Tuscaloosa Independent Monitor* encouraged conflict, urging the murder of Judge Blackford because there existed "no other but the Ku Klux code" that could reach such men.[75] It became clear Blackford's life could not be protected, and his Democratic contacts told him so directly. Sleeping in concealment, guarded by black supporters, Blackford concluded that it might be opportune to relocate. After private negotiations, A. C. Jones, editor Harvey and planter grandees raised some $5,000 to buy out Blackford's property, on the condition that he never return.[76] Before departure, Blackford held one final meeting with leading freedpeople in Colonel Harvey's office. Many had been threatening to leave if the judge was forced out, but Blackford assured them his departure was voluntary, and that they were safe where they were.[77] This final service to his planter colleagues complete, Judge Blackford departed local politics.

Afterward, things settled down in Hale County, as the local leadership reasserted support for the rule of law, while planters in the vicinity passed supportive resolutions.[78] The governor appointed a Democratic moderate to succeed Blackford, and the new probate judge urged restraint. A last spasm of violence occurred in August 1871, with Klansmen shooting into a plantation prayer meeting. One freedman was killed in a subsequent attempt at retaliation.[79] This raid concluded Klan actions in Hale County, which largely ceased throughout the region in the face of federal prosecution and the changing political exigencies of the situation. The *Tuscaloosa Independent Monitor* itself rejected further violence, and even the Republican sweep of local elections in November prompted little trouble. By 1872, the Klan essentially had disbanded in the west Alabama cotton belt.

How, then, does one evaluate the role of planters and their economic objectives in the Klan outbreak? For some time scholars have stressed agricultural motives for the terror. For example, Jonathan Wiener argued that the Klan in the Alabama black belt was "an instrument of the planter class, rather than the poor whites."[80] In such areas it "worked in pursuit of the goals of the planters," especially to preserve the plantation system, rather than being narrowly political in intent. However, if Hale County is any indication, planters' economic grievances were not the social force propelling agrarian violence. The timing is wrong: the Klan episode coincided with the recovery of the plantation system. The point is of wider applicability, for throughout the region decentralizing production and a rising price of cotton meant improving economic prospects. Given the circumstances, shortage of workers was planters' abiding concern, and few described night riding as strengthening their position. Even in the political sphere, the need for stability and the railroad promotion campaign disposed rich planters toward moderation. Elite commitment to law and order was opportunistic, as Blackford's abandonment demonstrated; still, the region's wealthy planters were not the primary source of political violence. One has to look elsewhere for the Klan's motivation, toward the exigencies of Democratic politics, and toward the social grievances of smaller farmers who saw the freedpeople primarily as rivals—rather than as the indispensable plantation labor force.

NOTES

1. Eric Foner, *Reconstruction: America's Unfinished Revolution, 1863–1877* (New York, 1988), 124, 128, 425, 433.
2. U.S. Bureau of the Census, *Compendium of the Ninth Census*, 24–25.
3. Anon. to Mr. Lever, August 11, 1865, Lever Family Papers, Southern Historical Collection, University of North Carolina.

4. W. H. Tayloe to H. A. Taylor, October 21, 1865, reel 22, no. 175, Tayloe Family Papers, in Kenneth M. Stampp, ed., Records of the Ante-Bellum Southern Plantations from the Revolution to the Civil War, microfilm, Series M, Part 1 (hereafter Tayloe Family Papers).

5. Sarah Woolfolk Wiggins, ed., *The Journals of Josiah Gorgas, 1857–1878* (Tuscaloosa, 1995), 176.

6. John Parrish to Watson, June 20, 1867, Watson Papers, Duke University.

7. John Parrish to Watson, June 20, 1867, Watson Papers, Duke University.

8. D. Drake to P. B. Cabell, June 20, 1867, Cabell Papers, UVA.

9. *Testimony Taken by the Joint Select Committee to Inquire into the Condition of Affairs in the Late Insurrectionary States* (Washington, D.C., 1872), *House Reports*, 42nd Cong., 2nd Sess., no. 22, vol. 10, p. 1487 (hereinafter cited as *KKK*).

10. Parrish to Watson, December 29, 1867, Watson Papers, Duke University.

11. G. A. Farrand to Charles Pierce, December 2, 1867, Letters Received by the Assistant Commissioner for Alabama (M 809), Records of the Bureau of Refugees, Freedmen and Abandoned Lands, RG 105, National Archives.

12. J. A. Wemyss to Watson, October 10, 1867, Watson Papers, Duke University.

13. Paul Cameron to ?, December 24, 1867, Mordecai Manuscript, Southern Historical Collection, University of North Carolina.

14. A. Beuners to Sereno Watson, September 3, 1867, Watson Papers, Duke University.

15. George Hagins to Watson, September 8, 1867, Watson Papers, Duke University.

16. A. Beuners to Sereno Watson, September 3, 1867, Watson Papers, Duke University.

17. John H. Parrish to Watson, November 7, 1867, Watson Papers, Duke University.

18. W. W. Gwaltmey to Tayloe, August 5, 1867, reel 14, no. 164, Tayloe Family Papers.

19. Richard Ransom and Robert Sutch, *One Kind of Freedom: The Economic Consequences of Emancipation* (Cambridge and New York, 1977), 56–71, 87–98.

20. J. A. Wemyss to Watson, March 4, 1868, reel 15, no. 547, Watson Papers. In Kenneth M. Stampp, Records of the Ante-Bellum Southern Plantations, Series F, Part 1.

21. W. O'Berry to Cameron, May 10, 1868, Cameron Papers, UNC.

22. W. W. Gwaltmey to Tayloe, May 4, 1868, reel 14, no. 226, Tayloe Family Papers.

23. W. O'Berry to Cameron, October 20, 1867, Cameron Papers, UNC.

24. H. Watson to Mother, December 26, 1869, reel 15, no. 709, Watson Papers. In Stampp, Records of the Ante-Bellum Southern Plantations, Series F, Part 1.

25. John Parrish to Henry Watson, April 16, 1868, Watson Papers, Duke University.

26. *Greensboro Beacon*, March 28, May 23, 1868.

27. W. W. Gwaltmey to Tayloe, March 25, 1868, reel 14, no. 222, Tayloe Family Pa-

pers. Gwaltmey wrote his absentee employer that in person he could "tell you much, which it is difficult on paper to explain satisfactorily." The comment might suggest some knowledge of terrorist activities, though this is speculative.

28. W. W. Gwaltmey to Tayloe, September 26, 1868, no. 226, reel 14, Tayloe Family Papers.

29. L. L. Singleton to P. B. Cabell, August 26, 1868, Cabell Family Papers, University of Virginia.

30. Parrish to Watson, March 11, April 16, 1868, Watson Papers, Duke University.

31. J. A. Wemyss to Watson, June 2, 1868, Watson Papers, Duke University.

32. Wemyss to Watson, November 24, 1868, reel 15, no. 594, Watson Papers.

33. Parrish to Watson, December 2, 1868, reel 15, no. 600, Watson Papers.

34. J. Wemyss to H. Watson, November 24, 1868, Watson Papers, Duke University.

35. John H. Parrish to Watson, August 12, 1869, Watson Papers, Duke University.

36. Henry Watson to Stollenwerck, May 19, 1869, reel 15, no. 641, Watson Papers.

37. H. A. Stollenwerck to Watson, October 22, 1869, Watson Papers, Duke University.

38. George and Peter Hagins to Watson, March 27, 1869, Watson Papers, Duke University. The 1870 Hale County manuscript agricultural census lists George Hagins operating a $10,000 farm with 850 improved acres and 133 in woodland.

39. A. C. Jones to P. C. Cameron, January 23, 1869, Cameron Family Papers, UNC.

40. A. C. Jones to Cameron, October 6, 1869, Cameron Family Papers, UNC.

41. Singleton to Cabell, January 5, February 5, 1870, Cabell Papers, University of Virginia.

42. P. B. Cabell to W. R. C. Cocke, March 28, 1870, Cabell Papers, University of Virginia.

43. O'Berry to Cameron, May 16, 1872, Cameron Family Papers, UNC.

44. A. C. Jones to Cameron, December 11, 1869, June 27, 1870, Cameron Papers, UNC.

45. Thomas T. Munford to Tayloe, January 3, 8, 1870, Tayloe Family Papers, reel 17, nos. 449, 554.

46. *Greensboro Beacon*, January 15, 1870, see also January 29 and February 15, 1870.

47. *Greensboro Beacon*, January 15, 1870.

48. *Greensboro Beacon*, April 9, 1870.

49. *KKK*, v. 9, pp. 1301–2.

50. *KKK*, v. 9, p. 1288.

51. *Tuscaloosa Monitor*, September 7, 1869.

52. Gavin Wright, *Old South, New South: Revolutions in the Southern Economy* (New York, 1986), 17–50.

53. John H. Parrish to Watson, May 4, 1869, Watson Papers, Duke University.

54. A. C. Jones to Cameron, October 6, 1869, Cameron Papers, UNC.

55. A. C. Jones to Cameron, June 27, 1870, Cameron Papers, UNC.

56. *Greensboro Beacon*, July 3, 17, 1869.

57. *KKK*, vol. 10, p. 1531.

58. *KKK*, vol. 10, p. 1482.

59. *KKK*, vol. 10, p. 1531.

60. William Stanley Hoole, ed., *Reconstruction in West Alabama: The Memoirs of John L. Hunnicutt* (Tuscaloosa, 1959), 51.

61. *Tuscaloosa Independent Monitor*, May 11, 1869.

62. *Greensboro Beacon*, May 29, 1869.

63. *KKK*, v. 10, p. 1485.

64. *Tuscaloosa Independent Monitor*, September 7, 1869.

65. *Tuscaloosa Independent Monitor*, October 19, 1869.

66. *Tuscaloosa Independent Monitor*, September 28, 1869.

67. *Greensboro Beacon*, February 4, 1871.

68. An impressionistic measure of this appears in the index to the Congressional investigation, which reports eleven dead in Greene County, eight in Tuscaloosa, twenty-six in Sumter, but only one dead in Hale County (*KKK*, v. 8, xviii).

69. *Greensboro Beacon*, January 28, February 4, 1871.

70. *Greensboro Beacon*, February 11, 1871.

71. *KKK*, vol. 10, pp. 1530–31.

72. *KKK*, vol. 10, p. 1486.

73. A. C. Jones to Watson, 14 August 1870, Watson Papers, Duke University.

74. *KKK*, vol. 10, p. 1504.

75. *Tuscaloosa Independent Monitor*, February 14, 1871.

76. *KKK*, vol. 10, p. 1492.

77. *KKK*, vol. 10, p. 1296.

78. *Tuscaloosa Independent Monitor*, May 3, 1871.

79. *Greensboro Beacon*, August 26, 1871.

80. Jonathan M. Wiener, *Social Origins of the New South: Alabama, 1860–1885* (Baton Rouge, 1978), 61. Candor requires the admission that the author makes much the same case in Michael W. Fitzgerald, *The Union League Movement in the Deep South: Politics and Agricultural Change During Reconstruction* (Baton Rouge, 1989), especially chap. 7.

Federal Enforcement of Black Rights in the Post-Redemption South: The Ellenton Riot Case

Lou Falkner Williams

T he question of writing history," Francis Wilkinson Pickens Butler wrote looking back on the election of 1876 in South Carolina, "depends to a great extent on who does the writing as to a true version of the time." Concerned that a recently published history of Republican governor Daniel Chamberlain's administration in South Carolina would be mistaken for fact, Butler, who was the son of Matthew C. Butler—the leader along with Martin W. Gary and the Tillman brothers of the shotgun policy that redeemed the state for white supremacy in 1876—prepared his "true history" of the straight-out campaign to set the record straight. There was no such thing as "Re-construction" in South Carolina, according to Butler, only "De-struction" until Wade Hampton's redshirts ran "Chamberlain and his crowd of mercenary, place-seeking vandals" out of the state. "There are always two sides to every question," Butler continued. God forbid that posterity should believe the carpetbaggers' "malignant, dastardly arraignment of the white people who were forced to defend themselves and their families from rioting negroes." [1]

The Ellenton Riot—the most vicious demonstration of racial violence in Reconstruction South Carolina—and the ensuing legal efforts to bring the perpetrators to justice demonstrate that Butler's perception of election violence as a matter of self-defense was typical of white South Carolinians.[2] When violence broke out between the races, whatever the circumstances, whites were preconditioned by race to view blacks as the aggressors. In white minds, racial atrocities were inevitably the result of lawlessness and aggression on the part of African Americans. Recognizing this instinctive reflex on the part of whites helps us to understand why the local justice system in South Carolina failed absolutely to bring redress for the wrongs suffered by black citizens. It illuminates as well the reasons why the best efforts of the federal government could not sustain a rule of law sufficient to maintain a "free ballot and fair count." Black and white South Carolinians had dramatically different perceptions of reality where election violence was concerned.

Encouraged by the successful redemption of other southern states, white South Carolinians determined in 1876 to rescue the state from its "oppressors" and return it to those who should rightfully govern—the property-owning, tax-paying, educated white citizens. The vast majority of the state's white population had simply never acknowledged the legitimacy of the Republican state government. Blacks were inferior creatures in white minds, created to serve the superior race, not to vote—and certainly not to govern. Laissez-faire constitutional principles added to the white determination to redeem the state. Whites believed that men of rank and position were the only ones able to rise above the race and class interests that informed the Republican state government and to work for the good of all South Carolinians.[3]

Insisting on the inherent legitimacy of their cause, many whites refused to recognize that political violence was the cornerstone of redemption. The Ellenton Riot manifested some of the most barbarous treatment of African Americans of the entire Reconstruction era, yet white South Carolinians either condoned the violence or kept their mouths shut. Where political crimes were concerned, as Belton O'Neal Townsend wrote anonymously, white South Carolinians as a rule "palliate it, smooth over everything, . . . indulge in loud generalities about their good feeling towards the negro," and "charge the blame on the murdered victims." Refusing to recognize the immorality of their racial values, white South Carolinians denied the truth both to themselves and to outsiders.[4]

Although racial prejudice and constitutional principles united white South Carolinians, they were nonetheless divided on the methods they proposed to redeem the state in 1876. The difficulty was that the state had a large black majority completely devoted to the Republican party. Persuasion had failed absolutely to lure blacks into the Democratic fold when whites tried it in the election of 1870. But violence, intimidation, and fraud had provoked a strong federal response. Whites needed to choose their weapons carefully. Conservative Democrats in the low country considered a fusion policy of co-operation with the Republican administration of Daniel H. Chamberlain the best strategy. Chamberlain was the reform-minded "carpetbag" governor from Massachusetts who had surprised Democrats and Republicans alike with his determination to clear away the worst excesses of the Republican era and run an honest government for the benefit of both races. Chamberlain's even-handed distribution of the patronage had turned out unqualified office holders and earned him a great deal of favor among white Democrats. It had also replaced many of the Republican trial justices, responsible for local jus-tice, with Democrats who were inclined to white perceptions of reality when racial problems surfaced. Chamberlain was intent on maintaining good rela-tions with influential Democrats—so intent that he neglected his black con-stituency and divided his own party. When he was unable to block the elec-tion of several state judges who were considered totally incompetent by Democrats and thoughtful Republicans alike, Chamberlain lost the support of many Democrats and even the reform-oriented Republicans who had ini-tially considered fusion a good idea.[5]

Outside the low country, whites generally preferred a "straight-out" Democratic campaign from the beginning. Perhaps it was the lower per-centages of African Americans in their midst that persuaded whites in the midlands and up-country that they could win. These whites had a strong tra-dition of violence and vigilante justice. They would not shrink from using whatever means were necessary to carry the election. Nowhere was this tra-dition stronger than in the western counties along the Georgia border. Edge-field County—"Bloody Edgefield" it was called—had established a well-known tradition for violence as far back as the Revolutionary War. Whether the violence resulted from the Celtic tradition of honor, transported to the New World by Scotch-Irish settlers, as some historians have speculated, or was the result of frontier violence and a Regulator movement that had inured the district's settlers to violence, Edgefield men had little regard for human life. The homicide rate was high—four times that of New York City—and newsmen reported an unusual proportion of men with their eyes gouged out or their ears or noses bitten off as a result of fighting. While the lower classes brawled, Edgefield planters were quick to defend their honor in the code duello.[6] Aiken County, where the Ellenton Riot raged for over a week during the heated election campaign in September 1876, had been a part of Edgefield County and nearby Barnwell County until 1871.

The western counties were as well known for political extremism as for violence. The area had produced a disproportionate number of the state's leaders in the antebellum years, fire-eating advocates of nullification and secession who helped push the state into the Civil War. Preston Brooks of Edgefield is remembered for his brutality on the U.S. Senate floor when he caned Massachusetts Senator Charles Sumner for a speech dishonoring Brooks's cousin, Senator Andrew Pickens Butler. "Bloody Edgefield" laid down its arms in 1865 only to take them up again against the African Americans who lived among them. The county was a hotbed of Ku Klux Klan violence during Reconstruction—one that had yet to feel the restraining power of federal intervention. And it was the Democratic extremists of Edgefield County, "hot heads and reckless hearts" like Martin W. Gary, Matthew C. Butler, and young Ben Tillman who established the shotgun policies that redeemed the state for white supremacy in 1876. When the Ellenton Riot commenced in 1876, Edgefield County rifle clubs under the leadership of Benjamin Tillman rushed to the scene to assist the redshirts of Aiken and Barnwell Counties.[7]

Martin Gary managed to capture the state Democratic party from the fusionists when he persuaded Confederate hero Wade Hampton to run for governor on a straight-out ticket. Hampton was the perfect candidate: patrician by birth, the ranking Confederate officer in South Carolina, loved and respected by his men. Hampton campaigned in conciliatory terms while his straight-out followers established force as the bedrock of the Democratic program. A genuine moderate on racial issues, Hampton had advocated limited suffrage for blacks soon after the Civil War. Now he pledged to "know no race, no party, no man, in the administration of the law." Hampton honestly believed that his moderation on racial issues persuaded some 16,000 black Republicans to vote the Democratic ticket in 1876, "but every active worker in the cause knew that in this he was woefully mistaken," Ben Tillman later recalled.[8]

While Hampton promised reconciliation, his straight-out supporters pursued another course. Political violence and the threat thereof played a significant role in the redemption of South Carolina. All over the state rifle and sabre clubs allegedly organized for "social purposes" eagerly joined Hampton's gubernatorial campaign. These paramilitary "red shirt" armies—so called as a gesture of defiance toward the northern tradition of "waving the bloody shirt" to gain support for the Republican party—were tightly organized, equipped with up-to-date rifles, trained, drilled, and led by experienced Confederate officers. According to historian Francis B. Simkins, it is safe to say that the number of redshirts "actually under arms included a majority of the white male population able to ride." Edgefield had thirty-nine rifle companies with an average of fifty men in each company. Aiken County where the Ellenton Riot began had twenty-nine, an army of 3,400 in these two counties alone, spoiling for a fight.[9] Thousands of redshirts rode with Hampton wherever he campaigned; the idea was to present a show of force that would arouse the white population to the fever pitch of the secession crisis and strike fear in the hearts of black voters. Torchlight parades, martial bands, booming cannons, and the bloodcurdling sound of rebel yells swelled the hopes of white South Carolinians and signaled to the black population that a new day had arrived. Hampton's redshirts by the hundreds rode into Republican meetings demanding equal time, bullying the speakers, and terrorizing the Republicans.[10]

Not content with this show of force, straight-outs choreographed opportunities to use violence to underscore their message of terrorism. Redeemers insisted that black aggression provoked the whites to violence, but Justice Department records tell a different story—one with which Ben Tillman later concurred. Whites preferred a fight to a peaceful settlement of problems in order to provide a concrete example of the force that lay behind the redeemer efforts. "It had been the settled purpose of the leading white men of Edgefield to seize the first opportunity that the negroes might offer them to provoke a riot and teach the negroes a lesson," Tillman recalled; "as it was generally believed that nothing but bloodshed and a good deal of it" could redeem the state "from negro and carpetbag rule."[11]

An attempted robbery on Friday, September 15, in Silvert on Township, Aiken County, furnished the pretext the rifle clubs in Edgefield and Aiken desired. The Ellenton Riot is the prime example of a small incident turned into a full-blown race riot. The trouble allegedly began with an attempted robbery when two black men walked into the home of Alonzo Harley, a white man, and attacked his wife with a stick. Hardly the fragile flower of southern womanhood, Mrs. Harley managed to deflect the blow with her broom, screamed for help, then grabbed her husband's unloaded gun and ran the men off her property. According to Mrs. Harley's statement to the Senate Investigating Committee, she was "not much hurt." The story that newspapers circulated, however, was that she and her young son were seriously injured, perhaps beyond hope of recovery in his case. It included—in typical southern style—an attempted rape. White men from nearby took off in hot pursuit of two suspects, Peter Williams and Frederick Pope, who had allegedly been seen in the area earlier that day. They "took care of" Williams without benefit of warrant, shooting first and then asking Mrs. Harley for identification. She said she had never seen Williams before, a story she later changed. Leaving Williams in the road to die, the whites rode off to obtain a warrant for Pope.[12]

What happened next depends upon the race of the witness. Blacks and whites were predisposed by race to interpret the riot in a very different manner. Finding one of their number "shot to pieces" for no reason they could understand, local blacks were naturally alarmed. Whites had mounted an escalating campaign of threats and intimidation for weeks preceding the riot. Black men outnumbered whites about three to two around Silverton, which was considered a major Republican stronghold. If they could "kill out all the educated niggers" and break up the local Republican clubs, whites figured, "there would be no one to lead the others." Circulating "dead lists" of targeted Republican leaders, whites had threatened all summer to kill "all the leading radical niggers" so that they "could rule the balance." Scores of blacks testified that whites had vowed to "kill the last one" of the black Republicans. Whites meant to "have the election if they had to have it at the muzzle of their guns." According to black testimony, the white men of Edgefield and Aiken had sworn they "were not going to be governed by Lincoln law no longer. They had been waiting for God Allmighty to change the niggers' minds so long, and he hadn't done it, and now they concluded to change it themselves." Blacks had good reason to take these threats seriously; Democrats from Edgefield and Aiken counties had staged the Fourth of July riot in nearby Hamburg to demonstrate the violence that undergirded the Democratic campaign. Several members of the black militia had been shot down mercilessly in Hamburg, and the redshirts had made a travesty of the state's attempts to bring the killers to justice. Fearing the worst, black citizens of Silverton armed themselves as best they could and congregated in the swamp that night for self-defense.[13]

In the white version of the Ellenton affair, it was blacks who were the aggressors and whites the victims. Having taken the precaution of obtaining an arrest warrant for Frederick Pope, whites mounted a "small posse" to search out the suspect. When the blacks refused to turn over Pope—and blacks insisted to a man that Pope had never been with them—the posse retired and sent for reinforcements. With the black community up in arms against them, white people had no choice but to put down the disturbance. Whites insisted that their participation in the rioting was an entirely lawful attempt to serve the warrant. The constable had asked for their assistance; the violence that followed was an unfortunate consequence of black insurrection. Thus the Democrats played to traditional white southern fears—the need to protect defenseless white women from the criminality of black men and the fear of insurrection. In many white minds—and certainly for the record—it was a matter of self defense.[14]

Who shot next after the initial shooting of Peter Williams is uncertain, but the Ellenton Riot raged over a thirty-mile radius in Aiken and Barnwell counties for a full week before the bloodletting finally subsided. Blacks were unorganized and unprepared. It was often a matter of bird shot against high-powered Winchesters, according to Justice Department records, but blacks shot back. They were "learning the law of retaliation," as state attorney general William Stone put it. Such evidence of black assertiveness only enraged the whites.[15]

On Saturday, the day after the disturbance began, a small group from each side was chosen to "parley." Persuaded that Pope was not with the group of blacks hiding in the swamp, whites agreed to disperse. It seemed that the danger was past. By this time, however, white rifle clubs were pouring into the area. Riding around in a threatening manner, these men made no pretense of attempting to serve a warrant; indeed, U.S. government records suggest that they were unaware of the alleged assault and robbery. These rifle clubs seem to have come on other business: rifle clubs from Aiken and surrounding counties had previously arranged to meet on Saturday, expecting to break up the Republican clubs in the vicinity scheduled to meet that day. Few Republicans turned out, however. When an estimated three hundred mounted whites galloped up to the church where Republicans were meeting, the twenty or so blacks fled for their lives. Disappointed whites took off after them and rode around the county in groups of about twenty looking for trouble. Skirmishing between the groups continued on Sunday and Monday.

Whites shot down any blacks who had the misfortune to get in their way.[16] Aiken County was an armed camp.

The rioting spread to Ellenton, an Aiken County community on the Savannah River, when a group of blacks removed some railroad tracks and derailed a train to stop the flood of white recruits coming on the Port Royal Railroad from Augusta, Georgia. Whites fanned out in the neighborhood, shooting all the blacks they could find without determining whether they had derailed the train or not.

While these events were taking place, another group of eighty to a hundred blacks huddled together in the swamp near Rouse's bridge, where they had congregated on Friday. Approximately eight hundred mounted whites, commanded by Colonel A. P. Butler, who was soon to be elected a state senator, and George W. Croft, county chairman of the Democratic party, surrounded them on Tuesday morning "like frightened sheep await[ing] their doom" and began to shoot them down like animals. Federal troops arrived in the nick of time to save the besieged blacks from certain massacre. The rifle club members did not "conceal nor attempt to conceal their chagrin at being deprived of their opportunity of killing colored people." Although the rifle clubs agreed once again to disperse and make their way home, they continued their orgy of killing for several more days.[17]

It is impossible to determine exactly how many blacks died in the Ellenton Riot. Estimates range from 15 to 125. While some of those who were shot down were among the blacks who had taken up arms to defend themselves from their white neighbors, many more were at home minding their own business. A ninety-year-old black man was shot dead in a cotton field, for example; another victim was a "deaf and dumb" boy who was completely unaware of the rioting. Simon Coker, a dignified black Republican legislator with no idea that he was personally in any danger, was kidnapped at a train station, taken into the countryside, then shot in a field. Ironically, Coker had counseled a group of blacks who sought his advice concerning the armed white men to return to their homes and avoid trouble. Newspapers circulated the story, however, that Coker had personally led a company of rioting black militia. After filling Coker with bullets, the redshirts stole Coker's watch, ring, and studs. Government records indicate that some of the dead were mutilated—their ears carried home for souvenirs. "A correct and full account of the *bloody affair* will never be known to the public," a local white resident reported to his employer. Some two thousand whites, "determined to kill all the negroes they could find with arms . . . did so without keeping any account." He considered the overall effect of the riot positive: "The negroes *generally* have been greatly benefitted. All seem in a good humor, are quiet, obedient, & submissive." The Republican leaders who had not been killed had fled the area, and "everything is perfectly quiet." The Democratic clubs, meanwhile, had passed resolutions to protect all the black men who would "come in [to the Democratic Party] and behave themselves." [18]

With the majority of the whites in arms and blacks hiding in the woods and swamps for fear of their lives, there is little wonder that the local justice system would not—or could not—put a halt to the violence and protect the tormented blacks. As the rifle clubs established their control over the state, Chamberlain was completely unable to meet the emergency with the state's resources. Indeed, as Francis Simkins wrote, Chamberlain was little more than "governor of the state house." The governor's mail had warned him that trouble was brewing before the rioting began in mid-September. "All is not quiet in our hellish county," H. N. Boney, a Republican probate judge had reported from Edgefield. White Democrats were riding through the countryside "striking terror" among Republicans and "seeking a fuss." Boney expected an outbreak at any time. A similar request for protection came from Blackville in Barnwell County where Republicans were forced to submit to "insults and abuse" from the Butler party. Democrats in Barnwell boasted that the Hamburg murders would never be prosecuted and "that they can kill a thousand Niggers and dify [*sic*] Chamberlain's carpetbag government." The state militia was in complete disarray; only a few ragged bands of black militia remained at the governor's disposal. Their guns, trial justice Frank Arnim wrote from Hamburg, were scattered around the countryside, many of them in Augusta.[19]

Letters and telegrams to Chamberlain while the rioting took place demonstrate the futility of state intervention. The whites were all armed, Sheriff Jordan of Aiken County telegraphed the governor, but he had seen no blacks under arms. He was "powerless to disband them," he stated, because the white men were "all on the other side," and blacks were sure to be killed if he used them for such a purpose. When the rioting spread to Barnwell County, Sheriff Patterson and at least one trial justice rode with the redshirts rather than working to protect their black victims. "What are we to do," trial justice Frank Arnim implored from Hamburg. With no known leader, the little town—predominately black—was in a "general panick" with five to six hundred armed riflemen camped nearby. "While I am willing to sacrifice my life and to use my ability as a soldier in the interest of rights of humanity, civilization, and to enforce the laws when violated," Arnim continued, "I am not willing to throw myself in the breach for any party, or any set of men, without I am sustained by such party or such set of men." Arnim was one of a very few white men willing to support Governor Chamberlain's administration and protect the black Republicans. Chamberlain recognized, moreover, that "to call upon the colored Republicans alone to suppress this lawlessness and terrorism would be to invite or precipitate a conflict, the result of which would be to increase, rather than suppress, the lawlessness and terrorism which now exist." [20]

Chamberlain's only recourse seemed to be to call on the federal government for help. Chamberlain telegraphed General Ruger for the federal troops who arrived in time to save the day at Rouse's Bridge. Although the rifle clubs promised the federal troops to return to their homes, Chamberlain's mail from Barnwell County demonstrates that small groups of redshirts continued killing blacks wherever they could find them. Blacks fled from their homes and hid in the woods for safety. Chamberlain appealed to federal marshals and the federal district attorney, David Corbin, to investigate. [21] "Terrorism reigned supreme," according to the marshals who urged the governor to request more federal troops. Chamberlain appealed to President Grant to increase the government forces in South Carolina to maintain peace and secure a fair election. [22] Angrily insisting that Chamberlain had called for troops in a time of "profound peace," whites castigated the governor for requesting federal aid. The chairman of the state Democratic Executive Committee, A. C. Haskell, declared "it is our right that you call upon us" to enforce the laws before appealing to the federal government, a policy Chamberlain considered as "unnatural and unfaithful" as sending "wolves to guard sheep." Chamberlain's authority continued to wane across the state as scores of leading citizens and public officials—some of whom were allegedly Republicans—published cards insisting that peace prevailed throughout the state. [23]

Federal district attorney, David T. Corbin, detested among white South Carolinians as "Ku Klux Corbin" for his vigorous prosecution of the Klan, spent weeks investigating the atrocities committed in the Ellenton Riot. Convinced that the atrocities were part of a Democratic conspiracy to suppress the Republican vote, which brought them under the purview of federal law, Corbin "determined to commence prosecutions in the United States Courts against these white men engaged in this business." The state government, he reported, was "as powerless as the wind to prevent these atrocities." Corbin issued warrants for over a hundred suspects and began preparing the cases for prosecution. Democratic papers screamed that the arrests, which commenced in late October, were part of a Republican plot to suppress the Democratic vote; suspects who were locked up in jail at election time could not go to the polls. Supreme Court Chief Justice Morrison Waite and Circuit Judge Hugh Lennox Bond, who would hear the cases jointly, decided to postpone: "A trial of these cases in the midst of the present excitement could do no good as far as verdicts," Waite wrote.[24]

While the federal courts sought to bring white terrorists to justice, state criminal courts in Aiken and Barnwell counties investigated and charged the black participants. In a classic case of blaming the victims, the grand jury presentment for Aiken County charged about one hundred blacks with riot, assault, and even murder. Men charged with federal offenses served as witnesses for the county grand jury. The events described in the county court records bear little resemblance to those described in U.S. Justice Department records; in the county courts blacks were the criminals and whites the persecuted minority. The conflicting evidence in the various accounts of the Ellenton Riot suggests that the reality of the situation was so distorted that many whites genuinely believed that blacks were the aggressors.[25]

By the time the Ellenton cases came to trial in May 1877, the election was over and President Rutherford Hayes had removed the last of the federal troops from South Carolina, forcing the Chamberlain administration to vacate the state house. The redshirts had triumphed. The removal of the troops was a bow to reality. Having gained control of the entire state, the redeemers were willing to take the statehouse by force if necessary. Hayes lacked the troops to prop up a government that could not stand in its own right, and public opinion no longer supported the military occupation of South Carolina. Nevertheless, the president expected the Hampton administration to fulfill its obligation to protect the rights of black citizens.[26]

The Ellenton Riot cases were the first important civil rights cases to be tried after the Supreme Court's pinched interpretation of the Fourteenth and Fifteenth Amendments and federal Enforcement Acts in *Slaughterhouse*, *U.S. v. Cruikshank*, and *U.S. v. Reese*—and thus an important gauge of fed-

eral authority left standing in the wake of these previous civil rights decisions.[27] The chief justice arrived in Charleston full of hope for the "New Departure," Hayes's southern policy that combined reconciliation with southern whites and respect for black rights. Reality set in quickly; the political
atmosphere in South Carolina was still thick with tension. The *Charleston
News and Courier*, the state's leading Democratic newspaper, was downright
hostile to the court proceedings. Daily coverage vilified Judge Hugh Bond
and the prosecuting attorneys, ridiculed the witnesses, praised the defense,
and completely denied the injustices that had been committed. "The people
here," Waite wrote his wife during the trials, "are further from reconstruction than they have been since the war. They have received the first fruits
of success over what they assume to have been their enemies, and they have
gone back to their original idols."[28] In truth, white South Carolinians had
never abandoned their "original idols."

Bond, Waite's partner on the bench, was already well acquainted with the
racial mores of white South Carolinians. Bond had presided over the Ku
Klux Klan trials in 1871–1872 when the U.S. government had convicted numerous Klan members. Democrats in South Carolina despised Bond for his
determination to bring the Ku Klux Klan to its knees. But Bond was not the
radical South Carolinians perceived him to be. While he had found ample
authority in the Enforcement Acts to bring Klan members to justice, he
had given a cool reception to indictments inviting a judicial interpretation
that nationalized the Bill of Rights and allowed common law crimes to come
under the purview of the national courts. Bond had agreed to a division of
opinion in two of the Klan cases to allow the Supreme Court an opportunity
to interpret the Reconstruction Amendments and Enforcement Acts. But his
own construction of the Fourteenth and Fifteenth Amendments, like that of
the chief justice, held firmly to traditional notions of dual federalism.[29]

The Supreme Court ducked the South Carolina Klan cases and chose
instead to interpret the Fourteenth Amendment for the first time in the
Slaughterhouse Cases. Choosing a case about white butchers instead of black
freedmen effectively depoliticized the explosive legal questions involved in
civil rights enforcement and enabled the High Court to decide some of the
controversial issues without hearing the Klan cases at all. A broad national-
istic interpretation of the Fourteenth Amendment in these cases would have
expanded the authority of the national government to protect its citizens. Instead the cases defined a federal system little changed; *Slaughterhouse* left the

basic rights of citizenship where they had always been, under the protection of the states. The Court's narrow interpretation of national rights in *Slaughterhouse* was bad news for black Americans.[30]

Chief Justice Morrison Waite continued the High Court's emasculation of the Reconstruction amendments in *U.S. v. Cruikshank* and *U.S. v. Reese*, dramatically curbing the federal government's ability to step in when the state failed to protect its black citizens. Ku Klux Klan violence in South Carolina and throughout the South had spurred Congress in the first Enforcement Act of May 31, 1870, and the Ku Klux Klan Act of 1871 to provide statutory authority for federal intervention when the states were unable—or unwilling—to maintain the rights of the former slaves. Although the Fourteenth Amendment forbade discriminatory *state* action, Congress recognized that individual discrimination against the freedmen was often the problem. Reasoning that a state's lack of action to protect its citizens was a kind of state action, Congress produced laws that prohibited private interference with the right to vote. Targeting paramilitary organizations like the Klan and the rifle clubs, the Enforcement Acts outlawed conspiracy to deprive citizens of their civil rights. Conspiracy charges had proved the most effective means of prosecuting the Ku Klux Klan, and it was under the conspiracy provisions of the Enforcement Acts that the Ellenton cases were brought.[31]

In *Cruikshank* and *Reese* Chief Justice Waite ruled that the national government had exceeded its authority in the Enforcement Acts. *Cruikshank* involved federal efforts to convict the white men who had murdered around one hundred black Republicans who occupied the local courthouse in Colfax, Louisiana, following a disputed state election in 1872. The massacre was clearly not a matter of state action, but federal attorneys tried Cruikshank on a thirty-two-count indictment that charged—among other things—conspiracy to interfere with the franchise and conspiracy to hinder black citizens from their First and Second Amendment rights to assemble peaceably and to bear arms.[32] Waite found the indictment faulty on all counts. Following *Slaughterhouse*[33] the chief justice described a federal system of national and state governments that are separate and distinct; the Fourteenth Amendment had not altered the basic relationship between the national government and the states. Waite threw out the counts that alleged deprivation of First and Second Amendment rights. For protection of their individual rights citizens must "look to the states." The Fourteenth Amendment provided that *no state* should deprive a person of liberty; it added "nothing to the rights of one citizen as against another." Waite found the law objectionable, because it applied to individuals rather than to the state. The state had not failed to protect the rights of citizens, according to Waite; with no state action, the federal government had no right to interfere.[34] If the state courts would not—or could not—enforce the rights of black citizens, *Cruikshank* demonstrated, whites could get away with murder. Federal authority to protect United States citizens shriveled in the hands of the chief justice.

Waite interpreted the Fifteenth Amendment for the first time in a companion case, *U.S. v. Reese,*[35] where he left federal authorities a little more room to maneuver. The case involved a state voting official's refusal to allow an African American to vote. The Fifteenth Amendment did not confer a positive right to vote, Waite ruled, but it did invest the people with a new constitutional right, "exemption from discrimination in the exercise of the elective franchise on account of race, color, or previous condition of servitude." He struck down sections 3 and 4 of the First Enforcement Act because of overbreadth. These sections were not confined to interference against the franchise on account of race but prohibited "*every* wrongful refusal to receive the vote of a qualified elector." Although he had seriously limited federal authority to protect the franchise, Waite did not buy the defense argument that the Fifteenth Amendment could be applied only in cases of overt state action. He left standing the sections of the Enforcement Act that explicitly prohibited voter discrimination because of race. Thus the decision suggested that both private individuals and state officials could be punished for denying the franchise on racial grounds.[36]

Prosecuting attorneys David Corbin and William Stone carefully considered the decisions in *Cruikshank* and *Reese* as they prepared the Ellenton cases.[37] In previous Enforcement Act cases Corbin had deliberately framed indictments to support a broad nationalization of federal rights under the Fourteenth and Fifteenth Amendments. He had argued vigorously that the Fourteenth Amendment made the Bill of Rights applicable to the states, that the national government could punish individuals who abridged the rights of citizens, that the Fifteenth Amendment bestowed a positive right to vote, and that the federal government could charge ordinary crimes in conjunction with civil rights offenses.[38] *Cruikshank* and *Reese* had destroyed many of Corbin's expansive notions of federal power. This time there would be no such constitutional experimentation. The job of the federal attorneys was to take and hold whatever ground the nation's high court had not already conceded to the states.

The prosecution brought a five-count indictment in *U.S. v. Andrew Pickens Butler, et al.* that adhered closely to Waite's decision in *Reese* as well as the counts Judge Bond had allowed in the South Carolina Klan cases. The first three counts charged Colonel Andrew Pickens Butler, leader of the rifle clubs who instigated the Ellenton disturbance, Captain George W. Croft, chairman of the Democratic Party in Aiken County and another leader in the riots, and ten others with conspiracy to prevent David Bush, a victim of the riots, "by force, intimidation, and threat" from exercising his legal right to vote for a member of Congress. Bush was one of the black Republicans Butler and his followers had murdered. These counts were drawn on the conspiracy provisions of the Ku Klux Klan Act (repassed in 1874 as section 5520, Revised Statutes).[39] They did not allege race as the motive for the conspiracy, because, as Corbin explained, the counts did not depend "on any law which was intended to enforce the provisions of the fifteenth amendment. . . . The right to vote is a right secured to the people by the constitution of the U.S.; it is a right which the Congress can regulate and protect."[40] The key here is that these counts alleged violations of the right to vote for federal officials. The fourth and fifth counts, framed under section 6 of the Enforcement Act of May 31, 1870 (section 5508, Revised Statutes), charged conspiracy to "injure, oppress, threaten, and intimidate" Bush in the free exercise of the right to vote—following *Reese*—"on account of race and color."[41]

Despite the defense team's best efforts to quash the entire indictment, the bench sustained four of the five counts—good news for civil rights enforcement efforts in the post-Reconstruction era. Presiding jointly over the two-headed circuit court, Waite and Bond threw out the first count because it did not follow precisely the language of the statute. They upheld the other four without comment. The implication was that the judges believed Article 1, section 4 of the Constitution justified legislation like the Klan Act under which the first three counts were framed. Judge Bond had sustained a similar count in the Klan trials, maintaining that Congress had the power to protect voters at federal elections even before the Reconstruction amendments were passed. The fourth and fifth counts had alleged race as the motivation for the conspiracy as *Cruikshank* and *Reese* had indicated they must.[42] Thus the counts stood. Although the Supreme Court had significantly narrowed the scope of federal authority to protect the civil rights of black citizens when justice failed at the state level, federal law was still sufficient to bring civil rights offenders to justice. Now the federal prosecutors needed a jury that would convict.

Finding an impartial jury proved to be a difficult task in Redemption-era South Carolina. When the circuit court opened in April 1877 tension ran high. The state's leading newspaper kept up a steady barrage of criticism designed to nullify the government's chances for successful prosecution. "The Ellenton affair," the editor wrote, "was in a few words the effort of a body of white citizens to effect an arrest for which there was a warrant, and to suppress, as a lawful posse, the resistance of an organized body of armed Negroes." Far from being "rioters and lawbreakers," the Ellenton prisoners were "peacemakers and conservators of the peace." The prosecution was "neither more nor less than a political persecution engineered by Mr. D. T. Corbin," who had "bribed and deceived a large number of ignorant negroes" into perjuring themselves as witnesses; "on this trumped up evidence about one hundred and fifty respectable persons were arrested and bound over to the United States Court."[43] White South Carolinians looked to the Charleston paper for the news; it must have been difficult for them to remain unprejudiced when the editor was himself so biased. The *Courier* claimed, also, that the Republicans had packed the grand jury and rigged the list of petit jurors to enable the prosecution to choose jurors who could be bought.[44]

The deep division between black and white South Carolinians surfaced during the selection of the jury. Federally appointed jury commissioners had made up a list, "fairly drawn from both parties," of five hundred men "of good reputation" from all sections of the state. It is unclear exactly how the Republican commissioners chose the names they submitted. They could not have come from voter registration lists, because the state legislature had steadfastly resisted the idea of requiring voters to register, an omission that enabled voters to cast their ballots at any precinct in the county, literally inviting fraud. From the list of five hundred, the clerk of the court, in the presence of District Judge George S. Bryan, had drawn the names of the twenty-three grand jurors and thirty-seven petit jurors who were summoned for duty. The defense challenged the array of both grand and petit juries, claiming, among other things, that the Republican jury commissioners and court officers who served the writs of venire were not "indifferent persons" as required by federal statute.[45]

The voir dire process demonstrated that few South Carolinians could honestly claim to be impartial. Race had preconditioned their perceptions of the truth where racial problems were concerned. One white man claimed that he had not formed any opinion concerning the guilt or innocence of the defendants, but he did not think it fair that the government had brought white men to trial while the blacks involved in the riot went free. "That does not prove bias or prejudice," defense attorney Leroy Youmans insisted, "but it is what might be expected from any fair-minded man." Ordering the juror to stand aside, the chief justice disagreed.[46] Another juror, a prominent Charleston banker and former Confederate officer, admitted some sympathy for the defendants, but insisted that he had "no prejudice against the government." Corbin, however, recalled seeing the man's signature in the *Courier* with a group of Charleston businessmen and clergy who stated "that no such offenses as these charged ever took place in this state." The juror was unable to recall "exactly" what he had signed, if anything. The court subpoenaed the *Courier* to bring the newspaper, so that Corbin could find the document. The issue was mysteriously missing, however, so the prosecution lacked the evidence to exclude the juror. Corbin then, as the *Courier* put it, "fired off the last run which he had held in reserve." Establishing that the juror had served in the Confederate Army, Corbin asked if he was conscripted or coerced in any way. He proudly replied that he had volunteered. Corbin then challenged for cause, citing the statute that disqualified Confederates from serving on juries. The defense objected furiously, insisting that the amnesty proclamation had removed all such disabilities. Waite ruled, however, that because the statute had been repassed in the Revised Statutes, it was a permanent disqualification.[47] Black men who reported for jury duty were no more impartial than the whites. The defense produced a witness who had ridden on the train to Charleston with one of them. The witness had overheard the juror say "that all those grand rascals in the Ellenton cases ought to be convicted and sent to Sing Sing." The juror was disqualified.[48]

A jury of six white men and six black was eventually impaneled. The *Charleston Courier* insisted that the jury was packed with jurors willing "to remain for months" to draw their "three dollars per diem and vote every time against innocent men." Several of the jurors had served previously in the Ku Klux trials, according to the newspapers, and all but one of the whites had "tended in the past toward Republicanism." The *Courier* labeled one of the jurors a "filthy looking negro ignoramus" straight from the cotton field—

the worst ever seen on a jury. The editor of the *Courier*, like most white people in South Carolina, obviously still considered blacks incapable and unworthy of jury duty. All was not lost, however; the Charleston paper confidently admonished the white jurors to "do their duty." The jurors took the special oath required by the Ku Klux Klan Act that they had not "counselled, advised or voluntarily aided" the conspiracy, while the opposing sides squared off to prove their opposing versions of what happened in the riot.[49]

The prosecution, for its part, had to prove a conspiracy to deprive black Republicans of their right to vote. Because there was no direct proof of conspiracy, the government relied entirely on circumstantial evidence. Emphasizing that the Ellenton violence was politically motivated, around sixty witnesses described an escalating program of threats and intimidation beginning as early as May 1876 and culminating in the September riots. White Democrats had threatened to turn blacks off their lands and run them out of the country if they continued to support the Republican party. Vowing that they would "carry this election if we have to wade knee deep in blood," whites had circulated "dead lists" of Republicans whom they planned to murder. The choice was "to live as Democrats or die as Republicans."[50] Witnesses related the bloody details of about twenty separate murders. Their stories, the chief justice wrote his wife, "are almost beyond belief." Waite could hardly "comprehend such a state of society. Negroes . . . shot down in cold blood without any cause or provocation." Unfortunately, however, the defendants were not on trial for murder. The burden of proof was on the prosecution to connect the murders to a politically motivated conspiracy.[51]

Playing directly to the traditional racial fears of white South Carolinians, the defense planned its strategy to demonstrate that the entire Ellenton affair had been a matter of self-defense. Two black male criminals had broken into the home of a "defenseless" white woman and beaten her brutally.[52] Clearly the white men had no choice but to arrest the offenders. The rifle clubs called out under Colonel Butler were a lawful posse, complete with warrant, deputized to uphold the law of the land. By refusing to turn over the suspect, the blacks had started the riot. The ensuing violence was the natural result of such black lawlessness. Numerous witnesses testified that white women and children in the area had huddled together in fear because the blacks were out of control. Defense witnesses denied altogether that the conflict was connected with the upcoming election.[53]

Each side had presented its own perception of reality. "More unprovoked murder was never proven than has been done in some of these cases," Waite wrote his wife. Indeed the defense did not even bother to deny the material facts concerning the homicides. The entire case hinged on the question of motivation. In their concluding arguments—six hours per side—the attorneys reiterated their main points. For the prosecution it was a clear-cut case of conspiracy to deprive black citizens of the suffrage. It could not be proved by any written agreement, for the conspirators had not put their plan in writing, "but by their acts." The murders proved the conspiracy.[54]

Leroy Youmans, a prominent Democratic attorney, closed for the defense. His address, the *Courier* enthused, "for soundness of reasoning, apt citation of authority, withering sarcasm, happy illustration, literary finish, and earnest, fervid, overpowering eloquence has seldom been equalled." That the defense argument "has seldom been equalled" seems clear. Youmans was downright insulting to the federal government, the prosecuting attorneys, the government witnesses, and even the victims. "From start to finish," he insisted, the entire trial had been nothing but a political persecution, "the last gasp of those who wished to obtain revenge for their defeat in the election." Youmans attacked the prosecution's strategy and rudely compared the prosecution's witnesses—all black—to circus animals willing to perform for their trainers. He then attacked the prosecution's strategy. Finally the defense attorney drove home his main point: "The things alleged must correspond with the things proved." There was no direct evidence of conspiracy, because there was no conspiracy. "The whole country was occupied by armed negroes"; thus the "white people were compelled to assemble in self-defence." Youmans was eloquent and persuasive; white jurors were bound to be impressed. Even the chief justice admitted privately that the "defence has made a strong case against their liability—under this indictment."[55]

Although Waite's jury charge—his first—was scrupulously fair to both sides, he leaned heavily in the direction of dual federalism.[56] First he explained the various counts of the indictment. To convict under the second and third, the jurors must find that the defendants had conspired to prevent Bush from voting for a member of Congress or to injure him for having voted. Conviction on these counts did not depend upon race as the motivating factor. The "controlling element" in the fourth and fifth counts, however, was race: "It is not enough that the defendants may have conspired against him on account of his political opinions, or on account of his support or advocacy of any political party." That was, in effect, what was charged in the second and third counts, but in the fourth and fifth the object of the conspiracy must be to interfere with the franchise "on account of race or color, without regard to . . . political belief or association."[57]

"The real controversy before you," Waite continued, is "the existence of the alleged conspiracy." There was no direct proof. Since the defendants were not on trial for murder, the evidence should be considered only "so far as they legitimately tend to prove the crime charged." Murder, he emphasized, was not an offense against the United States. Punishment for homicide "has been committed by the laws to other courts than this"—the states. Waite encouraged the jurors to consider carefully the circumstances of the time and "the rumors which, acting as prudent men, [the defendants] would then have reasonable cause to believe were true." This remark seemed to justify the whites' claim that they were acting in self-defense. Waite then carefully explained that the defendants had a warrant for the arrest of Frederick Pope and that one of them had been deputized as a special constable for his arrest. He had every right to order a posse to his assistance. Waite emphasized that a posse had the right to wound and even kill "those who resist, taking care to commit no unnecessary violence or to abuse the power legally vested in them." If the object of the defendants was to execute the warrant and suppress the riot, they were innocent of any federal crime. If, on the other hand, the "real purpose" had been to effect a conspiracy, then the defendants were guilty. To warrant a conviction for conspiracy on circumstantial evidence, however, the evidence must not only support the theory of the guilt of the defendants, but be "entirely inconsistent with any other rational conclusion."[58] State law, as explicated by the chief justice, was clearly on the side of the defendants.

Federal law seemed weak by comparison. That a number of black citizens had been killed was "not enough to enable the government of the United States to interfere for their protection." That duty belonged to the state alone. Nevertheless, Waite acknowledged, the federal government did have some authority in this case. It was the "absolute duty" of the United States to "interfere" to protect its citizens "when an unlawful combination is made to interfere with any of the rights of national citizenship secured to citizens of the United States by the national constitution." It is noteworthy—and doubtless indicative of Waite's understanding of federal-state relations—that he chose the word "interfere" rather than "intervene." His perception of federal intervention as interference with the state's prerogative demonstrates his adherence to the principles of dual federalism. Waite admonished the jury to forget the claims that the trial had been "instituted and carried on for political purposes." It was political only in the sense that a conspiracy had allegedly interfered with the political rights of U.S. citizens. It was the duty of the jurors to "lift yourselves above the political arena and render your verdict regardless of popular clamor or partisan excitement."[59] Or race—he might have added.

After deliberating for over thirty hours the jury deadlocked. Their only point of agreement was on the innocence of one of the defendants. The chief justice ordered a mistrial. The government attorneys were deeply disappointed. They had demonstrated "almost beyond question," as district attorney Stone reported to the attorney general, that the "main object of the whites was to affect the election." Stone expected to convict "at least some of the defendants on trial." Waite was not so sanguine. "They are not likely to agree," he had predicted to his wife; rumor had it there would be a ten to two split for conviction.[60] The editor of the *Charleston Courier* understood white South Carolinians better than either the district attorney or the chief justice. The defendants had no reason to fear, according to the paper; to the "unprejudiced observer" it was clear from the evidence and the character of the witnesses that the defendants were "entitled to a verdict of acquittal without the jury leaving the box." Only "partisan zeal" could have moved the government attorneys "to hope for a conviction on such evidence before a jury with so many intelligent [read white] members." The *Courier* expected the white jurors to "do their duty," and they did. It was six to six, race against race. The jury took several votes during the time they were out; no one ever changed his mind. The white jurors attempted to convince the blacks to "free themselves" from the "party lash." By voting with the whites they could "bring about the desired reconciliation among the races."[61] But it was not to be. Black South Carolinians held a vastly different perception of what happened at Ellenton than that of the whites. As many as one hundred black citizens had been brutally murdered in the Ellenton Riots. Blacks recognized that they were persecuted for their political beliefs, yet the white jurors— even the Republicans—had preferred to believe that the perpetrators acted in self-defense.

Federal enforcement efforts in South Carolina did not end with the Butler case. Federal attorneys continued to prosecute voting rights cases well into the 1880s. Although the Supreme Court in *Cruikshank* and *Reese* had seriously diminished federal remedies for the failure of state and local law enforcement, the Butler case had demonstrated that it was still possible to frame an indictment that would stand up in court. Federal authorities could step in to protect the rights of African Americans when the local justice system let them down. The law was sufficient to convict. But the case manifested also the difficulties the federal government faced in South Carolina. The social and political environment was downright hostile to enforcement efforts. Whites inevitably perceived federal enforcement as political persecution. Newspapers discredited the integrity of black witnesses and jurors, insisting that both were "for sale." Federal attorneys faced batteries of highly skilled trial lawyers ready to donate their services for the cause of white supremacy. Most important, the federal attorneys found it virtually impossible to impanel an impartial jury. "The law is plain," Lucius Northrop, the South Carolina district attorney, complained in 1879, "the facts are plainer, but I can't make a white democratic juror believe colored witnesses nor force him to vote [to convict]." [62] Black and white jurors in Redemption-era South Carolina held fundamentally different perceptions of reality where racial violence was concerned—a problem that resonates in the American justice system today.

NOTES

1. Francis Wilkinson Pickens Butler, "True Story of the Hamburg Riot," Francis Wilkinson Pickens Butler Papers, South Caroliniana Library, University of South Carolina, Columbia, S.C. (cited hereafter as SCL). On Chamberlain see Walter Allen, *Governor Chamberlain's Administration in South Carolina: A Chapter on Reconstruction in the Southern States* (New York: G. P. Putnam's Sons, 1888).
2. Historians have paid scant attention to the Ellenton Riot, but see Mark M. Smith, "'All Is Not Quiet in Our Hellish County': Facts, Fiction, Politics, and Race—The Ellenton Riot of 1876," *South Carolina Historical Magazine* 95 (April 1994): 142–55; George Rable, *But There Was No Peace: The Role of Violence in the Politics of Reconstruction* (Athens: University of Georgia Press, 1984), 173–75.
3. Lou Falkner Williams, *The Great South Carolina Ku Klux Klan Trials, 1871–1872* (Athens: University of Georgia Press, 1996), 8–10, 13–15. On laissez-faire

constitutionalism as a component of southern resistance to Reconstruction, see Michael Les Benedict, "The Problem of Constitutionalism and Constitutional Liberty in the Reconstruction South," in *An Uncertain Tradition: Constitutionalism and the History of the South*, ed. Kermit L. Hall and James W. Ely, Jr. (Athens: University of Georgia Press, 1989).

4. A South Carolinian [Belton O'Neal Townsend], "South Carolina Morals," *Atlantic Monthly* 39 (April 1877): 470–71. Townsend was a native white South Carolinian who wrote anonymously. His articles are valuable, even-handed sources.

5. For information on Chamberlain, see Richard N. Current, *Those Terrible Carpetbaggers* (New York: Oxford, 1988), 333–66. For the power struggle over the election of state judges, see Peggy Lamson, *That Glorious Failure: Black Congressman Robert Brown Elliott and the Reconstruction in South Carolina* (New York: Norton, 1973), 220–27. Francis Dawson, editor of the *Charleston Daily News and Courier*, the state's most influential newspaper, was the most avid supporter of Democratic cooperation with Chamberlain. See E. Culpepper Clark, *Francis Warrington Dawson and the Politics of Restoration: South Carolina, 1874–1889* (Tuscaloosa: University of Alabama Press, 1980), 34–69.

6. On Edgefield's tradition of violence, see Richard Maxwell Brown, *Strain of Violence: Historical Studies of American Violence and Vigilantism* (New York: Oxford University Press, 1975), 71–90. For information on homicide rate, see H. V. Redfield, *Homicide North and South: Being a Comparative View of Crime Against the Person in Several Parts of the United States* (Philadelphia: Lippincott, 1880), 9–109. Redfield was a correspondent for the *Cincinnati Commercial*. For general information on southern violence, see Edward L. Ayers, *Vengeance and Justice: Crime and Punishment in the Nineteenth Century American South* (New York: Oxford University Press, 1984); Bertram Wyatt-Brown, *Southern Honor: Ethics and Behavior in the Old South* (New York: Oxford University Press, 1982). On the Celtic tradition, see David Hackett Fischer, *Albion's Seed: Four British Folkways in America* (New York: Oxford University Press, 1989), 605–15. Fox Butterfield has traced African American urban violence to the violent tradition of honor in rural Edgefield County; Butterfield, *All God's Children: The Bosket Family and the American Tradition of Violence* (New York: Alfred A. Knopf, 1995).

7. Butterfield, *All God's Children*, 14–18; Benjamin R. Tillman, "The Struggles of '76: Address Delivered at the Red Shirt Reunion, Anderson, S.C., August 25th, 1909" (printed pamphlet), SCL, pp. 14–28.

8. For Hampton's campaign promises to the blacks, see "Free Men! Free Ballots!! Free Schools!!! The Pledges of Gen. Wade Hampton, Democratic Candidate for

Governor to the Colored People of South Carolina," Green Files, Miscellaneous Records Freedmen, 1876 Speeches, South Carolina Department of Archives and History, Columbia, S.C. (hereafter cited as SCDAH). On the Hampton campaign, see Francis B. Simkins, "The Election of 1876 in South Carolina," *South Atlantic Quarterly* 21 (October 1922): 224–40; Hampton M. Jarrell, *Wade Hampton and the Negro: The Road Not Taken* (Columbia: University of South Carolina Press, 1950), 158–73; Alfred B. Williams, *Hampton and His Red Shirts: South Carolina's Deliverance in 1876* (Charleston: Walker, Evans, and Cogswell, 1935); William J. Cooper, Jr., *The Conservative Regime: South Carolina, 1877–1890* (Baltimore: Johns Hopkins University Press, 1968), 28; George C. Rable, *But There Was No Peace: The Role of Violence in the Politics of Reconstruction* (Athens: University of Georgia Press, 1984), 163–77. Tillman, *The Struggles of '76*, 28. See also Michael Perman, "Counter Reconstruction: The Role of Violence in Southern Redemption," in *The Facts of Reconstruction: Essays in Honor of John Hope Franklin*, ed. Eric Anderson and Alfred A. Moss, Jr. (Baton Rouge: Louisiana State University Press, 1991), 132–33.

9. Francis B. Simkins, "The Election of 1876 in South Carolina," *South Atlantic Quarterly* 21 (October 1922): 336–37.

10. Jarrell, *Wade Hampton and the Negro*, 158–73; Williams, *Hampton and His Red Shirts*, 161–63. See also Simkins, "Election of 1876," 225–40, 335–51.

11. For a redeemer history of South Carolina see John S. Reynolds, *Reconstruction in South Carolina, 1865–1877* (Columbia, S.C.: State Company, 1905: reprint, New York: Negro Universities Press, 1969), 344–47. Tillman, "The Struggles of '76," 14, 17. Tillman claimed he had personally taken part in four race riots during the election of 1876. D. T. Corbin to Alphonso Taft, October 9, 1876, R. W. Wallace to A. Taft, October 18, 1876, D. H. Chamberlain to U. S. Grant, October 11, 1876, all in Department of Justice, Source Chronological Files for South Carolina, Letters Received by the Department of Justice, Record Group 60, M 947, National Archives (cited hereafter as SCF).

12. The various accounts of the riot tell wildly conflicting stories. For a Democratic newspaper account, see *Columbia Register*, October 14, 1876. The Senate Investigating Committee produced three volumes of testimony on the election of 1876 in South Carolina, along with a fourth volume, which was the committee's majority report. U.S. Congress, Senate, *South Carolina in 1876: Testimony as to the Denial of the Elective Franchise in South Carolina at the Election of 1875 and 1876*. Sen. Mis. Doc. 48, 44th Cong., 2d Sess. (Washington: U.S. Government Printing Office, 1877), 3 vols. and Senate Report. On the riot see D. T. Corbin to Alphonso Taft, October 9, 1876, SCF; Smith, "'All Is Not Quiet in Our Hellish County,'" 142–55; Rable, *But There Was No Peace*, 173–75. See *South Car-*

olina in 1876, 1: 927–28; Senate Report, pp. 179–81; deposition of Addison Hattinger in T. H. Blackman, "Report of the Late Riot in Aiken County South Carolina," October 7, 1876, Daniel H. Chamberlain Papers, SCDAH.

13. Senate Report, pp. 169–78; *South Carolina in 1876*, 2: 291–95.

14. *Columbia Register*, October 14, 1870. For evidence that white women during the course of the riot believed they were in imminent danger of attack from insurrectionary blacks, see Sara Anna Walker, "Ellenton Riot," n.d., Sara Anna Walker Papers, SCL.

15. For the report of the U.S. district attorney in South Carolina, see D. T. Corbin to Alphonso Taft, October 9, 1876; William Stone to Alphonso Taft, October 21, 1876, both in SCF; Senate Report, pp. 204–5.

16. Testimony conflicts wildly. See, for example, Senate Report, p. 178. David T. Corbin to Alphonso Taft, October 9, 1876, SCF; *South Carolina in 1876*, 3: 518–19.

17. D. T. Corbin to Alphonso Taft, October 9, 1876; in SCF; *South Carolina in 1876*, 3: 179–222, 521–22.

18. F. E. Thomas to J. H. Aycock, September 21, 1876, September 25, 1876, September 27, 1876, J. H. Aycock Papers, SCL. Thomas, the resident manager of a turpentine camp, wrote a series of letters to his employer, Aycock, keeping him informed about the disturbance. It is unclear from the letters whether Thomas was a participant. Ben Tillman reported that the best informed white men estimated between 80 and 125 blacks killed. Tillman, *Struggles of '76*, 66.

19. Simkins, "Election of 1876," 337; Frank Arnim to Chamberlain, September 8, 1876; H. N. Boney to Chamberlain, September 7, 1876; Samuel Jones to Chamberlain, August 18, 1876, all in Chamberlain Papers, SCDAH.

20. Frank Arnim to Chamberlain, September 18, 1876, D. T. Corbin to Chamberlain, October 9, 1876, Chamberlain Papers, SCDAH; Chamberlain to A. C. Haskell, October 4, 1876, in Allen, *Governor Chamberlain's Administration*, 388.

21. Allen, *Governor Chamberlain's Administration*, 418. For descriptions of the continuing violence, see, for example, the letter of E. J. Black, a trial justice in Barnwell County, who reported that Democrats would not allow him to get close enough to a murder victim to hold an inquest. See also A. D. Cooper to Chamberlain, September 28, 1876, and D. T. Corbin to Chamberlain, October 9, 1876, all in Chamberlain Papers, SCDAH.

22. David T. Corbin to D. H. Chamberlain, October 9, 1876; T. H. Blackwell to D. H. Chamberlain, October 7, 1876; Chamberlain to U. S. Grant, October 8, 1876, all in Chamberlain Papers, SCDAH.

23. A. C. Haskell to Daniel H. Chamberlain, September 28, 1876, Chamberlain Papers, SCDAH; "A Vindication of the People of South Carolina: The Charge of Lawlessness Denied, Testimony of the State Judiciary, County Officers, and Pri-

vate Citizens," [October 1876], pamphlet, SCL; Chamberlain to A. C. Haskell, October 4, 1876, in Allen, *Governor Chamberlain's Administration*, 387. See also A South Carolinian [Belton O'Neal Townsend], "The Political Condition of South Carolina," *Atlantic Monthly* 39 (February 1877): 184–85; Columbia *Register*, October 12, 1876.

24. Corbin to D. H. Chamberlain, October 9, 1876, Chamberlain Papers, SCDAH; Corbin to Alphonso Taft, October 9, 1876, SCF; "Aiken Items," *Columbia Register*, October 31, 1876; Waite to Bond, December 25, 1876, Morrison Waite Papers, Library of Congress (LC), Washington, D.C.

25. Presentment of Grand Jury, May Term, 1877, Journal, Aiken County Court of General Sessions, SCDAH; Robert Aldrich to Charles Devens, April 24, 1878, SCF.

26. T. Harry Williams, ed., *Hayes: The Diary of a President, 1875–1881* (New York: David McKay, 1964). See also Ari Hoogenboom, *Rutherford B. Hayes: Warrior and President* (Lawrence: University Press of Kansas, 1995), 304–10.

27. 16 Wall 36 (1873); 92 U.S. 542 (1876); 92 U.S. 214.

28. Waite to Mrs. Waite, May 20, 1877, May 24, 1877, Waite Papers, LC. *Charleston Daily News and Courier*, May 15–June 4, 1877. Although the *Courier* was extremely one-sided, its extensive daily coverage contains trial materials not available elsewhere. See also C. Peter Magrath, *Morrison R. Waite: The Triumph of Character* (New York: Macmillan, 1963), 158–60.

29. For an analysis of Bond's constitutional scruples on civil rights enforcement, see Williams, *South Carolina Klan Trials*, 51–52, 71–76; Corbin's constitutional experimentation in the Klan trials in ibid., 60–66. *U.S. v. James W. Avery*, 13 Wall 251 (1872); *U.S. v. Elijah Ross Sapaugh*, Supreme Court Appellate Case Files, no. 6482, National Archives.

30. 16 Wall 36 (1873).

31. U.S. Statutes at Large, 16, 140–46; U.S. Statutes at Large, 17, 13–15. The Enforcement Acts were repassed by Congress in the Revised Statutes, 1874, sections 5506–5532.

32. 92 U.S. 542 (1876).

33. 16 Wall 36 (1873).

34. 92 U.S. 542 (1876), 549–54. For an excellent analysis of *Cruikshank* see Robert J. Kaczorowski, *The Politics of Judicial Interpretation: The Federal Courts, Department of Justice, and Civil Rights, 1866–1876* (New York: Oceana, 1985), 14–17. See also Michael Les Benedict, "Preserving Federalism: Reconstruction and the Waite Court," *Supreme Court Review* (Chicago: University of Chicago Press, 1979), 39–79.

35. 92 U.S. 214 (1876). For background information on *Reese* see William Gillette, "Anatomy of a Failure: Federal Enforcement of the Right to Vote in the Border

States During Reconstruction," in *Radicalism, Racism, and Party Realignment: The Border States During Reconstruction*, ed. Richard O. Curry (Baltimore: Johns Hopkins University Press, 1969): 265–304.

36. 92 U.S. 214 (1876), 216–21, 242–43.

37. Corbin had resigned his position as federal district attorney when he was elected to the U.S. Senate by the Republican state government after the election of 1876. The Senate refused to seat Corbin; the seat went instead to General Matthew C. Butler, the choice of the Democratic state government. Because Corbin had extensive experience in Enforcement Act cases, the attorney general appointed him associate counsel. William Stone, Corbin's brother-in-law and law partner, meanwhile, had been appointed federal district attorney. Stone had been state attorney general during the Chamberlain administration. William Stone to Charles Devens, April 23, 1877, May 10, 1877, and D. T. Corbin to Charles Devens, May 3, 1877, all in SCF. Both Corbin and Stone had originally come to South Carolina as Freedman's Bureau Agents. R. H. Wallace, a native white Republican and assistant federal district attorney for South Carolina, was the other prosecuting attorney.

38. Williams, *South Carolina Klan Trials*, 62–66; United States Circuit Court, *Proceedings in the Ku Klux Klan Trials at Columbia, S.C. in the United States Circuit Court*, November Term, 1871 (Republican Printing Company, 1872; reprint, New York: Negro Universities Press, 1969), 58–68, 146–50 (cited hereafter as *Proceedings*).

39. Attorney general Charles Devens had instructed Stone to prepare only a few cases for trial—those involving influential citizens who led the rifle clubs and "in which all the questions of law are likely to arise." William Stone to Charles Devens, April 22, 1877, SCF.

40. The original indictment is in Criminal Case Files, United States Circuit Court for South Carolina, roll no. 927, National Archives, East Point, Georgia. See also *U.S. v. Andrew P. Butler, et al.*, 25 Federal Cases 213 (1877), 214. A partial transcript for the trial has survived in the Source Chronological Files, rolls 8 and 9. Prosecution's discussion of counts in transcript, roll 8, pp. 51–53. Butler, ironically, did not stand trial in the case that bears his name. As a member of the state senate which was in session during the trial, Butler was excused to stand trial later. The cases were nolle prossed in 1881.

41. *U.S. v. Butler*, 25 Federal Cases 213 (1877), 214–15.

42. Opinion on the motion to quash in Criminal Journal, pp. 268–69. For Judge Bond's Opinion on the Motion to Quash in the Klan trials, see *Proceedings*, p. 92. The Supreme Court later made a similar ruling in *Ex parte Yarbrough*, 110 U.S. 651 (1884).

43. *Charleston Daily News and Courier*, March 26, 1877, March 30, 1877, April 23, 1877, April 28, 1877, May 14, 1877, May 15, 1877.

44. *Charleston Daily News and Courier*, April 28, 1877.

45. *U.S. v. Butler*, 25 Federal Cases, 214–15; Criminal Journal, U.S. Circuit Court, District of South Carolina, National Archives, East Point, Georgia, p. 232; Transcript, SCF, roll 8, pp. 71–82; *Aiken Courier Journal*, June 14, 1877; *Charleston Daily News and Courier*, May 16, 1877, May 17, 1877, May 18, 1877.

46. Transcript, roll 8, pp. 71–72, SCF.

47. Ibid., pp. 72–76. *Charleston Daily News and Courier*, 18 May 1877; Section 820, Revised Statutes (1874).

48. Transcript, pp. 79–82. *Charleston Daily News and Courier*, May 18, 1877.

49. The jury foreman, George W. Williams, was a leading Charleston banker and a Democrat. *Aiken Courier Journal*, May 31, 1877, June 14, 1877; *Charleston Daily News and Courier*, June 4, 1877; 17 U.S. Statutes at Large 13, section 5; repassed as Section 822, Revised Statutes (1874). Signed oath is in the trial record, *U.S. v. Butler*, roll 927, Criminal Case Records, National Archives, East Point, Georgia.

50. David T. Corbin, Opening Remarks, transcript, roll 8, SCF; *U.S. v. Butler*, 25 Federal Cases 213 (1877), 217–20.

51. Waite to Mrs. Waite, May 20, 1877, May 27, 1877, Waite Papers.

52. *South Carolina in 1876*, 1: 927–28.

53. *U.S. v. Butler*, 25 Federal Cases 213 (1877), 220–23.

54. Closing arguments in transcript, roll 9, SCF. *Charleston Daily News and Courier*, May 30, 1877, June 1, 1877; Waite to Mrs. Waite, May 27, 1877, Waite Papers.

55. *Charleston Daily News and Courier*, June 1, 1877; Waite to Mrs. Waite, May 27, 1877, Waite Papers.

56. Waite was relieved when his jury charge was well received on all sides. The *Courier* called it "A Clear, Dignified and Impressive Address." William Stone, U.S. district attorney for South Carolina, reported, "the charge stated the law as strongly in our behalf as we could wish while at the same time no exceptions were taken by the defendants." See Waite to Mrs. Waite, June 1, 1877, June 5, 1877, Waite Papers; Stone to Charles Devens, June 1, 1877, SCF; *Charleston Daily News and Courier*, June 2, 1877. On this point, see also Magrath, *Morrison Waite*, 162–63.

57. *U.S. v. Butler*, 25 Federal Cases 213 (1877), pp. 223–24.

58. Ibid., pp. 224–25.

59. Ibid., p. 226.

60. *Aiken Courier Journal*, June 14, 1877; William Stone to Charles Devens, June 1, 1877, SCF; Waite to Mrs. Waite, June 1, 1877, Waite Papers.

61. *Charleston Daily News and Courier*, May 29, 1877, May 30, 1877, June 4, 1877.
62. Lucius Northrop to Charles Devens, November 24, 1879, SCF. For an overview of federal enforcement efforts in the South after redemption, see Robert Goldman, *"A Free Ballot and a Fair Count:" The Department of Justice and the Enforcement of Voting Rights in the South, 1877–1893* (New York: Garland, 1990).

African American Communities, Politics, and Justice: Washington County, Texas, 1865–1890

Donald G. Nieman

Reconstruction witnessed revolutionary changes in public life in America. During the late 1860s and early 1870s, congressional Republicans sounded what Illinois Senator Lyman Trumbull called "the trumpet of freedom," adopting a sweeping program of constitutional amendments and legislation guaranteeing citizenship, civil equality, and political rights to the freedmen. Yet many historians have discounted Reconstruction's revolutionary nature. Frequently, they have argued that the changes were largely illusory. The sweeping phrases of the Fourteenth Amendment guaranteeing equal citizenship and the Fifteenth Amendment's extension of the right to vote did little, they contend, to alter the grim realities of African American life. Such critics point out that even though black votes temporarily transformed the political landscape of the South, bringing Republicans to power, the vast majority of Republican officeholders were white men who used their authority to promote programs that marginally benefited blacks. And even this was short-lived; by 1877, white Democrats had reestablished control throughout the South.[1]

Moreover, there is widespread agreement among scholars that the Republican Reconstruction program was fundamentally flawed. Rejecting programs to guarantee blacks meaningful access to landownership, Republicans sought to guarantee former slaves freedom and opportunity by granting them political rights and legal equality. Most scholars agree that this approach was short-sighted because it failed to afford black southerners the economic basis necessary to achieve substantive freedom and left them vulnerable to domination by white planters. As a result, during the late nineteenth century, black agricultural laborers and sharecroppers existed in a sort of limbo between slavery and freedom. They remained desperately poor and dependent on white landowners, much as their slave forebears had been. Despite the sound and fury in Congress and the state legislatures, these scholars conclude, the changes in the lives of African Americans were quite meager.[2]

This analysis is certainly not without merit, especially in emphasizing the relationship between property ownership and substantive freedom. Nevertheless, it fails to appreciate the radical consequences of political and legal equality in a caste-bound society just emerging from slavery. In communities across the South, emancipation and congressional Reconstruction policies helped transform public life and private relationships in profound ways, creating a vibrant biracial democracy, transforming the legal system, and nurturing an assertiveness on the part of African Americans that was essential to freedom.

These changes, of course, did not happen simply because they were mandated by Congress. Rather, they occurred because bold, courageous, and ambitious individuals in hundreds of southern communities took advantage of the opportunities opened by congressional policy and forged a competitive, democratic political order. African Americans played a crucial role in this process. They eagerly grasped the rights of citizenship, registering and voting in numbers that shocked and alarmed southern whites. Moreover, a remarkable group of black leaders quickly emerged as active political players and shaped the direction of political change in their communities. Indeed, it was the activism and assertiveness of black leaders and the black rank and file that made Reconstruction at the grass roots something more profound than one set of white elites replacing another.

If we are to understand the force of the winds of change sweeping the South during Reconstruction, we must look to the grass roots—to individual communities—for that is where Radical Reconstruction had its most radical consequences. This essay will focus on a single community, Washington County, Texas, examining the role of African Americans in creating a vibrant biracial democracy in Washington County, a democracy that survived the collapse of Reconstruction in Texas in 1873 and that profoundly affected the lives of blacks and whites alike.

Located in the Brazos River Valley midway between Houston and Austin, Washington County possessed fertile soil that made it one of the state's leading cotton producers.[3] Blacks provided much of the labor for the cotton crop and accounted for approximately 52 percent of the county's population from 1860 through 1890.[4] This small black majority, which was concentrated on the rich loamy soils of the eastern half of the county, persisted in the face of heavy German immigration. The German-born population, which settled mainly on prairie lands in the western part of the county, grew from slightly over one thousand in 1860 to almost thirty-five hundred in 1890, when one in four residents of Washington County was of German extraction.[5] Although the county was predominantly rural and agricultural, Brenham, the county seat, became a flourishing cotton marketing center whose population grew from one thousand in 1860 to more than five thousand twenty years later.[6]

Although many of its sons went off to war, Washington County, like most of Texas, did not experience the devastation and dislocation that the Civil War brought to many other southern communities. Nevertheless, in the war's aftermath, it quickly felt the consequences of the war's most momentous result—emancipation. As word of emancipation and Confederate defeat reached the county and U.S. troops and a representative of the Freedmen's Bureau established a federal presence in Brenham by the fall of 1865, African Americans quickly asserted their freedom and independence. During the fall of 1865, as planters entreated them to enter labor contracts for the coming year, many blacks remained aloof, explaining that they believed the government would compensate them for their labor during slavery by dividing the plantations among them on January 1. Although visions of "forty acres and a mule" were quickly dashed, black workers repeatedly challenged restrictive work rules that planters attempted to impose.[7]

Washington County blacks also asserted their independence by creating community institutions. Autonomous African American churches—many of which had had an underground existence during slavery—blossomed in the months and years following the war. Members of these congregations mustered their meager resources to build modest churches or to refurbish dilapidated structures purchased from whites. These buildings not only served the spiritual needs of Washington County blacks; they were also centers of community life. In at least one instance, a church doubled as a schoolhouse. Indeed, rather than waiting for northern benevolent societies or the Freedmen's Bureau to provide schools, Washington County blacks began to create their own. In early 1867, the Bureau agent at Brenham reported that local blacks would soon "have a small building ready . . . for a school which will accommodate about twenty scholars—also a place provided for the teacher to live in." But bigger plans were in the works: "they are building a schoolhouse capable of holding a large number of scholars," the agent commented, "but as it is being done by contributions of labor and material it . . . progresses slowly."[8]

Whites were alarmed by this assertiveness and determined to preserve the old ways, all too frequently through violence. Despite a strong federal presence in Washington County, bureau and army officials reported twenty blacks murdered by whites between 1866 and 1869, a figure that one agent admitted was on the low side. Violent assaults were simply too common for federal officials to tally. Although most planters told their slaves they were free and contracted with them to work for wages, others clung tenaciously— even violently—to slavery. Irving Randle, the son of a Chappell Hill physician and planter, shot a freedman named Albert for "asking if he was free and being told no said he could not believe it as all of the rest of the blacks were." The freedman's arm was shattered and required amputation. Randle's action, while perhaps extreme, was by no means unique. "Threats on the part of planters to shoot their employees and violent and abusive attacks upon them, are an every day occurrence," the local Bureau agent noted in September 1866.[9]

Nor was violence simply a result of conflict between planters and freedmen over the nature of free labor. Whites also directed their wrath at blacks' emerging community institutions. At Independence, for example, a band of whites brandishing pistols burst into a black Baptist church and drove worshipers from the building, pistol-whipping several members of the congregation.[10]

Between 1865 and 1867, as the antebellum elite regained control of local government, whites also used law to curb black freedom. Justices of the peace routinely apprenticed black orphans to whites, bypassing black relatives and providing labor-starved planters with a cheap, tractable source of labor. Local officials also sought to assuage whites' concern about the prevalence of guns among the freedmen. In late 1865, local officials organized a "county police" that confiscated freedmen's firearms. Moreover, justices of the peace and their constables routinely used prosecution for petty offenses such as vagrancy, disturbing the peace, disorderly conduct, and malicious mischief as means to discipline plantation workers. "The civil law is badly administered," the Bureau agent reported in early 1867. "I am constantly engaged rescuing freedmen from its clutches for petty offenses while serious offenses [perpetrated by whites] are posponed [*sic*] and the offenders get every advantage by the delay."[11]

Far from being intimidated by these manifestations of white power, Washington County blacks continued to challenge white authority. They repeatedly lodged protests against the apprenticing of black children and demanded that the Bureau agent have black apprentices released and placed in the homes of relatives. They also crowded the Bureau office in Brenham to file complaints against employers who cheated them. And in the case of an agent who was unresponsive, they complained to Bureau headquarters in Galveston. The result was an investigation that led to a strong reprimand and suggested that the freedmen understood bureaucracy and knew how to use it to advantage.[12]

African Americans also struck back at whites who threatened or attacked them. In July 1868, the Bureau agent reported that Brenham had been in "a high state of excitement" because of an altercation between whites and freedmen. Several whites attempted to break up a meeting held by blacks, and when they fired into the crowd, the freedmen fired back. Later, a white man went to the premises of a freedwoman and threatened her with a gun when he was ordered to leave. Enraged, a group of freedmen arrested the man and turned him over to the post commander. Nor was this an isolated incident. On a number of occasions, African Americans forcefully resisted and even made citizen-arrests of whites who menaced them.[13]

Blacks also frustrated planters' efforts to establish work rules and a pace of labor reminiscent of slavery. They did so principally by collectively refusing to obey their employers' directives. Unable to overcome this resistance, frustrated planters requested help from the despised Freedmen's Bureau. "Men who do not favor the Bureau keeping control at heart [i.e., in principle]," noted an agent from Brenham, "do so from necessity and policy and recognize the fact that their only hope of controlling their labor is through the influence of the friend of the freedpeople." Blacks also used the chronic shortage of labor to force planters to accept sharecropping arrangements that gave black workers greater freedom from white supervision. Blacks "find themselves anxiously courted to go to work on some terms or other," one white observer grumbled. "The condition is that they are to do entirely as they please, as to the working of the crops and the disposition of their time being always insisted on."[14]

Their world already badly shaken, Washington County whites found it turned upside down in the spring and summer of 1867. In March, Congress passed the Reconstruction Act, giving adult black males in Texas and the other unrestored states the right to vote. The act authorized the army to register black voters, supervise adoption of new state constitutions, and conduct elections for state and local officials to implement the new constitutions. The process outlined by the Reconstruction Act took longer to implement in Texas than elsewhere: voters did not elect delegates to the state convention until February 1868; the convention took one year to complete its work; and elections for state and local officials did not occur until November 1869.[15]

Although a long road lay ahead, Radical Reconstruction came quickly and dramatically to Washington County. In April 1867, General Charles Griffin announced the opening of registration in the state and promptly appointed Peter Diller, Louis Edwards, and Benjamin O. Watrous to serve as registrars in Washington County. All three were prominent members of the county's emerging Republican Party. Diller was a Texas Unionist,[16] and Edwards a discharged U.S. Army officer.[17] Watrous, a freedman, was a leader in Brenham's African American community. A thirty-nine-year-old preacher, he was the founder of a flourishing church and the driving force behind the town's first black school.[18]

The three began their work in June 1867 and met with an enthusiastic response from the freedmen. Indeed, blacks were so eager to enroll that when registration opened in Brenham, many freedmen from outlying areas refused to await the registrars' arrival in their neighborhoods and trekked to the county seat to enroll. This enthusiasm persisted in the face of whites' interference. Many planters threatened to fire employees who registered, and when registration began in the village of Washington, in the northeastern part of the county, three white men attacked the registrars, shooting and wounding Edwards and Watrous. Nevertheless, eager to claim the mantle of citizenship and have a voice in how their communities were governed, African Americans continued to enroll.[19]

Blacks not only registered but quickly became involved in politics. In May 1867, a black delegate from Washington County, Scipio McKee, traveled to San Antonio to attend one of the first Republican mass meetings held in Texas. He returned with information about the Reconstruction Act and the winds of political change that were sweeping the state. By the time the registration process got under way a month later, black leaders in several communities were apparently holding political meetings to explain the registration process and to mobilize their neighbors.[20]

Sometime during the following months, Washington County blacks organized a chapter of the Union League in Brenham. Under the lead of Benjamin Watrous, the organization enjoyed sustained growth. By early 1868, the league held regular monthly meetings that attracted large numbers of freedmen from the surrounding countryside. Indeed, in May 1869, a member casually noted that two thousand league members had attended a recent meeting, an astonishing figure given that the county's entire black population was twelve thousand.[21] Moreover, during 1868, league members who lived outside Brenham established several new chapters, including a vital club in the village of Chappell Hill.[22] The league's expansion and its regular meetings drew former slaves into the political process, taught them about voting and government, and allowed them to debate personalities and issues. Although a few whites began to join in early 1868, the league remained a predominantly black organization and spawned a remarkable group of African American political leaders.[23]

Although blacks constituted the Republican Party's core constituency, they were joined by a small group of whites in a biracial coalition. As in other parts of the South, the county's white Republicans were drawn from native Unionists, old-line southern Whigs, and discharged U.S. Army personnel who had decided to remain in the South.[24] Republicans also attracted a substantial portion of the county's large and growing German population. Many Germans had strongly supported the Confederacy. Others, however, were Unionists whose hostility to the planter elite had grown as a result of wartime repression of Germans in the area, and many of them joined the Republican Party. By the 1870s, a significant number of Washington County's Germans voted Republican, contributing several hundred votes to the roughly 2,500 votes the party typically polled. Moreover, throughout the 1870s and early 1880s, as German immigration continued, many of the newcomers aligned themselves with the Republicans.[25]

A diverse group, most of the county's white Republicans were attracted to the party because of their hostility to the Democratic elite, not because they supported black suffrage as a matter of principle. Blacks, they assumed, would provide the votes that would lift the party to victory, while whites took positions of leadership. During the late 1860s, white Republicans jostled with one another for preference and won appointments to local offices when army officials used their powers under the Reconstruction Act to replace un-cooperative local officials.[26] White Republicans also proved reluctant to make concessions to African Americans on matters of public policy. Thus Frank Wood, a planter and former Whig who was appointed county judge by the army, steadfastly refused to add the names of African Americans to the jury list between 1867 and 1869.[27]

Yet white Republicans quickly learned that their black allies were not clay on the potter's wheel. A remarkable group of black leaders, active in the Union Leagues, quickly challenged white hegemony and gained a strong voice in party councils. These men drew their political strength from lead-ership in the African American community and close identification with the black masses. Of twelve black leaders active in the Union League and the early Republican Party who can be identified in the 1870 census, many were leaders in community institutions.[28] Even though only one of the twelve listed his occupation as "preacher" in the census, at least two others headed churches.[29] Moreover, three, including one of the preachers, were active in establishing schools.[30]

The county's black leaders could also identify with the problems and as-pirations of their neighbors. All but one were former slaves. Although two were in their early twenties, most (eight) were over thirty-five and had grown to manhood as slaves. Nor did they represent an economic elite. Although the group included several artisans, a farmer, and a minister, a majority (seven) listed their occupation as "farm laborer," as did the vast majority of the county's freedmen. Several owned small amounts of property, and there was one substantial property holder, Theodore Stamps, a farmer who had been free before the war and who owned $600 in taxable personal property and $1,300 in real estate. But like their neighbors, most black leaders owned neither taxable personal property (seven) nor real estate (eight). Although able to identify with their neighbors, these men were nevertheless set apart by their ability, force of character, and drive. By 1880, all four of the men who reported themselves as laborers in 1870 and who could be identified in the

1880 census had achieved substantial occupational mobility. Two had become teachers, one a stonemason, and one a lawyer.

From the beginning, these men played a prominent role in Republican politics. The county's Union Leagues drew officers from their ranks, starting with Benjamin Watrous, who became the first president of the Brenham League in 1867. Because the league represented the mass of Republican voters, it came to exercise real power in the party. In 1868, with the backing of the league, Benjamin Watrous was elected as one of the county's two delegates to the constitutional convention. In 1869, Matthew Gaines, who had become a leading force in the Brenham Union League, easily won election to a four-year term in the Texas state senate.[31]

Gaines's election opened the way to a sharp challenge to white primacy in the party. A farm laborer and preacher from the western portion of the county, Matt Gaines was a forceful, charismatic, and militant leader. He resented white Republicans' continued domination of state and county offices and used his position to demand that the party give blacks a fairer share of the nominations. In 1871, Gaines challenged the renomination of Congressman William Clark, a white carpetbagger, and pressed unsuccessfully for the nomination of Richard Nelson, a black Galveston justice of the peace. "We are entitled to the candidate; we do all the voting and are entitled to the offices," he told an audience of three thousand at Brenham. "Shall we turn the mill forever and let someone else eat the meal?"[32] A year later, Gaines demanded that African Americans be nominated for both of the county's seats in the general assembly. Although Gaines fell short of his goal, one of the seats did go to a black man, twenty-seven-year-old Allen Wilder of Chappell Hill.[33]

Matt Gaines's influence was intense but short-lived. In 1873, he was convicted of a specious charge of bigamy in Fayette County. The Texas Supreme Court reversed the conviction and Gaines won reelection to the Senate in November 1873. Democrats now controlled the legislature, however, and when Seth Shepard, Gaines's Democratic opponent, challenged the outcome, Senate Democrats denied Gaines his seat. Gaines remained active in local Republican politics and continued to press for a more prominent role for African Americans. But he never again was a dominant force among Washington County Republicans.[34] Nevertheless, his demand for greater equity within the party left an important legacy. Black leaders became more assertive and came to play a more forceful role in party affairs. Moreover, white

Republican leaders and officeholders, aware that their power depended on black leaders and voters, proved more responsive to black concerns and the claims of black leaders.

The black leaders who succeeded Gaines lacked his uncompromising militance. They worked with white Republican leaders to hold together a biracial political coalition in which African Americans were the most important element, but whites—especially Germans—were crucial to the party's success. Nevertheless, throughout the 1870s and 1880s, black delegates were in the majority at county nominating conventions and black Republican leaders served as chairmen of the county executive committee.[35] As a result of this growing influence, blacks' share of the nominations for countywide office grew throughout the period. They never received nominations in proportion to their numbers and were never nominated for such prestigious offices as sheriff or county judge. However, they won the bulk of the nominations for state legislature and, increasingly, nominations for such countywide offices as treasurer and clerk of court. After 1876, when a new constitution created a county commission with broad fiscal and administrative authority, African Americans consistently won two of the four seats.[36]

During the 1870s and 1880s, black leaders' strength continued to depend on the influence they enjoyed within their communities. As the Republican Party gained strength, the Union League passed from the scene during the early 1870s. But politics continued to play a vital role in the county's black communities. During election years, African Americans held frequent local political meetings as well as precinct conventions to nominate delegates to the Republican county convention, which selected candidates for county office. These gatherings were derisively labeled "owl meetings" by the Democratic *Brenham Banner* because they often met at night when black workers who formed the party's rank and file could attend. Community leaders took leading roles in these meetings and had to win support if they hoped to retain their clout in county politics. Moreover, prospective candidates for county office appeared to speak and answer questions, attempting to win the endorsement of local leaders and the delegates who would attend the county convention.

These meetings were centers of a vibrant African American political culture that had deep roots in community institutions. Gatherings in Brenham were usually held in Camptown or Watrousville, the town's black neighborhoods, while in the countryside they generally met at black schools and churches. Sometimes, politics and religion shared the bill. In July 1884, for example, blacks held a "religious, Sunday School, and political gathering" near the home of George Rucker, a black preacher who lived near Burton. According to the *Brenham Banner*, "In the forenoon there was preaching and praying and in the afternoon political affairs absorbed the attention of voters present."[37] Brass bands, which were an important part of black community life, also regularly participated in political meetings and rallies, especially in Brenham. Prior to a Republican meeting in Watrousville in 1878, the *Banner* reported, "the streets were enlivened by the appearance of the colored brass band, in a wagon, discoursing excellent music."[38]

Political meetings were often festive occasions, and they brought entire communities—men, women, and children—together. When the nominating convention for the twelfth senatorial district (which included Washington and four other counties) met in Brenham in 1884, "there were almost as many colored people in town as on Saturdays," the *Banner* noted, "and among the crowd there were a good many colored ladies." Rallies in Brenham frequently attracted crowds of 1,500 to 2,000 persons, and even in isolated rural communities attendance was often impressive. In 1878, a Republican barbecue sponsored by blacks in the isolated Coles' Creek community drew between three and four hundred persons.[39]

Although these meetings were often devoted to eating, drinking, and political hoopla, they also had a substantive side. Rival candidates often made speeches and took questions from the audience, attempting to win support for their candidacies. Occasionally, the questions were pointed, and the criticisms of white and black leaders were sharp. Thus, at one meeting at Harris Spring, a disgruntled voter told a black politician from Brenham that "the rural roosters knew who they wanted to support" and the "city chaps" were wasting their time. According to the *Banner*, the critic complained that the speaker and his friends only "came among them when they wanted their votes . . . and then not in the interest of the colored people but only in the interest of white office seekers and he regard[ed] them more as enemies than friends."[40] Such hostility appears to have been rare, but it does suggest that owl meetings were not cakewalks for Republican leaders.

Politics was, then, an important part of community life. Blacks not only turned out for meetings; they demonstrated a passion for politics, especially in election years. "At the present time nine out of every ten colored men are active politicians," noted a reporter in October 1886. "Wherever two colored men are gathered together they are talking politics."[41] Ordinary black men also demonstrated their commitment to the political process by putting their lives on the line to preserve it. In 1875, a group of whites attacked a Republican meeting near Independence, pistol-whipping several white leaders and threatening black women and children who were present. Two black men— David Graves, "a colored Baptist preacher" and "an esteemed and outspoken Republican," and William Wares—were shot down when they attempted to drive the whites away with shotguns.[42] In 1886, black men in the Graball community, fearing foul play by the Democrats, posted an armed guard around the house where the precinct's votes were tallied. When a group of disguised whites broke into the house shortly after midnight to steal the ballots of the overwhelmingly black precinct, Polk Hill, a local sharecropper, opened fire with his shotgun, instantly killing one of the bandits, Dewees Bolton, the son of the Democratic candidate for county commission.[43]

How do we explain this vibrant political culture, this passion for politics and public life? On one level, of course, political participation was of enormous symbolic importance to African Americans. It was an affirmation that, although they had been chattels who had possessed "no rights that a white man was bound to respect," they were now free men and citizens. To participate in political discussion, question candidates, influence nominations, and cast votes that decided who would become sheriff or county judge or justice of the peace was to assert that you and those like you counted.

But political participation was more than a symbolic act; it had tangible consequences. For African Americans, political influence translated into opportunities for public sector employment, a source of income that had been reserved for whites. In Washington County, Republican officials appointed blacks to a range of positions, including cattle and hide inspector, deputy sheriff, jailer, bailiff, deputy assessor, and notary public.[44] Republicans also opened public works jobs to black artisans and laborers, hiring them to construct bridges and work on major public works like the jail, which was constructed in 1871, and the county courthouse, which was completed in 1884. Republicans also improved delivery of social services for blacks. They not only opened pauper relief programs to blacks as well as whites but also adopted policies that were sensitive to the needs of the elderly, the handicapped, and the widows and orphans who were unable to support themselves. Instead of insisting that paupers live at a county poor farm, Republican county commissioners provided monthly payments that allowed them to remain in the community. Republican policy contrasted sharply with that of their Democratic successors. Four years after Democrats had regained control of the county, the *Brenham Banner* crowed that by requiring paupers to live on the county farm, the county commission had reduced the cost of poor relief from $2,700 to $700 per year.[45]

African Americans also benefited from Republican law enforcement policies. Even though planters continued to complain of a labor shortage, vagrancy prosecutions were no longer used as a means to compel blacks to work on terms set by planters. In 1878 a planter living near Independence grumbled that there were "a great many colored gentlemen and ladies in the neighborhood, . . . [but] with few exceptions they evince no disposition to go to work." They were holding off, he explained, hoping "to catch planters in a straight and then [work] for a limited time by the day. They then expect to wait until next cotton picking time, when all the negroes make an 'African fortune' and become independent." [46] Republican officials rebuffed calls for enforcement of the vagrancy law in these situations, allowing black workers to use their leverage against planters to gain the most favorable terms—and the most independence—possible. That, of course, was not the case where Democrats were in control. Republicans also ended the practice of apprenticing black orphans to white planters, instead allowing relatives to raise and care for them.

Black political power had its most striking effect on the administration of criminal justice. Under the Democrats, the criminal justice system became an engine of oppression, best characterized by the bluesman's barbed comment:

> White folks and nigger in great Co't house
> Like a Cat down cellar wit' no-hole mouse.[47]

In Washington County, however, Republican rule brought dramatic changes to the system. Elected Republican officials who took office early in 1870 placed African Americans on the jury rolls. As a result, blacks came to play a prominent role on both grand juries (which had authority to indict) and petit juries (which tried cases). Between 1870 and 1884, while Republicans controlled the criminal justice system, African Americans constituted over thirty percent of those who served on petit juries.[48]

Participation on juries gave ordinary people a role in public life. Service on the grand jury carried considerable prestige in rural America in the nineteenth century. Grand jurors not only decided whether there was probable cause to indict persons accused of crime but also investigated county finance, the operations of county government, road maintenance, and the like. Petit jurors tried individual cases and, under Texas law, determined the sentences of those whom they found guilty. Moreover, because criminal trials were often of vital interest to the public and therefore generally well attended, petit jurors played a highly public role.[49]

Black jurors also had a salutary effect on the criminal justice system. With blacks sitting on grand juries, a black person was less likely to be indicted—to be placed in jeopardy in the telling words of the law—simply because a white man suspected him of crime and pressed charges. Moreover, when African Americans were placed on trial, black jurors were less likely to accept the testimony of whites as gospel and to discount evidence offered by blacks. Indeed, during the years Republicans controlled criminal justice, the conviction rates of black and white defendants were virtually the same. Sentencing also became more equitable. In most major categories of felony, blacks and whites received remarkably similar sentences.[50]

White criminal justice officials—judges, sheriffs, district attorneys, and justices of the peace—also treated blacks equitably. For persons charged with crime, the ability to post bond was of vital importance. The district court held only two or three brief terms in the county each year, and if they could not post bond, those charged with crime might spend months in jail awaiting trial, much to the detriment of their economic prospects and the well-being of their families. Republican officials, taking into account their poverty, set bond at modest levels for blacks (substantially lower than for whites accused of the same crimes). Moreover, they readily allowed black property owners to sign surety bonds for black defendants, enabling them to win release without turning to white landowners, who often exacted onerous terms from those whom they bailed out of jail. As a result, black defendants were released on bond at about the same rate as whites. Decisions made by prosecutors also had important consequences for defendants. District attorneys had broad authority to dismiss cases when they believed there was inadequate evidence to convict, and Republican district attorneys used this authority equitably. They dismissed prosecutions against African American defendants at virtually the same rate as in cases against whites.[51]

One case illustrates the striking changes in criminal justice during the 1870s and 1880s. In December 1880, Alexander Mason, a black drayman, killed Ferdinand Bohnenstengel, a German bar and grocery keeper who had lived in Brenham for eight years. When Mason entered Bohnenstengel's shop, Bohnenstengel demanded that Mason retract statements he had made about him. Mason refused, left the store cursing, and remained outside the shop, daring Bohnenstengel to come after him. When the enraged merchant approached Mason with a buggy whip, the black man first warned him to stop, then picked up "a piece of board . . . about six feet long and weighing eight or ten pounds," and struck Bohnenstengel. The next day the shop-keeper died. Because whites were outraged by the killing—the *Brenham Banner* carried a lengthy story on the altercation under the headline "A WHITE MAN KILLED BY A NEGRO"—Mason promptly fled. Two months later, however, he sent a messenger to local officials and explained that he was ready to surrender. Mason was then taken into custody by a black deputy sheriff and brought before Republican justice of the peace Stephen Hackworth for a preliminary examination. The county attorney agreed that it was not a case of first-degree murder, and Hackworth set bail at $1,250, which Mason promptly posted. One month later, a jury of seven blacks and five whites acquitted Mason. Bohnenstengel was not a prominent citizen, but he was a white man, and, as the *Banner* headline suggested, the white community viewed Mason's action as an outrage. Nevertheless, the system afforded the black drayman justice.[52]

Mason's case was not an isolated example. Freedmen were convicted in only three of six black-against-white murder cases that went to trial (four other cases were not prosecuted). This was a lower conviction rate than in black-against-black murder cases. And blacks were convicted in only two of the four black-against-white attempted murder cases that went to trial, again a lower rate than in black-against-black cases. Thus, with freedmen present in the jury box, blacks who used force against whites in self-defense escaped retribution. While this might seem insignificant in light of the small number of cases involved, it was undoubtedly important to the black community. Large numbers of black men and women attended court and spoke with their friends about what went on there. Cases like that of Mason unquestionably attracted attention and suggested that whites' assumption that it was never justifiable for a black man to raise his hand against a white no longer had the imprimatur of law. This encouraged blacks to be more aggressive in defending their rights and, in the process, further eroded the foundations of white dominance.[53]

The open, competitive political process that flourished in Washington County in the 1870s and 1880s and that transformed public life in ways unimagined a few years before did not last forever. During the late 1870s and early 1880s, Democrats exploited Germans' antipathy to blacks and won growing German support. In 1884, they further diminished German support for the Republicans by intensifying charges of Republican corruption when the county treasurer (who, ironically, was a German) defaulted. Democrats spearheaded formation of a so-called People's Party, which claimed to unite public-spirited men to restore honesty to local government. As a result, all but one of the People's Party candidates won narrow victories in 1884, breaking the Republicans' grip on the courthouse.[54] Two years later, Democrats—still operating under the banner of the People's Party—retained their grip on power in another extremely close election by stealing the ballots cast in three heavily Republican precincts. In the aftermath of the election, they permanently crippled the party by lynching three black Republicans and driving from the county three prominent white Republicans.[55] Republicans suffered a final blow in 1888, when Joe Hoffman, the county assessor and only Republican to survive the People's Party onslaught in 1884 and 1886, was assassinated two months before the election.[56]

Republicans did not easily crumble. After defeat in 1884, they launched a powerful challenge to the Democrats in 1886. Had the stolen ballots been counted, they probably would have won. No relief could be expected from the state legislature or state courts, which were firmly in the hands of Democrats. Consequently, Washington County Republicans turned to the national government, prevailing on their allies in the U.S. Senate to conduct a major investigation of the 1886 election. Several dozen Washington County residents went to Washington, D.C., in 1887 to testify, and their testimony ran to over seven hundred pages of fine print. Yet with Democrats in control of the House of Representatives and the presidency, congressional Republicans were unable to pass new legislation to provide more effective remedies against lynching and electoral fraud.[57] Republicans also pressed the federal courts for redress. The U.S. attorney brought federal charges against Democratic county judge Lafayette Kirk and seven other prominent Washington County Democrats who were implicated in the theft of the ballots. Whites, however, sat on the juries who tried these men in the federal court in Austin, and the prosecution resulted in a mistrial and then in acquittal.[58] With Republicans in disarray and reeling in terror and Democrats in control of the electoral process and insulated from effective external control, democracy died in Washington County.

Yet the democracy that African Americans and their white allies forged, if transitory, was both remarkable and important. The Washington County experience testified to the power of ordinary people to affect the political process and to use politics to gain a larger measure of control in their communities. It also clearly demonstrates that something more than a kind of political musical chairs was going on in the Reconstruction South. Viewed from this vantage point, Reconstruction was something far more profound than one group of white elites replacing another. Across the South, African American communities that had taken root during slavery produced institutions and leaders that were powerful forces for democratic change. They brought to a caste-ridden society a vibrant democratic politics that made public life more open and public policy more equitable. This was a truly remarkable accomplishment. That it did not survive was tragic for the South as well as for African Americans. That it occurred, however, left its mark on African American culture, creating an impulse that would be felt in the civil rights struggles of the twentieth century.

NOTES

1. These themes characterize much of the postrevisionist writing on Reconstruction in the 1970s and 1980s. For works on Texas that take this approach, see Carl Moneyhon, *Republicanism in Reconstruction Texas* (Austin and London: University of Texas Press, 1980), and Randolph B. Campbell, "Grass Roots Reconstruction: The Personnel of County Government in Texas, 1865–1876," *Journal of Southern History* 58 (February 1992): 99–116. For other works reflecting this view, see Joe Gray Taylor, *Louisiana Reconstructed* (Baton Rouge: Louisiana State University Press, 1974); Jerrell H. Shofner, *Nor Is It Over Yet* (Gainesville: University of Florida Press, 1974); William C. Harris, *The Day of the Carpetbagger* (Baton Rouge: Louisiana State University Press, 1979); Mark W. Summers, *Railroads, Reconstruction, and the Gospel of Prosperity: Aid Under the Radical Republicans* (Princeton: Princeton University Press, 1984). An important study of South Carolina, where African Americans exercised considerable political influence, concluded that black politicians were drawn heavily from a literate, property-holding elite whose agenda was out of touch with the needs

of the black masses. See Thomas Holt, *Black over White: Negro Political Leadership in South Carolina During Reconstruction* (Urbana: University of Illinois Press, 1977).

2. William S. McFeely, *Yankee Stepfather: General O. O. Howard and the Freedmen* (New Haven, Conn.: Yale University Press, 1968); Louis Gerteis, *From Contraband to Freedman: Federal Policy Toward Southern Blacks, 1861–1865* (Westport, Conn.: Greenwood Press, 1973); Carol Bleser, *The Promised Land: The History of the South Carolina Land Commission* (Columbia: University of South Carolina Press, 1969); Eric Foner, "Thaddeus Stevens, Confiscation, and Reconstruction," in *The Hofstadter Aegis: A Memorial,* ed. Stanley Elkins and Eric McKitrick (New York: Alfred A. Knopf, 1974), 154–83; Jonathan Wiener, *Social Origins of the New South, 1860–1885* (Baton Rouge: Louisiana State University Press, 1978); Wiener, "Class Structure and Economic Development in the American South, 1865–1955," *American Historical Review* 84 (October 1979), 970–92; Leon Litwack, *Been in the Storm So Long* (New York: Alfred A. Knopf, 1979); Jay R. Mandle, *The Roots of Black Poverty* (Durham: Duke University Press, 1978); Pete Daniel, "The Metamorphosis of Slavery, 1865–1900," *Journal of American History* 66 (June 1979): 88–99.

3. U.S. Census Office, *Report on Cotton Production in the United States* (2 vols.; Washington, 1884), vol. 1, 101–2.

4. U. S. Census Office, *The Statistics of the Population of the United States . . . Compiled from the Original Returns of the Ninth Census* (3 vols.; Washington, 1872), vol. 1, 372–73; U.S. Census Office, *Compendium of the Eleventh Census: 1890* (3 vols.; Washington, 1892–97), vol. 1, 511. According to the 1860 census, only three free blacks resided in Washington County in that year. Because the number of free blacks present in the antebellum period was so small and there is no evidence that other blacks who had been free before the Civil War migrated to the county after the war, the term freedmen has been applied generally to black men in postwar Washington County. U.S. Census Office, *Population of the United States in 1860 . . .* (Washington, D.C., 1864), 478–79.

5. *Statistics of the Population . . . Ninth Census,* vol. 1, 322; *Compendium of the Eleventh Census,* vol. 1, 511, 654–55, vol. 2, 672. The German-born population is calculated by combining those listed in the 1890 census figures as having been born in Germany (3,217) and in Austria (204). Census Office tabulations referring to the 1890 population do not give the number of persons who were German-born and the children of German-born parents, only the numbers of persons who were foreign-born and the children of foreign-born parents (8,615). On the assumption that the percentage of Germans in the categories of foreign-born and children of foreign-born reported in the 1890 census were equal to the percentage of Germans among the total foreign-born population (85 percent),

7,323 residents of Washington County were natives of Germany or the children of German-born parents in 1890. This is 25 percent of the county's total population (1890) of 29,157.

6. *Statistics of the Population . . . Ninth Census*, vol. 1, 274; *Compendium of the Eleventh Census*, vol. 1, 401.

7. *Galveston Daily News*, September 14, 1865; William H. Sinclair (Galveston) to Lt. J. T. Kirkman, February 26, 1867 (reel 8), Capt. Edward Collins (Brenham) to Kirkman, August 3, 1867 (reel 21); Collins, February 1, 1868 (reel 24), Texas Bureau Records.

8. Capt. Edward Collins (Brenham) to Lt. J. T. Kirkman, March 24, 1867 (reel 4), Collins to Lt. J. P. Richards, December 31, 1867 (reel 23), Records of the Assistant Commissioner for the State of Texas, Bureau of Refugees, Freedmen, and Abandoned Lands, 1865–1869 (Washington, D.C.: National Archives Microfilm Publication, M821) reel 4 (hereinafter cited as Texas Freedmen's Bureau Records).

9. "Record of Criminal Offenses Committed in Texas, 1865–1868," Texas Freedmen's Bureau Records (reel 32); "Abstracts of Crimes Committed in Counties of Texas, January 1869–March 1870," Office of Civil Affairs, District of Texas and the Fifth Military District, Record Group 393, National Archives (hereinafter cited as Civil Affairs); Lt. James C. Devine (Brenham) to Lt. Lemuel Morton, September 17, 1866, Texas Freedmen's Bureau Records (reel 32).

10. Capt. Edward Collins (Brenham) to Lt. J. T. Kirkman, April 1, 1867 (reel 32), Collins to Kirkman, March 4, 1867 (reel 4), Texas Freedmen's Bureau Records (reel 4).

11. F. P. Wood (Brenham) to Lt. Chas. A. Vernon, August 8, 1868 (reel 16), Lt. B. J. Arnold (Brenham) to Capt. C. C. Morse, December 2, 1865 (reel 17), Arnold to Morse, January 16, 1866 (reel 17), Capt. Edward Collins (Brenham) to Lt. J. T. Kirkman, May 4, 1867 (reel 20), William Sinclair (Galveston) to Kirkman, February 26, 1867 (reel 8), Texas Freedmen's Bureau Records.

12. F. P. Wood (Brenham) to Capt. C. S. Roberts, August 25, 1868 (reel 13), Wood to Lt. Charles Vinson, December 3, 1868 (reel 16), Wood to Lt. Charles Vernon, August 8, 1868 (reel 16), Capt. Edward Collins (Brenham) to Lt. J. T. Kirkman, August 3, 1867 (reel 21), Collins to Kirkman, September 29, 1867 (reel 21), Capt. Edward Miller (Millican) to Kirkman, June 26, 1867 (reel 4), Collins to Kirkman, June 26, 1867 (reel 4), Gen. A. Doubleday (Galveston) to Kirkman, July 31, 1867 (reel 5), Texas Freedmen's Bureau Records.

13. F. P. Wood (Brenham) to Lt. C. E. Moss, July 6, 1868 (reel 16), Texas Freedmen's Bureau Records. For other examples of black resistance, see *Galveston Daily News*, April 4, 1866, April 23, 1868, August 26, 1869.

14. William H. Sinclair (Galveston) to Lt. J. T. Kirkman, February 26, 1867 (reel 8),

Texas Freedmen's Bureau records (first quote); *Galveston Daily News*, December 18, 1867 (second quote).

15. 14 *Statutes at Large of the United States* 428; 15 *Statutes at Large* 2, 14. For the tortured progress of Reconstruction in Texas, see Moneyhon, *Republicanism in Reconstruction Texas*, 61–128.

16. Statement of Peter Diller, undated (reel 11), Texas Freedmen's Bureau Records; Diller to Capt. Edward Collins, April 29, 1867 (reel 5), Letters Received and Registers of Letters Received, District of Texas and the Fifth Military District, 1865–1870, Record Group 393, National Archives Microfilm Publication, M1193 (hereinafter cited as District of Texas).

17. L. E. Edwards (Brenham) to Gov. E. M. Pease, April 30, 1868, June 23, 1868, Governor's Papers, Texas State Archives (hereinafter cited as Governor's Papers).

18. 1870 Census of Population, Washington County, Texas, p. 76; Capt. Edward Collins (Brenham) to Lt. J. T. Kirkman, June 4, 1867 (Reel 20), Contract with Benjamin Watrous, June 15, 1868, F. P. Wood (Brenham) to Capt. C. S. Roberts, September 10, 1868, September 22, 1868, October 9, 1868 (reel 16), Texas Freedmen's Bureau Records.

19. Capt. Edward Collins (Brenham) to Lt. J. T. Kirkman, June 26, 1867 (Reel 4), June 30, 1867 (reel 7), Capt. Edward Miller (Millican) to Kirkman, June 26, 1867 (reel 21), Report of F. P. Wood, August 31, 1868 (reel 27), Texas Freedmen's Bureau Records; Lt. W. H. Crowell (Brenham) to Lt. C. E. Morse, November 28, 1867, and enclosures, Civil Affairs.

20. Moneyhon, *Republicanism in Reconstruction Texas*, 63; Capt. Edward Collins (Brenham) to Lt. J. T. Kirkman, June 26, 1867 (reel 4), Texas Freedmen's Bureau Records.

21. Benjamin Watrous (Brenham) to My Friend, February 12, 1868, Stephen A. Hackworth (Brenham) to Gov. E. M. Pease, May 28, 1869, Governor's Papers; *Galveston Daily News*, February 8, 1868.

22. Report of F. P. Wood (Brenham), August 31, 1868, Texas Freedmen's Bureau Records; J. H. Johnson et al. (Chappell Hill) to His Excellency Gov. Davis, June 30, 1870, Governor's Papers.

23. L. E. Edwards (Brenham) to E. M. Pease, April 30, 1868, J. D. McAdoo (Brenham) to Pease, June 13, 1868, J. J. Stockbridge et al. to E. J. Davis, March 5, 1870, Aaron Neely et al. (Brenham) to Davis, June 29, 1870, Matthew Gaines (Brenham) to E. J. Davis, March 6, 1870, Governor's Papers.

24. On the hardcore Unionists (those who had opposed secession *and* refused to support the Confederacy, see statement of Peter Diller, undated (reel 11), Texas Freedmen's Bureau Records; Diller to Capt. Edward Collins, April 29, 1867 (reel 5), District of Texas; George P. Webber (Brenham) to E. M. Pease, Febru-

ary 1, 1867, Governor's Papers; "Thos Dwyer and M. A. Healy," and "Thos Dwyer," Texas vol. 1, p. 280, R. G. Dun and Co. Collection, Baker Library, Harvard University Graduate School of Business Administration (hereinafter cited as Dun Collection). On former Whigs who had opposed secession but had generally supported the Confederacy after secession was a *fait accompli*, see *Brenham Banner*, July 17, 1883; Thomas J. Lockett to E. M. Pease, September 18, 1867, Governor's Papers; *Brenham Banner*, May 1, 1880; *Austin Daily State Journal*, February 15, 1872; C. G. Campbell (Vine Grove) to Gen. E. R. S. Canby, April 12, 1869 (reel 24), District of Texas. On discharged U.S. soldiers, see B. J. Arnold (Brenham) to Gen. J. J. Reynolds, September 25, 1868 (reel 11), District of Texas; Arnold to E. J. Davis, June 29, 1870, Governor's Papers.

25. William Schlottman to E. J. Davis, n.d. (probably January 1871), Governor's Papers; *Senate Miscellaneous Documents*, 50 Cong., 2 Sess., no. 62: *Testimony on the Alleged Election Outrages in Texas* (Serial 2616; Washington, D.C.: Government Printing Office, 1889), 156–69, 486–89, 591, 619.

26. "List of Civil Officers Elected or Appointed in Texas," Civil Affairs.

27. Minutes, Washington County District Court, I, 712, District Clerk's Office, Washington County Courthouse, Brenham, Texas; F. P. Wood (Brenham) to Gen. J. J. Reynolds, April 27, 1868 (reel 9), District of Texas; *Austin Daily State Journal*, December 6, 1870.

28. The names of sixteen African Americans who were active in the Union League and the Republican Party between 1867 and 1870 were culled from newspapers, correspondence, petitions, and Freedmen's Bureau and Army records. Of these, twelve were located in the 1870 census of population for Washington County. Information on age, occupation, literacy, and property ownership comes from the census.

29. Only Benjamin Watrous gave his occupation as "minister" to the census taker. Matthew Gaines and John H. Johnson, who were listed as farm laborers, also served as ministers. On Gaines, see Merline Pitre, *Through Many Dangers, Toils, and Snares: Black Leadership in Texas, 1865–1900* (Austin, Tex.: Eakin Press, 1985), 157–65. On Johnson, see *Brenham Banner*, October 23, 1884.

30. Agreement with Benjamin Watrous, June 15, 1868, Agreement with Charles Childs, October 1, 1868, both accompanying F. P. Wood (Brenham) to Capt. C. S. Roberts, December 29, 1868 (reel 16), Texas Freedmen's Bureau Records; *Austin Daily State Journal*, March 12, 1870.

31. B. O. Watrous (Brenham) to Gen. J. J. Reynolds, March 21, 1868 (reel 9), District of Texas; Watrous to Mr. Friend, February 12, 1868, Governor's Papers; Moneyhon, *Republicanism in Reconstruction Texas*, 236–47; *Galveston Daily News*, October 15, 1869.

32. Pitre, *Through Many Dangers*, 157–65, esp. 161; *Austin Daily State Journal*,

April 25, 1871; *Brenham Semi-Weekly Banner*, August 11, 1871, August 15, 1871 (quote).

33. J. R. Burns (Brenham) to J. P. Newcomb, July 14, 1872, Newcomb to Burns, July 28, 1872, James P. Newcomb Papers, Barker Texas History Center, University of Texas, Austin.

34. *Austin Daily State Journal*, February 14, 1872; *Brenham Banner*, August 2, 1873; *Brenham Banner*, June 11, 1874, April 23, 1875, April 30, 1875, November 26, 1875, July 12, 1878, August 15, 1884, August 17, 1884; Pitre, *Through Many Dangers*, 163–65.

35. *Austin Daily State Journal*, April 16, 1871; *Brenham Banner*, February 4, 1876, August 16, 1878, August 25, 1878, August 19, 1880, August 6, 1882, August 22, 1884, September 19, 1884, August 13, 1886.

36. The ratio of black Republican nominees to offices elected on a countywide basis is as follows: 1870 (1:4), 1873 (3:7), 1876 (5:16), 1878 (6:16), 1880 (5:16), 1882 (5:16), 1884 (6:16), 1886 (6:16). Election Returns, 1860–1892, County Clerk's Office, Washington County Courthouse, Brenham, Texas.

37. *Brenham Banner*, July 26, 1884. For other indications of black community institutions serving as the venues for these meetings, see *Brenham Banner*, August 8, 1878, July 16, 1880, July 20, 1882, August 28, 1886, September 18, 1886.

38. Ibid., August 25, 1878.

39. Ibid., August 15, 1884 (quote), November 5, 1876, July 12, 1878, August 9, 1878.

40. Ibid., August 12, 1880 (quote), August 5, 1880, August 18, 1880, August 13, 1882, August 29, 1884.

41. Ibid., October 26, 1886.

42. Affidavit of R. A. Harvin, July 15, 1875, affidavit of W. S. Decker, July 14, 1875, affidavit of Stephen Hackworth, July 18, 1875, affidavit of Daniel Hunt, July 15, 1875, affidavit of Adolph Secrets, July 13, 1875 (quote), affidavit of John W. Gee, July 20, 1875, affidavit of Phillip Baker, July 13, 1875, all accompanying Edmund J. Davis to Edwards Pierrepont, July 20, 1875, Box 675, Source-Chronological File, U.S. Department of Justice, Record Group 60, National Archives.

43. *Testimony on Alleged Election Outrages*, passim.

44. J. C. Cain to Edmund J. Davis, March 9, 1871, Governor's Papers; *Brenham Banner*, April 27, 1883, September 2, 1884, September 7, 1884, January 8, 1885. Of the 135 persons appointed deputy sheriff between 1870 and 1884 whose race can be determined, 31 (23 percent) were black. Record of Official Bonds, 1868–1875, and Record of Official Bonds, 1879–1883, County Clerk's Office, Washington County Courthouse, Brenham, Texas; Record of Official Bonds, 1876–1881, Washington County Records, Texas A & M Archives, College Station, Texas.

45. *Brenham Banner*, July 17, 1877, January 9, 1878, August 15, 1878, November 4, 1888.

46. Ibid., January 11, 1878.

47. Lawrence Levine, *Black Culture and Black Consciousness: Afro American Folk Thought from Slavery to Freedom* (New York: Oxford University Press, 1977), 251.

48. Donald G. Nieman, "Black Political Power and Criminal Justice: Washington County, Texas, 1868–1884," *Journal of Southern History* 55 (August 1989), 398–402. Between 1870 and 1884, court records give the names of persons who served on 159 petit juries. Of the 1,908 persons who sat on these panels, the 1870 and 1880 censuses permit identification of the race of 1,312. Of these (jurors who can be identified by race), 876 (67 percent) were white and 436 (33 percent) were black.

49. Ibid., 406, 418.

50. Ibid., 402–8, 413–19.

51. Ibid., 408–13.

52. *Brenham Banner*, December 19, 1880; February 3, March 12, April 3, 1881.

53. In ten cases in which blacks were charged with murdering whites, six went to trial and three ended in convictions. For the presence of large numbers of blacks in the courtroom, see *Brenham Banner*, February 2, August 2, 1878, March 27, 1883, April 9, 1884.

54. See *Brenham Banner*, December 11, 1873; February 25, March 3, 1876; August 22, 1882; August 31, September 4, October 26, 29, November 4, 8, 11, 1884; *Testimony on Alleged Election Outrages*, 6, 13, 169, 216, 242, 380–91, 401–5, 455, 468. The large-scale defection of Germans was critical. Because the black majority was slim and the black population very young, the number of black and white males of voting age was roughly equal. Indeed, the 1890 census would show that among males over twenty-one years old, whites exceeded blacks by 250. *Compendium of the Eleventh Census*, vol. 1, 805. With diminishing German support, Republicans, who had few other white supporters, found their hold on power tenuous.

55. *Brenham Banner*, November 6, 1884; *Testimony on Alleged Election Outrages*, passim; Rudolph Kleberg to A. H. Garland, March 4, December 21, 1887; anonymous, Brenham, Washington County, Texas to the attorney general of the United States, September 3, 1889, File no. 87-1293, Box 305, Central Files, Department of Justice, Record Group 60 (National Archives and Records Service, Washington, D.C.); *Brenham Banner*, November 4, 5, 6, 7, 9, 14, December 3, 7, 8, 19, 1886.

56. *Brenham Banner*, September 8, 1888; *Congressional Record*, 50 Cong., 1 Sess., vol. 19, pt. 9, 8523–34 (September 12, 1888).

57. *Alleged Election Outrages*, passim.
58. Rudolph Kleberg to A. H. Garland, March 4, 1887, December 21, 1887, anonymous, Brenham, Texas to the attorney general of the United States, September 3, 1889, File no. 87-1293, Central Files, U.S. Department of Justice, Record Group 60, National Archives.

Black Political Leadership: Warren County, Mississippi

Christopher Waldrep

The first generation of black leaders expected to use the same legal and political tactics and strategies once used by antebellum whites. White leaders—not the blacks—planned a sharp departure from past practices. Whites used racial tribalism to rally their followers, moving away from the kind of competitive political discourse that had characterized the antebellum South. Losing faith in law, they learned to rely on mobbing instead. Through Reconstruction, blacks retained a faith in constitutionalism, which even today seems quintessentially American, while whites tried a new tangent.

Vicksburg, county seat of Warren County, Mississippi, is an excellent place to examine black leadership in the years after the Civil War. Vicksburg attracted a host of articulate African American spokesmen. Since blacks made up 70 percent of Warren County's population, those leaders could reasonably expect to speak their minds and still get elected. And Warren County blacks must have expected to find at least some sympathy for their cause among local whites. Warren County whites had tolerated a large population of free and poorly supervised blacks in their midst and opposed secession. If blacks could win power anywhere in the Deep South, this was the place.

Freed slaves wanted to adjudicate quarrels much as whites had before emancipation. By crowding into the courts operated by the Freedmen's Bureau and the offices of black justices of the peace, ordinary blacks "voted" for existing legal institutions. Whenever possible, they took pleasure in the formal, courtlike settlement of things that had always previously been resolved informally. When blacks gathered in conventions, they spoke a language of constitutionalism, even when no lawyers were present. The occasional dissenter criticizing the Constitution or the law met a solid wall of opposition.[1] Instead, emancipated black southerners sought access to the very due process that whites had used against them in slavery.

Historians who depict black political activity as revolutionary echo the thinking of Reconstruction-era white conservatives. Even though Irish, white laborers, and various other factions had organized along ethnic lines for many years, Conservatives saw black political activity as inherently radical and criticized black politicians for forming black-only organizations. Black Vicksburgers actually tried to reach out to whites. Thomas W. Cardozo announced that black Vicksburgers wanted to forge a coalition with "Jews and Germans, and a few Irish," and his newspaper, the *Plain-Dealer*, championed the rights of farmers and laborers regardless of race. Cardozo wrote that "the sooner the colored people of the nation cease to look upon themselves as peculiarly set apart from the other elements of our citizens, the better it will be for all citizens." The goal, Cardozo insisted, was recognition simply as American citizens.[2]

Once they started politicking, blacks developed rivalries that resembled those in the white community. Antebellum white Vicksburg had long been plagued by factionalism and political infighting, a problem exacerbated by the arrival of so-called carpetbaggers. The same tensions appeared among black politicians. The Civil War had brought 30,000 freed-slave refugees to the Vicksburg area and many stayed through Reconstruction, becoming politically active. Aspiring politicians from Vicksburg resented those from out of town, and Mississippians from outside Warren County took exception to those from other states. Thomas Cardozo, born in Charleston, South Carolina, wrote that Peter Crosby of Clark, Mississippi, "dislikes men of other states to aspire to position in this state." As Cardozo slyly observed, "Perhaps, however, this is only the case when the men get in his way."[3] By 1867 ex-slave Albert Johnson and Thomas W. Stringer had emerged as the leading black politicians in Vicksburg, and the pair fueded much like antebellum white politicians. Johnson denounced Stringer as "disloyal" and Stringer condemned Johnson as "one of the most perfect knaves, black or white, that can be found in the State of Mississippi." Unlike Johnson, Stringer could not invoke his long residence in Mississippi, but he claimed to have opposed slavery for thirty-four years. Reminding readers that he was a minister of the gospel of Christ, Stringer urged blacks to be controlled by the word of God, and "not by the rule of Mr. A. Johnson."[4]

In 1868, Vicksburg sent both Stringer and Johnson to the constitutional convention, where they joined sixteen other black delegates. Stringer appeared as an articulate voice at the convention, serving on several important committees and opposing Conservative efforts to derail the convention. Stringer objected to Conservative efforts to make every delegate pay his own way, as he did when Conservatives sought to distract the Convention from its work by offering frivolous resolutions. When one Conservative delegate proposed a resolution to make the new bill of rights forbid interracial marriage, Stringer, a product of such a union himself, led the unsuccessful effort to table the proposal. Only ten delegates—not including Johnson—voted with him. Stringer played a key role in persuading the convention to go on record in support of congressional efforts to impeach President Andrew Johnson. Stringer also played a positive role in shaping the proposed constitution, proposing language for the new bill of rights that would have eliminated racial restrictions on suffrage.[5]

Black efforts to reach out to white Republicans foundered on white racism. Blacks meeting at Vicksburg's Apollo Hall asked "those in favor of Reconstruction" to attend, but the audience turned out to be almost entirely black. Blacks advertised another public meeting as open to "All persons who are interested in the reconstruction of Mississippi" but, apparently recognizing that few whites would attend, scheduled it at the colored Baptist Church.[6] Cardozo antagonized whites when he campaigned in the black community, promising to reward supporters with patronage. He would, he said, employ only "our colored young men as my deput[ies]." This was nothing new; politicians had been playing a similar game for years, but now, for the first time, blacks stood as the beneficiaries.[7]

The leader of white Republicans, a former Union army officer and Warren County Sheriff named Charles E. Furlong, showed little interest in black rights. Alert black Republicans could hardly have missed the obvious signs of Furlong's disloyalty to the Republican Party. Even as he led the Republicans, Furlong maintained ties to the most conservative elements in Vicksburg society. As a result, white conservatives defended him from criticism. Nonetheless, blacks loyally, some said slavishly, turned out to vote for him. When the Warren County Republican Party met in August 1871, Furlong's followers began chanting their man's name, but black Republicans spoke up as well. As he had done so often before, Furlong moved to placate his black supporters without offending his white friends. In this case, he stepped aside and allowed ex-slave Charles W. Bush to serve in the largely ceremonial post of president of the nominating convention.[8]

Furlong's balancing act offended some in Vicksburg. Unfortunately, the best evidence of black discontent with Furlong comes from an extremely biased white source. Furlong had awarded the county's lucrative printing contract to the Democratic paper, angering the white-owned Republican *Times*. As a result, the *Times* began describing Republicans' meetings as chaotic, disorderly, disgraceful and "indescribably ridiculous." The *Times* goaded blacks to demand more from Furlong, reporting that Warren County blacks wanted more power in their party, repeatedly challenging Furlong in political meetings to get it.[9] In September the *Times* accused him of amassing a huge fortune from his office, adding that "now it is fairly the turn of the colored men to have it." The newspaper went on to doubt the sincerity of Furlong's Republicanism and to observe that he owned no property in the city and paid no taxes. Instead, the sheriff kept himself ready to migrate at a moment's notice. Quite accurately, the *Times* declared that "his aim is to make all he can out of the people of the county and then vanish from our midst."[10]

Just a week later the *Times* struck again. "Furlong," the paper roughly demanded, "Who is your candidate for Chancery Clerk of this county . . .? We claim that a colored man must either be chancery clerk or sheriff. How is that with you? Answer." In the same issue, the formal head of the Republican Party in Warren County read Furlong out of the party. John Rankin wrote that Furlong had "played hell becoming a Democrat."[11] The local Republican hierarchy undoubtedly called on Governor James L. Alcorn to remove Furlong and the *Times and Republican* pressured Alcorn with headlines such as "Furlong defies the Governor." Shortly thereafter Alcorn acquiesced and removed Furlong from office.[12]

In the election former slave George W. Boyd ran against Furlong. The *Times and Republican* endorsed Boyd, pointedly describing him as a life-long resident of Warren County and a loyal Republican.[13] Later the paper condemned Furlong as a criminal and perjurer.[14] Nevertheless, despite the *Times and Republican*'s efforts, the nominating convention picked Furlong over Boyd. The convention did nominate blacks George W. Davenport for chancery clerk, Thomas W. Cardozo for circuit clerk, and Peter Crosby for treasurer. In November Warren County's rank-and-file black voters once again elected Furlong sheriff.[15]

Furlong was not the only white Republican to frustrate Vicksburg's black leaders. Virtually all Vicksburg whites favored segregated seating in theaters and other public accommodations. On February 7, 1873, Governor Ridgley C. Powers signed into law Mississippi's civil rights bill.[16] Black Vicksburgers did not wait long to test the new law. In March a black minor city official purchased a ticket for the theater and refused to sit in the colored section. Whites quickly ousted him from his seat and the Democratic *Herald* hoped local blacks had learned their lesson: "the white people of Vicksburg do not intend to tolerate such impudence." The white Republican newspaper did not approve of the desegregation attempt either but sought to placate black Republicans by adding that "we have greater condemnation for the acts of those who, mob like, rushed to the assistance of the usher with drawn pistols."[17] In May another minor black official, this time a justice of the peace, challenged white Vicksburg's segregation policy. Sydney Brooks bought a ticket to hear Vermont poet John G. Saxe lecture at the YMCA and insisted on sitting in the white section. Arrested, he went before Judge Alexander Arthur. Though only a city judge and ostensibly a Republican, Arthur condemned the civil rights law as unconstitutional class legislation, concluding that it did not cover private associations like the YMCA.[18]

Just a day later Cardozo, Davenport, and Crosby, leaders of Warren County's black community by virtue of the 1871 election, issued a handbill.

Hail! Republicans! Rally!

Indignation meeting! to be held at the Courthouse to-morrow night, Friday, May 2—why hallo! What's the matter now? Why there's nothing the matter—but a fresh cut, why so? Because, hallucination has taken hold of one of our most trust Judges of literary merit. Well, how do you know? Because, he has stretched back one of his far reaching roots to the very cell of usurpation, and has thrown another under the funeral pile of corruption. Yes he has twisted another around the stake of absurdity. Respectfully Yours, T. W. Cardozo, G. W. Davenport, Peter Crosby, P. C. Hall, A. W. Dorsey, W. L. Merritt, L. H. Wilson, and others.[19]

At the meeting Peter Crosby spoke. The *Herald* described him as tall, intelligent-looking, and middle-aged. He spoke in a deliberate but rather impassioned tone, declaring that "we do not intend to be satisfied until we have all the privileges belonging to all citizens. We do not intend to be satisfied in part." After reading from the Declaration of Independence, he announced, "We want the whole hog or not."[20] The Democrats denounced the meeting. The Meridian *Mercury* hooted in derision at the white man and radical, "holding his office by favor of the Radical negro party."[21] The *Herald* made the point with doggerel:

> Judge Arthur is as fine a man
> As ever you did see,
> Though he did decide the "civil Rights"
> Unlawful for to be
> And although he was censured,
> And requested to resign,
> He hasn't yet forgotten how
> To law on cost and fine.
> Silence in the Court!
> The first man that laughs
> I'll fine him.[22]

The incident ultimately led to the unseating of the white Republican ring in Vicksburg. Peter Crosby had already served as Warren County coroner, ranger, and treasurer. Born into slavery, he seemed destined for higher office. Like so many Mississippi slaves who had become politicians, he worked as an artisan. In 1864 he had earned enough money by shoemaking to buy four mules and a carriage, which he used to transport his family to freedom. While he was serving in the Union Army, federal authorities seized his property. Despite that loss, in 1872 he and his wife had accumulated enough money to purchase a lot in Vicksburg. Crosby traveled the county making speeches on "the political issues of the time." One observer sourly commented that he had only proved himself "intellectually unable to do justice to the subject of his speech." Others, though, were more impressed.[23]

By 1873 Warren County blacks understood that they could win equal treatment under the law only by asserting themselves as a united bloc. Wishing for a color-blind society would not make one. Acting on this insight, blacks dominated the 1873 Republican ward meetings, which selected only three white men as delegates to the county convention.[24] Blacks so thoroughly controlled the convention that at one point Davenport argued for giving whites at least token representation.[25] Instead of pitting whites against blacks, the convention split along city-country lines. When country folk hoped to nominate G. W. Chavis for assessor, Crosby, who had already been nominated for sheriff, induced Chavis to withdraw by offering to make him deputy sheriff. In this era men crudely sought office to make money, and Crosby promised Chavis he could make more money as deputy sheriff than as assessor. Chavis's country supporters erupted in anger, shouting, quite accurately, that he had sold out.[26] The convention nominated Furlong for the state senate.

Blacks had reacted to whites' refusal to treat them fairly by insisting that some powerful positions go to African Americans. At the election in November Crosby easily defeated his Democratic opponent, 2,308 to 485.[27] Whites reacted badly to the new black militancy. Angry at his ouster from the lucrative sheriff's office for the less-than-profitable office of state senator, Furlong consorted with the Democrats. Some state Republicans thought Furlong should help Crosby by vacating the sheriff's office early, but Furlong declared that he would not give up his position as sheriff until the first of January, when, by law, he had no choice.[28]

Crosby imagined that he could function in roughly the same fashion as previous white sheriffs. But Crosby faced problems like no other sheriff. Whites, who, after all, paid most of the taxes that made government possible, did not recognize Crosby's legitimacy. Controlling the county's wealth gave whites one immediate lever over elected blacks. By law elected officials had to post a bond. All blacks elected to office confronted this problem. Justice of the peace G. Morris Smith and his constable petitioned the board of supervisors to reduce their bonds. Smith explained that he was a colored man and regular member of the Union League, an organization which, he reminded the supervisors, held "principles distasteful to the minds of a majority of the property holders."[29]

Crosby's election as sheriff energized Democratic opposition to Republican rule. Previously loyal white Republicans fled their party.[30] The all-white Taxpayers' League, dormant for years, came back to life, mutating into militia-like clubs. Although Warren County whites had been historically factionalized along political, economic, and ethnic lines, some whites now aspired to a new unity. An organization called the "People's Club" sought to enlist all white people in the county. A People's Club formed in each of Vicksburg's four wards as well as in rural districts surrounding the city.[31]

The best evidence of blacks' innate conservatism may be their business-as-usual approach to governing. Once in power they raised taxes and, in some cases, corruptly enriched themselves. Taxes had gone up under white Republican rule without exciting much response, but whites hunted for an excuse to criticize black Republican rule. Circuit clerk Thomas W. Cardozo added names to lists of witnesses to be paid out of taxes, writing the new names in a cramped hand between the names of the original and genuine witnesses. Cardozo pocketed the money issued to these additional "witnesses" himself.[32] Cardozo's successor in office, Alfred Dorsey, proved just as corrupt, failing to account for the tax money he collected. Chancery clerk George W. Davenport altered the official records in his office so he could issue himself larger checks than he deserved. When Cardozo's fraudulent witness certificates reached the state auditor, he refused to pay.[33] Hearing this, angry whites demanded to examine the county's books. Black officials first turned them away. Then, when the Board of Supervisors launched an investigation of the chancery clerk's office, someone mysteriously burgled the courthouse, stealing the incriminating records.[34]

Whites were unable to produce evidence against Peter Crosby but claimed that he had similarly stolen money when he served as treasurer and, as sheriff, had covered up the crimes committed by Cardozo, Dorsey, and Davenport.[35]

Crosby died in Warren County with one mule valued at $15 and a mare appraisers described as "almost worthless." Furlong spent his retirement years in posh New York hotels, making it his hobby to visit every city in the world with a population of over 100,000.[36]

Unable to prove Crosby guilty of anything, whites went after his bonds as tax collector and sheriff. Mississippi's law requiring public officials to put up a bond had the effect of forcing elected officials without property of their own to find men of property to ratify their service. By law public officials had to produce the names and signatures of property holders willing to pledge to pay any money the officials might lose or steal. Old white planters, outvoted by their former slaves, could still wield power through the bond. In effect, the law gave men of wealth a veto, or would have if public officials only solicited the local elite for their bonds. But blacks from outside Warren County could find no locally wealthy white man to sign their bonds. As one white man explained, Warren County property holders valued their old family servants and might sign a bond for them, but a black stranger from outside the county would have trouble finding anyone to sign his bond. For the sheriff, the sums involved made the problem of obtaining a bond especially difficult. Crosby had to find men willing to stake $100,000 of their own property on his service.[37] Nonetheless, Crosby came up with a bond.

Almost immediately whites attacked the new bond. The *Plain-Dealer* complained that "There is always some sly knave at work, endeavoring to give our officers in the county as much trouble as possible." George S. Yerger, who had supported Crosby by pledging $1,000, had suddenly and unexpectedly gone insolvent. Yerger wanted to notify the Board of Supervisors but the *Plain-Dealer* thought the board could avoid trouble by refusing to meet. "It is simply a smear," the newspaper maintained, "a contemptible trick upon Mr. Crosby."[38]

In April 1874, the circuit court convened in Warren County. By April 7 Crosby had assembled a grand jury and George Brown, the white Republican judge, delivered a blistering charge, reminding jurors of Cardozo's ghost witnesses, Dorsey's failure to account for the taxes he collected, and Davenport's forgeries, and urging them to root out local corruption. He undoubtedly recognized the danger in allowing white Conservatives to paint Republicans as corrupt. But after deliberation the grand jury refused to indict any local officials. One black and five white grand jurors wrote a "Minority Report" to the judge. The six jurors expressed sorrow and regret "that we are unable to sustain you in your noble efforts" to clean up the county. The dissenters claimed that most of the grand jury, "in the face of positive proof and direct testimony," had refused to perform their duty.[39] The Republican district attorney joined with the dissenters in denouncing the grand jury for failing to indict.[40]

Brown recognized this as a disastrous setback for the Republicans. The circuit court met only twice a year; it would be six months before another grand jury could indict Cardozo and the others. During those long months the idea that the law could not effectively fight Republican corruption would fester and grow. In fact, the Republicans had a far better record for rooting out corruption than the Democrats, but this was the critical moment. If the Republicans could not deliver justice now, nothing else mattered. Brown blasted the grand jury. "I am astonished and shocked," he thundered at them, complaining that they had acted "to shield crime . . . by skulking and protecting" criminals. Brown warned that if crime cannot be punished through the proper agencies established by law, the people will take its punishment into their own hands. If that happened, Brown said, the grand jury would share the blame. Brown expressed regret that he could not jail the grand jurors.[41]

Within months of Crosby's election, white militia companies challenged the new sheriff's authority. Rioting seemed inevitable. The governor of Mississippi, carpetbagger Adelbert Ames, fretted, writing his wife, "I have tried to get troops, but the President refuses." Ames heard talk that Ulysses S. Grant hoped to win a second term with the support of southern Democrats by allowing them a free hand in the South. Violence seemed so certain that white Conservatives moved their families out of Vicksburg to avoid the riot.[42]

Crosby tried to react as a white sheriff might under such circumstances, calling on his law-abiding constituents to support legitimate authority. On July 12, 1874, he published a proclamation calling for help in the *Vicksburg Herald*. He began by observing that an "unwonted excitement . . . likely to lead to breaches of the peace" plagued the community. It is the duty of the sheriff, he explained, to prevent lawlessness and to call on "all good men without regard to race, color, or previous condition" to promote peace. Crosby deputized sixty men and printed their names at the bottom of his proclamation. It is likely the sixty discovered they had been deputized only when they read Crosby's proclamation in the newspaper. Crosby appealed to reputable white men he thought likely to favor order, even order under a black-dominated local government. He included, for example, banker John A. Klein. A wealthy and influential Democrat, Klein's support would have granted Crosby legitimacy in the eyes of many whites. And Crosby probably thought it not unreasonable that Klein might support him. Under slavery Klein had been especially sympathetic to slaves, granting several of them so-called nominal status by allowing them to work unsupervised as artisans. Klein sometimes even allowed slaves who had illegally bought their freedom to use his name as their ostensible owner.[43] He had acted as Albert Johnson's agent and pretended owner. Without his help, Johnson might never have achieved the success he did in slavery and risen to a position of leadership after emancipation.

As Crosby tried to cross racial boundaries, appealing for help from whites, whites organized along racial lines. One sign of this can be found in the disappearance of dueling. Warren County had for decades been a mecca for duelists. Even the Civil War and the massive infusion of Yankees had not halted the ritual. As late as 1869, Union army veteran and Republican Frederic Speed announced that as a northerner he naturally disliked dueling, "but as I have cast my lot for the future in a community where, among gentlemen, this prejudice does not exist, I determined to . . . accommodate this bogus specimen of Chivalry."[44] But dueling stopped as blacks gained political power.

As whites formed an unprecedented racial bloc, blacks played the same kind of political games once common among whites in the antebellum era. On the eve of the election, Hannibal C. Carter attacked the Republican ticket as virtually defeated. He expressed regret that the election had been turned into a referendum on race. He had probably already begun plotting a political future outside the Republican party that would further divide black voters in 1875.[45]

Vicksburg's voting population was almost evenly divided between blacks and whites. Whites expected to win by turning out their troops en masse and by intimidating blacks. Whites charged that Crosby had tried to block white voting, but blacks charged more credibly that they had been afraid to vote for fear of white reprisals. White newspapers carried the names of blacks illegally registered to vote. Registrar George R. Walton saw less subtle forms of intimidation. A black Republican, he testified later that whites tried to intimidate him with loud cursing as he registered black voters. Transient white raftsmen pushed forward, wanting to vote. In one ward rowdy whites forced him to jump out a window; pursuing whites shouted, "Kill him; catch the yellow son of a bitch and bring him back." Walton had to ask some respectable whites he found on the street for protection.[46]

After the 1874 city elections, whites continued to disparage the criminal justice system. They assailed Judge Brown as a "wretched old man" who had encouraged blacks to burn Vicksburg if they did not win at the polls. In September the *Herald* reported that it was "perfectly apparent" that the Board of Supervisors intended to repeat its villainy of the last term and nominate grand jurors sympathetic to official corruption. When the Board of Supervisors met to nominate grand jurors for the fall term of the circuit court, members of the Taxpayers' League appeared to heckle their choices. The leaguers spoke disrespectfully and cowed some supervisors into withdrawing the names of men they had nominated for the grand jury. The league did not dictate who was nominated, but the grand jury produced by this process proved willing to move against corrupt officials, just as the taxpayers demanded.[47] During the November term this new grand jury indicted T. W. Cardozo for forgery and embezzlement. The jurors claimed that, as circuit clerk, he had amassed two thousand dollars from land sold by the state for back taxes and never reported it to the state auditor. His successor in office, Dorsey, had collected $1,800 in the same fashion and also failed to report it to the state auditor, as required by law. The jurors also charged that both Cardozo and chancery clerk George Davenport had forged warrants, pocketing county money.[48]

The *Daily Vicksburger* proclaimed all the defendants guilty. "If they can't be convicted," the paper said, "with the testimony against them, the law is a farce."[49] But local whites had long since lost confidence in their court.[50] And the *Vicksburger* complained of jury corruption.[51] Even white Republicans doubted a jury seated by Crosby would fairly try the sheriff's political allies.[52]

On December 3 the *Vicksburger* published an advertisement for runaways reminiscent of antebellum slave advertisements:

Runaways!
Two Niggers, Wash Davenport and Lewis Wilson!
The former is a high yaller nigger, about 5 feet 5 inches high.

The advertisement was signed "BY ORDER OF THE PEOPLE."[53]

On November 27 and December 2 the Taxpayers' League met in Temperance Hall.[54] The *Vicksburger* justified the second meeting with vigilante rhetoric: "the people felt themselves compelled to arise in their might and interpose their sovereign power between official thieves and plunderers and the interest and welfare of the city and county." Those assembled debated resolutions demanding the resignations of black county officials. When Harper Hunt objected to language hinting at violence, William H. McCardle "made an able answer to Col. Hunt's objection." The crowd decided to send a committee of ten to the courthouse to call for the resignations of Crosby, Davenport, Wilson, and Sydney Brooks, a justice of the peace.[55]

When Crosby and the other officials rebuffed the committee, the taxpayers formed another committee of three lawyers and two citizens to report whether all practicable legal remedies had been exhausted. The chair appointed lawyers Martin Marshall, Owen McGarr, A. M. Lea, and two men the *Vicksburger* identified only as Barnes and Fitzhugh. The committee met and returned with majority and minority reports. Three committeemen, McGarr, Lea, and Fitzhugh, thought all legal remedies had, in fact, not been exhausted. Davenport awaited trial and the Board of Supervisors could be called on to demand sufficient bond from Crosby.[56]

But two members of the committee, Marshall and Barnes, "represented that while *in theory* the law was ample for redress, yet practically it would fail to provide a proper remedy." George Barnes had been a Warren County planter for twenty years. In the Civil War he raised a regiment to fight the Yankees. Just twenty-four, Marshall, son of Vicksburg's top lawyer, represented a different generation.[57] Marshall and Barnes thought that such immediate evils required immediate remedy. They doubted Davenport could be convicted with Crosby picking the jury. The crowd unanimously adopted the minority report and the whole meeting adjourned to the courthouse. When the mob spied Davenport slipping down Monroe Street, they gave chase but he escaped. Crosby, however, remained in his office to confront the crowd. "The people have resolved that you cannot be sheriff of this county one hour longer," Charles Peine declared. Crosby talked for fifteen or twenty minutes before being interrupted by Martin Marshall. Marshall leaped atop a desk and whooped, "We have six hundred men; have we come to parley with this man? We came here for business." Marshall's appeal to the crowd broke Crosby's resistance and he signed a letter of resignation.[58]

That evening Crosby escaped Vicksburg on horseback. In Bovina he caught a freight train to Jackson, where the governor assembled a sort of kitchen cabinet of advisors to discuss how to react to Crosby's forced resignation. The attorney general thought Crosby should demand admission to his office and, if refused, call upon a posse to reclaim it. But others thought Crosby should not return to Vicksburg unaccompanied by a military force. Ames, who had asked for U.S. Army troops before and been rebuffed, stated positively he would not call for federal help.[59] Some of the white Republicans in attendance regarded Crosby as incompetent and worthless. Ames himself made it clear that he thought black leaders in Vicksburg needed to stand up for themselves. He lectured Crosby and other black Vicksburgers who had come to Jackson for help that he and other white men had faced bullets to free them. Now, he insisted, they should fight to maintain the freedom given them by whites or be exposed as unworthy of that freedom.[60] The meeting ended inconclusively but a U.S. Army captain named A. W. Allyn, who claimed to have blundered into the meeting by accident, said later that had he been Crosby he would have considered himself instructed by the governor to seize his office by force.[61]

While in Jackson Crosby supervised the preparation of a proclamation in the offices of the *Plain-Dealer*. Crosby claimed later that he did not order his proclamation published in handbill form, but it was. On Saturday, December 5, newsboys distributed it in Vicksburg and the next day black ministers read it from their pulpits.[62]

Ames dispatched his adjutant general to Vicksburg to investigate. A. G. Packer met with members of the Taxpayers' League, who insisted their only beef with Crosby was his bad bond. Meeting with Crosby, Packer found the sheriff insisting he could obtain a good bond. Packer urged him to do so. On the street local white leaders advised Packer that they believed Crosby was assembling a force to invade the city. Packer promised to try to halt such a plan if he could, and when he next saw Crosby, he told him "this thing has got to stop." The sheriff willingly agreed to send couriers out into the country to stop the impending invasion.[63]

At 4:30 A.M. on December 7, Erasmus R. Richardson, a Republican turned Conservative, rang the courthouse bell as an alarm to whites. This proved to be a false alarm, but it documented the unity whites had achieved. Ex-Confederates turned out to stand alongside their former Yankee enemies. Ex-Republicans joined with Conservatives. At 8:00 Richardson rang the bell again.[64]

This time Richardson's bell was no false alarm. Led by Andrew Owen, an army buddy of Crosby's from the Civil War, blacks approached the city. Vicksburg whites of every political stripe and ethnic group united to repulse them. Lawyer H. H. Miller led an informally organized white militia to defend Vicksburg. Confronting Owen, Miller presented his force as the embodiment of legitimacy and legality: "You are inside the corporate limits in violation of law as a band of armed men."[65] Owen also claimed to represent order, insisting he led his men into Vicksburg "under law."[66] After this exchange, Miller rode back to his command. He claimed later the blacks flourished their hats and cursed loud enough to create an immense noise. Witnesses disagreed as to who fired first. Miller said, "I think the firing was about as simultaneous as firing could be." Owen remembered the event differently. His men began to disperse and the whites fired on them as they tried to escape. Much the same happened when two other columns of blacks approached the city. No one knows how many men died that day. The city sexton buried sixteen men, all but two of them black. The mayor reported twenty-five to thirty killed in a fight on Cherry Street, another thirty to forty killed near the Pemberton monument, and fifteen to twenty killed on Grove Street.[67] After the riot, whites crowed that law had triumphed over lawlessness. The people of the city, the *Vicksburger* proclaimed, had vindicated the law and rebuked mob violence.[68]

In the days immediately after the Vicksburg riot, victorious whites decided to disarm local blacks, searching black Vicksburgers' homes for arms. On Tuesday night, December 8, rampaging white men went door-to-door in the black part of Vicksburg.[69] Ex-sheriff Furlong, now firmly allied with white Conservatives, went to William Wood's house to demand his gun. Wood's wife refused to hand it over, but later whites challenged Wood on the street, warning him he would be shot if he did not produce his gun, a musket he had "got new to save my own life." He turned it over.[70] Seven or eight white men crashed into John McPherson's house, turning over beds. His wife, confined to her bed "in a delicate condition," had a miscarriage in the excitement.[71] When Tom Bidderman, perhaps too unbalanced to understand the necessity of genuflection, admitted having a gun but refused to turn it over, whites shot and killed him.[72] When twenty whites with fixed bayonets burst into Lusinda Henry's home, they ripped up the floor, broke the bed down, tore the mattress open, and threw clothing on the floor. They found the gun her husband had hidden under the house and also stole $45 he had hidden.[73] Whites also arrested former deputy sheriff Charles H. Smith.[74] Crosby remained in town as this battle unfolded and whites quickly arrested him. They ended up using Packer to force a second resignation from Crosby. The adjutant general met with the sheriff and advised him to resign. Packer wrote the letter and witnessed Crosby's signature.[75] But U.S. Army troops returned Crosby to office.[76]

By the end of January Crosby had a new bond, his third, and announced himself ready to begin collecting taxes. U.S. Army troops still patrolled the streets and occupied the courthouse, but angry whites erupted in a storm of indignation. Knots of men could be seen on the streets talking about the latest development. From their perspective those who had stepped forward to defend their "city and families from outrage and the threatened torch and turpentine of the brutal negroes" had been outmaneuvered by the man who had ordered their homes outraged. White Vicksburgers confronted and demanded an explanation from every man on Crosby's bond. All denied they meant to be on Crosby's bond. They had understood that the lawyers' compromise would take effect. Crosby would remain as a figurehead, but a deputy would actually perform his duties. The *Vicksburg Herald* took pains not to disturb the new unity among whites. "We were glad," the *Herald* wrote, "to find some of the bondsmen expressing a determination not to qualify." The *Herald* reassured readers that the bond had been prepared from good motives and, therefore, no one should be reproached. The paper even expressed regret for the initial feeling of outrage some had expressed on learning that some white men had apparently deserted to Crosby. "We are all engaged in a common cause and struggling together to get out of the present trouble."[77]

In February Crosby produced still another bond. Now he clearly recognized he could not personally execute his office. He negotiated an agreement with J. P. Gilmer of Kemper County allowing Gilmer to act as de facto sheriff. Crosby's deputy and political rival, Washington Chavis, would continue in office, taking charge of the jail. All twenty-three bondsmen came from outside Warren County, mostly from Kemper County. Whites regarded Gilmer as a "radical Radical" but accepted his assurances that he intended to pour oil on troubled waters. "The white people of this county have never asked anything but a fair show," the *Herald* said, "and if Mr. Gilmer gives them that . . . he will receive their encouragement and support." A deal had been struck. Crosby signed a formal contract with Gilmer.[78]

But not all Warren Countians accepted the deal. Some whites described Gilmer's mission to Vicksburg as purely mercenary. Warren County's black population felt betrayed. They had elected their first black sheriff in 1873 and had been willing to lay down their lives for him in 1874. In 1875 it had become clear that he could be bought. Black Republicans convened an "indignation meeting" in the courthouse. The crowd demanded Crosby, who appeared to defend himself. The sheriff's office, he announced, functioned better under Gilmer than it had six months earlier. Crosby pointedly predicted that Gilmer would stand by him in times of danger and not desert him as his friends had in December. In case anyone doubted which friends he had in mind, Crosby then went on to denounce his own deputies for drawing $125 a month and crawling into cellars in times of danger. Deputy G. W. Chavis, everyone knew, had organized the meeting.

The black president of the Board of Supervisors, George Walton, denounced Crosby. Crosby sat and listened as Walton reprimanded him for signing away all his rights and betraying the black voters who had placed him in office. Walton even claimed he would prefer a Democrat to a mercenary like Gilmer. Crosby responded by denouncing Chavis rather than Walton. Gilmer, who was present, spoke as well, also attacking Chavis, and introduced himself to the mostly black audience as an ex-Confederate-turned-Republican.[79]

The deal between Gilmer, Crosby, and certain leading whites unraveled through the spring of 1875. In March the taxpayers met and vowed to pay no taxes to either Gilmer or Crosby. A few days later Chavis filed suit against Crosby, claiming the sheriff owed him $500 from his days as deputy. Crosby searched Vicksburg for Chavis to confront him, but when Chavis flourished a gun the sheriff backed away. In April the *Vicksburg Herald* announced that George Brown wanted to run for Congress and had made a deal to rig the juries in the trials of Davenport, Cardozo, and other black leaders in hopes of currying their support for his congressional ambitions.[80]

In the end Gilmer's mercenary lusts brought him down. Gilmer had been speculating in county warrants to supplement his income as deputy sheriff. A local pawnbroker named Rothschild sold him some warrants, which turned out to be the fraudulent warrants Davenport had circulated. Gilmer verbally chastised the pawnbroker and even threatened to whip him with cowhide. Arrested, Gilmer appeared before the mayor. But the mayor's authority carried little weight with the angry deputy, and upon release Gilmer immediately returned to Rothschild's shop with more threats and, this time, a pistol.[81]

On June 7, Peter Crosby accused Gilmer of shooting him in a Vicksburg saloon. The pair had fallen out, Crosby said later, over the appointment of deputies. More likely, they fought over the spoils of office. The shot fired into his head did not immediately kill Crosby, but newspapers reported the wound would certainly prove fatal. Apparently dying, Crosby swore out a warrant against Gilmer, accusing him of attempted murder. Vicksburg's black newspaper interviewed Crosby and reported that he had declared that Gilmer "had it done or did it himself."[82]

Crosby did not die and appeared at Gilmer's hearing before a justice of the peace, retreating from his original accusations. He and Gilmer had gone into the saloon together after clearing up whatever bad feelings had existed between the two. He and Gilmer had quarreled, but those differences had been entirely settled. Although he had been positive Gilmer had either shot him or ordered it done, he now admitted he could only see the perpetrator's arm and elbow. The justice dismissed the charges against Gilmer.[83]

Despite his testimony, Crosby's quarrel with Gilmer had been worked out after the shooting, not before. Crosby had fired Gilmer as deputy on June 5, but the deputy had refused to vacate the office. By July Crosby had located a white Vicksburger, Thomas C. Bedford, to serve as his chief deputy. Gilmer returned to Kemper County where a mob murdered him in 1877.[84] The Conservative *Herald* praised Bedford as an old Vicksburger of unquestioned integrity. He would, the paper reassured its readers, have full charge of the office. His bond included H. H. Miller, the same man who had led the military-style attack on Crosby's followers on December 7. Crosby continued as sheriff until October 28, 1875, when he resigned, but Reconstruction had been effectively ended in Warren County, Mississippi.[85]

White Conservatives succeeded in ousting the black president of the Board of Supervisors. Unlike Davenport or even Crosby, the head of county government, George Walton, had no reputation among whites for corruption. So whites challenged his election in circuit court. Although whites insisted they had no confidence in the courts and claimed Brown too biased to give them a fair trial, in the end they triumphed in Brown's courtroom. The Republican judge ordered Walton to step down in favor of J. Fred Baum, a business entrepreneur and white Conservative.[86]

Whites talked openly of carrying the 1875 election against all hazards.[87] Working-class Democrats formed a vigilante organization called the Modocs. One Warren Countian remembered the atmosphere in 1875 as "pregnant . . . with intimidation." Bodies of armed white men marched through Warren County, firing cannons every three or four hundred yards.[88] At night bands of men patrolled the county, stopping blacks on the highway and ordering them back to their homes. Blacks planned to celebrate the Fourth of July with speeches and a ceremonial reading of the Declaration of Independence in the circuit courtroom, but whites armed with pistols marched into the chamber. A scuffle broke out, and one of the invading whites fired his pistol. In the confusion, voices could be heard shouting, "Get out of here, you radical sons-of-bitches!" The crowd rushed for doors and windows. When the blacks had fled, more whites came into the courtroom, found Ben Allen, a Republican, on the floor, and beat him unmercifully; white boys threw spittoons at his head. Questioned afterwards, they insisted they had no objection to celebrating the Fourth, but objected to the presence of Cardozo, Davenport, and Crosby.[89] Blacks stopped holding public political meetings, meeting instead in swamps.[90] Some whites were not satisfied to drive black political activity underground; they meant to extinguish it entirely. The night before the Republican nominating convention, whites invaded Davenport's house. They could not find him, but satisfied themselves with killing his brother-in-law and burning the body.[91]

All this violence destroyed Republican influence over criminal justice in Warren County, even as Republicans continued to formally control the machinery of criminal justice. After 1874 the percentage of black grand jurors in Warren County sharply declined to 25 percent of the total. Through the remainder of the decade the redeemers kept the number of black grand jurors at about that level. These mostly white grand juries resisted returning many indictments based on black complaints and proved less receptive to the testimony of illiterates as well. Only 14 percent of complainants could not read or write. Thus, whites "redeemed" criminal justice even before they seized political power.

In their secret meetings at night, blacks debated what to do. Some argued against voting at all. By the summer of 1875 politically active blacks in Warren County realized that whites would never permit a black even to run for the sheriff's office. Some proposed nominating Bedford, the man serving as Crosby's deputy. Though Bedford was white and a Democrat, these black Republicans judged him a good citizen inclined to enforce the laws impartially. White Conservatives responded by attacking Bedford's supporters, shooting at least two, killing one. Modocs invaded Republican meetings to force an endorsement of their candidate. When the Republicans started to leave one meeting without endorsing any candidate, the Modocs fingered their pistols and announced no one could leave until they nominated or endorsed someone for sheriff. Some tried to jump out the windows, but in the end they endorsed the Democratic candidate, A. J. Flanagan.[92]

In 1875 white Conservatives swept into office, defeating those blacks brave enough to run against them. Whites had succeeded in organizing themselves as a racial bloc while blacks had factionalized in ways that recalled the splits common in the antebellum white community. The change can perhaps best be understood by comparing Vicksburg on the eve of the Civil War with the situation in 1874. At the end of 1859 whites imagined a nightmare scenario. "An attempt will be made very soon to get up an insurrection on a very large scale," one Vicksburger predicted. He claimed Vicksburg Irish would rob banks and then distribute to slaves 1,500 muskets, 1,000 rifles, and 2,500 pikes that abolitionists had hidden in a swamp. Irish and blacks would rise up together.[93]

The picture whites painted of this illusory insurrection indicates they feared a union of blacks and lower class whites, especially Vicksburg's Irish population. White Vicksburgers did not regard the Irish as fully "white." The "truly white" called the Irish "niggers turned inside out" and blacks "smoked Irish."[94] No wonder "white" Vicksburgers feared insurrection by blacks and Irish.

Fifteen years later Vicksburg Republicans thought such an alliance again possible. They nominated an Irishman named Martin Keary for mayor in hopes of cementing a union between Irish and black voters. But Irish-born Vicksburgers refused the bait, declaring that Keary had forfeited all claim he had upon the Irish "race" when he supported "negro rule." "Irishmen are *white men*," they declared.[95] The Irish merely recited a common theme. Whites "must accept, like men, the issue tendered by the negroes or slink like dogs and cowards." Those unwilling to slink must "unfurl the white banner" and "plant the white standard and invite all men of the Caucasian race to rally around it. Those who stand by and protect that standard, are WHITE men. *White* in color, *white* in heart, and *white* in deed!"[96]

After the riot on December 7, 1874, white Vicksburgers saw themselves as a solid unit, a racially defined community. Lawyer R. V. Booth described what happened as a "civic revolution," one that "swept the last vestige of carpetbag, negroe-Republican rule from Mississippi." That was quite an overstatement. As Booth himself wrote elsewhere, the Republicans, both black and white, remained a force long after 1875. Their presence in the body politic prompted whites to rewrite the state constitution in 1890 to eliminate black voting. But something dramatic had happened at the end of 1874, continuing through 1875. Whites had forged a new coalition, which severely reduced political, economic, and social differences within the white community.[97]

In the newly born community, law played a reduced role. When lawyer Roswell Booth wrote a historical sketch of Vicksburg, he conceded that the conduct of the outraged Vicksburgers who had lynched five gamblers in the 1835 gambling riots had been morally indefensible. Booth, after all, had decided to become a lawyer in the 1850s, a time when Vicksburgers had moved toward police regulation and away from extralegal collective action like the gambling riots. But now he added, "it must be remembered that 'desperate diseases require desperate remedies.'" Right or wrong, Booth now thought, the lynchers "taught a salutary lesson," and he observed approvingly that professional gamblers had never dared return to Vicksburg after the riots.[98] Booth's writings endorsed the vigilante spirit Vicksburgers had abandoned before the Civil War.

NOTES

A different version of this essay appeared in Christopher Waldrep, *Roots of Disorder: Race and Criminal Justice in the American South, 1817–80* (Urbana: University of Illinois Press, 1998).

1. Ben F. Cheney to Stuart Aldridge, April 21, 1865, in Ira Berlin et al., *The Wartime Genesis of Free Labor: The Lower South*, 886; Donald G. Nieman, "The Language of Liberation: African Americans and Egalitarian Constitutionalism, 1830–1950," in *The Constitution, Law, and American Life: Critical Aspects of the Nineteenth–Century Experience*, ed. Donald G. Nieman (Athens, 1992), 67–90; Philip S. Foner, George E. Walker, *Proceedings of the Black National and State Conventions, 1865–1900* (Philadelphia, 1986), 5–423.

2. *New National Era*, October 26, 1871, September 10, 1874, December 21, 1871.

3. *New National Era and Citizen*, August 2, 1873.

4. *Vicksburg Daily Herald*, June 4, 1867.

5. *Journal of the Constitutional Convention of 1868*, 7, 9, 46, 133, 134, 178, 199, 264.

6. *Vicksburg Daily Herald*, April 13, 19, 20, 21, 1867.

7. *National New Era and Citizen*, June 19, 1873.

8. *Vicksburg Times*, August 13, 16, 1871.

9. *Vicksburg Times*, August 13, 16, 1871.

10. *Vicksburg Times*, September 12, 1871.

11. *Vicksburg Times*, September 16, 1871.

12. *Vicksburg Times and Republican*, September 17, 1871.

13. *Vicksburg Times and Republican*, September 24, 1871.

14. *Vicksburg Times and Republican*, September 27, 1871.

15. *Vicksburg Times and Republican*, September 24, 27, November 10, 1871.

16. 1873 Miss. Acts 66; William C. Harris, *The Day of the Carpetbagger: Republican Reconstruction in Mississippi* (Baton Rouge, London, 1979), 446.

17. *Vicksburg Times and Republican*, March 3, 1873.

18. *Vicksburg Herald*, May 1, 1873.

19. *Vicksburg Herald*, May 3, 1873.

20. *Vicksburg Herald*, May 3, 1873.

21. *Meridian Mercury* quoted in *Vicksburg Herald*, May 8, 1873.

22. *Vicksburg Herald*, May 13, 1873.

23. Janet Sharp Hermann, *The Pursuit of a Dream* (New York and Oxford, 1981), 187; Warren County deed book MM, 250–52 (Chancery Clerk's Office, Vicksburg, Miss.).

24. *Vicksburg Herald*, August 13, 1873.

25. *Vicksburg Herald*, August 16, 1873.

26. *Vicksburg Herald*, August 16, 1873.

27. Blanche Ames, *Adelbert Ames, 1835–1933: General, Senator, Governor* (New York, 1964), 269–88.

28. *Vicksburg Herald*, November 4, 1873.

29. G. Morris Smith petition to Board of Supervisors, Board of Supervisors Papers, Natchez Trace Collection (Center for American History, University of Texas, Austin).

30. J. T. Rankin testimony, U.S. Congress, *Mississippi in 1875: Report of the Select Committee to Inquire into the Mississippi Election of 1875, with the Testimony and Documentary Evidence*, 2 vols. (Washington, D.C.: U.S. Government Printing Office, 1876), 1417.

31. John E. Hogan testimony, U.S. Congress. House, *Vicksburgh Troubles*, House Report 265, 43rd Congress, 2nd Session, 153; Moses Kellaby testimony, ibid., 197; Warren Cowan testimony, ibid., 342.

32. Alexander H. Arthur testimony, *Vicksburgh Troubles*, 256–57.

33. Alexander H. Arthur testimony, *Vicksburgh Troubles*, 259.

34. Alexander H. Arthur testimony, *Vicksburgh Troubles*, 265–67.

35. Luke Lea testimony, *Report of the Joint Special Committee Appointed to Investigate the Late Insurrection in the City of Vicksburg, Warren County* (Jackson, 1875), 16.

36. Peter Crosby estate file, 3727, Warren County Chancery Clerk's Office, Vicksburg, Miss.); Michael Fitzgerald, *The Union League Movement in the Deep South: Politics and Agricultural Change During Reconstruction* (Baton Rouge and London, 1989), 97; *New Orleans Daily Picayune*, March 31, 1886.

37. Luke Lea testimony, *Vicksburgh Troubles*, 308.

38. Vicksburg *Plain-Dealer* quoted in the *Vicksburger*, November 15, 1874.

39. "Minority Report" in *Vicksburgh Troubles*, 461.

40. L. W. McGruder testimony, *Vicksburgh Troubles*, 462.

41. L. W. McGruder testimony, *Vicksburgh Troubles*, 462–63.

42. Adelbert Ames to Blanche Ames, July 31, 1874, Adelbert Ames to Blanche Ames, August 2, 1874, in *Chronicles from the Nineteenth Century: Family Letters of Blanche Butler and Adelbert Ames*, vol. 1, ed. Blanche Butler Ames (Clinton, Mass., 1957), 692–95.

43. Andrew Black, claim 10362, box 207, Settled Case Files for Claims Approved by the Southern Claims Commission, 1871–1880, Records of the Lands, Files, and Miscellaneous Division, Records of the Accounting Officers of the Department of the Treasury (National Archives, Washington, D.C., hereinafter cited as SCC); John Cole, claim 116558, box 208, ibid.; Albert Johnson, claim 43532, box 210, ibid.; *Vicksburg Herald*, July 12, 1874.

44. *Vicksburg Times*, August 25, 1869.

45. *Vicksburg Herald*, July 31, 1874.

46. L. W. McGruder testimony, *Vicksburgh Troubles*, 463; George R. Walton testimony, ibid., 361–63; *Vicksburg Herald*, July 31, 1874.

47. *Vicksburg Herald*, July 18, 19, September 23, 1874; Luke Lea testimony, *Report of the Joint Special Committee Appointed to Investigate the Late Insurrection in the City of Vicksburg*, 28–29.

48. Grand jury indictment, November 1874, State v. Thomas W. Cardozo, case 528; grand jury indictment, November 1874, State v. Thomas W. Cardozo, case 529; grand jury indictment, November 1874, State v. Thomas W. Cardozo, case 531; grand jury indictment, November 1874, State v. Thomas W. Cardozo, case 532; grand jury indictment, November 1874, State v. Thomas W. Cardozo, case 533; grand jury indictment, November 1874, State v. Alfred W. Dorsey, case 543; grand jury indictment, November 1874, State v. Alfred W. Dorsey, case 544; grand jury indictment, November 1874, State v. Alfred W. Dorsey, case 545; grand jury indictment, November 1874, State v. Alfred W. Dorsey and E. E. Perkins, case 550; grand jury indictment, November 1874, State v. George W. Davenport, case 526; grand jury indictment, November 1874, State v. George W. Davenport, case 527; grand jury indictment, November 1874, State v. George W. Davenport, case 534; all in Warren County Circuit Court Papers (OCHM); Luke Lea testimony, *Report of the Joint Special Committee Appointed to Investigate the Late Insurrection in the City of Vicksburg*, 17.

49. *Daily Vicksburger*, October 17, 1874.

50. Alexander H. Arthur testimony, *Vicksburgh Troubles*, 273.

51. *Daily Vicksburger*, November 3, 1874.

52. Luke Lea testimony, *Vicksburgh Troubles*, 306.

53. *Daily Vicksburger*, December 3, 1874.

54. *Daily Vicksburger*, November 28, 1874.

55. *Daily Vicksburger*, December 3, 1874.

56. *Daily Vicksburger*, December 3, 1874.

57. *Vicksburg Daily Herald*, July 22, 1875.

58. Crosby testimony, *Vicksburgh Troubles*, 400–401; *Daily Vicksburger*, December 3, 1874.

59. W. W. Dedrick testimony, "Proceedings of Special [Mississippi House] Com-

mittee Appointed to Investigate Conduct of Gov. Ames, 1876," record group 47, vol. 51 (Mississippi Department of Archives and History, Jackson, hereinafter cited as Ames Investigation).

60. G. E. Harris testimony, Ames Investigation.
61. A. W. Allyn testimony, Ames Investigation.
62. Crosby testimony, *Vicksburgh Troubles*, 402.
63. A. G. Packer testimony, Ames Investigation; Peter Crosby testimony, *Vicksburgh Troubles*, 404–5.
64. Packer testimony, Ames Investigation.
65. H. H. Miller testimony, *Vicksburgh Troubles*, 16.
66. James M. Hunt testimony, *Vicksburgh Troubles*, 93.
67. Miller testimony, *Vicksburgh Troubles*, 16–17; Owen testimony, ibid., 108–10; J. Q. Arnold testimony, ibid., 460; O'Leary testimony, ibid., 4–5; Rable, *But There Was No Peace*, 148–49.
68. *Daily Vicksburger*, December 11, 1874.
69. In addition to the testimony cited below, see Harriet Gray testimony, *Vicksburgh Troubles*, 488; Thomas Brogden testimony, *Vicksburgh Troubles*, 398.
70. William Wood testimony, *Vicksburgh Troubles*, 175.
71. John McPherson testimony, *Vicksburgh Troubles*, 275.
72. Lucinda Mitchell testimony, *Vicksburgh Troubles*, 317.
73. Lusinda Henry testimony, *Vicksburgh Troubles*, 351.
74. Charles H. Smith testimony, *Vicksburgh Troubles*, 180.
75. Packer testimony, Ames Investigation.
76. *Vicksburg Herald*, January 19, 1875; A. J. Flanagan testimony, Ames Investigation.
77. *Vicksburg Herald*, January 26, 1875.
78. *Vicksburg Herald*, February 9, 1875.
79. *Vicksburg Herald*, February 17, 1875.
80. *Vicksburg Herald*, March 23, 27, April 27, 1875.
81. *Vicksburg Herald*, April 28, 1875.
82. Vicksburg *Plain-Dealer*, June 11, 1875.
83. *Vicksburg Herald*, June 27, 1875.
84. G. K. Chase to Charles Devens, April 29, 1877, Letters Received by the Department of Justice from Mississippi, Source Chronological File, southern Mississippi (National Archives microfilm M970).
85. Peter Crosby to Adelbert Ames, October 28, 1875, Governors' Papers box 99, record group 27 (Mississippi Department of Archives and History, Jackson); *Vicksburg Herald*, July 13, 14, 1875.
86. *Vicksburg Herald*, April 18, 1875. For Baum's political inclinations see Joseph Butler to Baum, July 15, 1871, Jacob F. Baum Papers, Natchez Trace Collection

(Center for American History, University of Texas, Austin, Texas). For Baum's commercial activities, see his papers generally.

87. G. M. Barber testimony, *Mississippi in 1875*, 1340.
88. W. F. Fitzgerald testimony, *Mississippi in 1875*, 1292.
89. W. W. Edwards Testimony, *Mississippi in 1875*, 1351–53; J. C. Embry testimony, ibid., 1304–7; M. G. Bennett testimony, ibid., 1386–87; George W. Stith testimony, ibid., 1394–97; J. T. Tankin testimony, ibid., 1407–12.
90. D. J. Foreman testimony, *Mississippi in 1875*, 1379.
91. W. F. Fitzgerald testimony, *Mississippi in 1875*, 1286–87.
92. S. H. Scott testimony, *Mississippi in 1875*, 1322–23; D. J. Foreman testimony, ibid., 1380; E. D. Richardson testimony, ibid., 1422.
93. "An Abolitionist" to Governor John J. Pettus, November 30, 1859, Governors' Papers, RG27 (Mississippi Department of Archives and History, Jackson).
94. Noel Ignatiev, *How the Irish Became White* (New York and London, 1995), 35–111.
95. Vicksburg *Herald*, July 28, 1874.
96. Vicksburg *Herald*, July 4, 1874.
97. R. V. Booth, "Glimpsing Backward," June 16, 1913, in private memoranda, vol. 8, 91 (Mississippi Department of Archives and History, Jackson).
98. R. V. Booth, "Historic Vicksburg," August 18, 1906, in private memoranda, vol. 5, 165–84 (Mississippi Department of Archives and History, Jackson).

CONTRIBUTORS

LAURA F. EDWARDS is associate professor of history at Duke University. She is author of *Gendered Strife and Confusion: The Political Culture of Reconstruction* (1997), *Scarlett Doesn't Live Here Anymore: Southern Women in the Civil War Era* (2000), and several articles on women, gender, and the law in the nineteenth-century South.

MICHAEL W. FITZGERALD is associate professor at St. Olaf College. His book *The Union League Movement in the Deep South* was published in 1989, and his articles have appeared in the *Journal of Southern History*, the *Journal of American History*, *Civil War History*, and other publications. He is currently completing a study of grassroots black activism in Reconstruction Mobile.

ARIELA GROSS is associate professor of law at the University of Southern California Law School. She is the author of *Double Character: Slavery and Mastery in the Antebellum Southern Courtroom* (2000) and several law review articles.

SALLY HADDEN is assistant professor of history and law at Florida State University. Her book on slave patrols in Virginia and the Carolinas will be published by Harvard University Press. Her next project is a study of law and legal culture in America's eighteenth-century cities.

TIMOTHY S. HUEBNER, an assistant professor of history at Rhodes College, is the author of *The Southern Judicial Tradition: State Judges and Sectional Distinctiveness, 1790–1890* (University of Georgia Press, 1999). He has published articles in several journals, including *Georgia Historical Quarterly*, *Virginia Magazine of History and Biography*, and the *Journal of Supreme Court History*.

DONALD G. NIEMAN is professor of history and dean of the College of Arts and Sciences at Bowling Green State University. His books include *Promises to Keep: African Americans and the Constitutional Order, 1776 to the Present* (1991); *To Set the Law in Motion: The Freedman's Bureau and the Legal Rights of Blacks, 1865–1868* (1979); *African-American Life in the Post-Emancipation South, 1861–1900* (12 vols., 1994); and *The Constitution, Law, and American Life: Critical Aspects of the Nineteenth-Century Experience* (1992).

JUDITH KELLEHER SCHAFER is the associate director of the Murphy Institute of Political Economy and an associate professor of political economy. She is the author of *Slavery, the Civil Law, and the Supreme Court of Louisiana* (1994).

CHRISTOPHER WALDREP is Jamie and Phyllis Pasker Professor of History at San Francisco State University. He is the author of *Night Riders: Defending Community in the Black Patch, 1890–1915* (1993) and *Roots of Disorder: Race and Criminal Justice in the American South, 1817–80* (1998).

LOU FALKNER WILLIAMS is associate professor of history at Kansas State University, where she specializes in constitutional history and history of the South. Her published works include *The Great South Carolina Ku Klux Klan Trials, 1871–1872* (University of Georgia Press, 1996). Currently she is completing a book on federal enforcement efforts in post-Reconstruction South Carolina.

INDEX